Parenting
for Humans

Parenting for Humans

How to parent the child you have, as the person you are

DR EMMA SVANBERG

Published by Sourcebooks
P.O. Box 4410, Naperville, Illinois 60567-4410
(630) 961-3900
sourcebooks.com

Originally published in 2023 in Great Britain by Vermilion, an imprint of Ebury
Publishing. Vermilion is part of the Penguin Random House group of companies
whose addresses can be found at global.penguinrandomhouse.com

Cataloging-in-Publication Data is on file with the Library of Congress.

Printed and bound in the United States of America.
VP 10 9 8 7 6 5 4 3 2 1

To my Square Family, the meaning of home

'Some people seem to think of a child as clay in the hands of a potter. They start moulding the infant, and feeling responsible for the result. This is quite wrong.'

Donald Winnicott

Contents

Introduction: Why Did We Think This Was
a Good Idea?   1

Part I The Myths and Legends of Parenting   15

  1 Unravelling Stories   17

  2 What Is a 'Parent'?   36

Part II Mapping Out Your Story   43

  3 Your Parenting Map   45

  4 Stories from Your History   58

  5 Stories from Your Childhood   67

  6 Stories from Your Babyhood   79

  7 Stories from Your Adulthood   98

Part III The Other Humans in Your Story   119

  8 Partners Who Parent   121

  9 Your Supporting Cast   150

 10 Stories from Society   164

Part IV The Story of Children   179

11 Tools for the Journey   181

12 Our Children's Map   203

13 Mapping Out Feelings   218

14 Family Stories   243

15 Children Are Mapmakers   250

The End   258

Further Reading   262

Influences   273

Acknowledgements   275

Index   277

Why Did We Think This Was a Good Idea?

W hen did you decide to become a parent?
Was it a conscious decision, or something that happened unexpectedly? Do you feel that you were always destined to be a parent, that it was an inevitable part of your life? Or perhaps something that you grappled with, and maybe still are?

When do you think you became a parent? Was it when you knew a child was going to be coming into your life – or did you only start to identify with that role months or even years after you first met them?

Did you think about what being a parent meant? What it is to begin a lifelong relationship with another human? Perhaps you had some stories in your mind about what parents are, and what they do. Stories you've been told since you were a baby yourself. Stories that have, perhaps, set up certain expectations for you about what 'good' parents do, how they behave, even how they feel inside and what they think about.

Maybe you haven't had much opportunity to think about those stories. Maybe you'd never really thought of them as stories. But they exist in all of us, in the form of ideals and assumptions. And they can lead to difficult feelings like loss, guilt and failure when our realities turn out to be quite different.

How about your child?

If you haven't met your child yet, how do you imagine they will be? Where have those ideas come from?

If you have a child in your life already, what ideas did you hold about them? Had you thought about what they'd be like before you met them? Did you assume that you would just 'know' them from the moment you met? Perhaps you had a baby already in your mind, one that had existed as a doll, or a stick or a train when you were tiny and carrying around a precious imaginary baby. Or perhaps you didn't think about what a child would be like at all, but more that it felt the right time to consider creating a family because, well, it just did and that's what people do, right?

We hold a lot of stories in us.

Stories about what it means to be a parent, what babies and children are like, stories about the relationship between parents and children. Sometimes these are positive stories from our own childhood that we wish to repeat. Sometimes they are based on our painful experiences, those stories we wish to forget about or rewrite completely. Sometimes these stories are buried deep within us, sometimes they exist closer to the surface.

But at some point in our parenting, we will find ourselves face to face with these stories – and the assumptions they contain. We might challenge them, and create new stories. Often, though, because we're human and changing stories is a hard thing to do, we hold tighter to them and wonder what we need to do differently to make that story a reality.

There's a good chance that one of those stories, or even many of them, are behind you picking up this book. A story like, 'If I can just figure out the right strategy to manage my child's behaviour, then life will feel easier again.' Or, 'Family life feels really hard and maybe this book will give me the answer to change that.' Or even, 'Maybe this is the book that will tell me what it is I'm meant to be doing because, frankly, I don't have a clue and everyone else seems to have it together and will someone *please* just tell me what to do because I'm drowning over here.'

We pick up parenting books because they appear to sell us that fantasy – that if we just do the thing or say the words or follow the instructions, everything will be easier. And, often, we put them down after the first few pages because they don't provide any easy answers.

But what if there aren't any easy answers? What if the story isn't just one story, but many – some of which contradict each other? What if we need to rip up the stories, and instead write our own? And keep coming back to them, editing them and adding new chapters as our children grow and our lives change?

Even in our adulthood, we might picture ourselves as heroes in our story – occasionally villains perhaps. Certainly we might wish for someone to come and rescue us (for parents, this may not be a knight in shining armour but a very kind fairy godmother).

Once we get to know ourselves better, unravel some of the stories we've brought along with us, challenge some ideals, consider a new story . . . then quite an amazing thing can happen. We start to see ourselves as we really are – good bits, bad bits and the many in-the-middle bits. Not heroes, just humans. And we start to see our children as they really are, too – the bits we love and the bits we find really annoying and all the bits we haven't really noticed. We bring our whole selves to our relationship with them, and they are encouraged to bring their whole selves to their relationship with us. That can feel a bit scary, but it can also be profoundly wonderful and make not just our relationships, but our whole lives feel richer.

This Isn't a Parenting Book (It's a Book about Parents)

I know that your heart may have sunk a little when I said there were no easy answers. I'm afraid I'm not going to be offering quick tips and easy solutions, because family life is long, and changes all the time, and the best solutions involve figuring out how *you* want to show up in *your* family. The rest will come and, let's face it, there's no shortage of books about parenting to give you some of those tips once you've finished with me.

Instead, I will be asking you a lot of questions – to help you find your own answers. And we'll be getting to know you, really well, and the things that influence you as a parent (and as a person). Through this process – just as when I see people in therapy – you'll gain insight and reduce pressure on yourself as a parent, which will help you find your own answers. While this won't provide a quick fix, I hope it will bring lasting change.

So, this is not a book about parenting. This is a book about parents. It's a book about *you*.

When we don't know ourselves well, we find it hard to apply all of the parenting knowledge we pick up from books, blogs, articles and podcasts to our lives. We can put a baby down to sleep beautifully but find it impossible to leave that baby lying there because of our own feelings of abandonment. We can recite a perfectly phrased response to a tantrumming toddler . . . through gritted teeth with tears stinging our eyes. We can try to timetable in special, one-on-one time with our child but find ourselves shouting because it hasn't gone how we wanted. And what that often leads to is feeling disconnected, and helpless, and that we're getting it all wrong, and we don't know what else to do. So then maybe we try something new – like picking up this book, for example.

All of the parenting advice in the world, all the understanding of child development and knowledge of sleep cycles, consistent boundaries, emotional validation – they can't truly help if you don't understand yourself and how you operate. Because parenting is not a tick-box exercise, or a recipe to follow. Parenting is a complex dance between multiple complicated and ever-changing human beings. It strips you naked and leaves you defenceless, all while getting to know a whole new person who initially can't do a thing for themselves and continues to surprise you on a daily basis, frequently on your own with only social media for moral support, and trying to figure out who *you* are now that you are, apparently, a parent.

This also means that you can get to know your real-life, actual child a little better. Because when we find ourselves looking for the answers that will make it all easier, we can lose sight of the child right in front of us. We have this idea that if we *just* found the right strategy, the right label, the right technique, the right line to say, perhaps even the right diagnosis – then everything would be OK. Then we'll have 'cracked it'. Whatever 'it' is – sleeping, feeding, eating five portions of fruit and veg, 'good' behaviour, a healthy relationship. We keep chasing that magic solution, and we never stop and look at what is going on right now in ourselves, in our children, and in our families.

But when we know ourselves – our own experiences, feelings, thoughts, beliefs, values, hopes and dreams – it is much easier to know others too.

So, while this book won't give you easy answers, parenting tips and tricks, or failsafe solutions, it will help you write a new story. A story that starts with you.

I'm Not a Parenting Expert

I'd like to make it clear right from the start that I'm not a parenting expert. In fact, I find the whole idea of having to listen to 'experts' when it comes to parenting can just amplify the idea that parenting is something we have to get right and do a particular way (which changes depending on who we are listening to). What I am trained in is not parenting tips, but models and approaches that help you to understand yourself and your relationship with your child better. Whether that is a child you are hoping to meet one day or a child who is already in your life.

I've worked with a lot of parents, as a clinical psychologist specialising in the perinatal period – that is, pregnancy, birth and the early years. And I've worked with parents and families in different ways for over 20 years. While many parenting books focus on the child, my training encouraged me to focus on the adult and what they bring to the parenting relationship. I've worked with parents in individual therapy, as couples, in groups, and – as my work expanded to campaigning and sharing information outside of traditional therapeutic spaces – I've been lucky enough to speak to thousands of parents online. So I'm bringing what I've learned from those parents into this book.

When people come to me for therapy, they are under huge pressure, often feeling desperate and looking for answers. A big part of my work with them is simply to slow things down. To support them in gaining insight into how they work and the challenges (from themselves and others) that they are up against. When that insight is gained, alongside some minimal general information about how children and adults tend to operate, people find their own solutions. And often there is a lot of trial and error, as people apply new ideas to their own life, their individual family and their unique situation. The longer I've worked, the less advice I give. Because creating meaningful change has to come from you, not me.

There are many different types of psychology and psychologists, and of course each individual interprets models slightly differently and is attracted to the approach they most relate to. I draw from diverse schools of thought, both within psychology and outside of it. And of course I bring my own lens to this, which is influenced by my own history and circumstances, and you will bring your lens too.

Psychology is a lot like Lego, with ideas building on foundations from long ago. Rarely are they truly new – some of the core concepts in this book began back with Freud in the 1920s. I won't be adding any exciting models, catchy acronyms or quick-fix ideas, because I'd be doing you a disservice by implying that there is a specific 'way' or set of beliefs (a new one, invented by yours truly, of course) that will solve your problems.

Instead, I'll be letting you know about some of the core concepts that I use in my everyday work, gathered together from others – psychologists, psychiatrists, psychotherapists, educators, campaigners, researchers, authors. And, just like I do with my clients, I'll be asking you questions and sitting by you as you figure out how this applies to your own life, your story from the past, present and future.

I'm a human, talking to you as a fellow human. Psychology can feel complex and hard to navigate from the outside. But my work is just about relationships. It focuses on understanding how we learn to relate to others, and how we then pass that way of relating on to our children. I've learned to guide people through discovering their story and, just as I do in my clinical work, I'd like us to enter this process with a blank page and a genuine curiosity to see what comes next. Explorers together on a quest for insight.

This Is a Slow Process

I want to start us off right. This is not going to be a quick process. Reading this book is going to get you thinking about a lot of different things; some of them are going to be difficult to read and think about, and others will be easier. Hopefully, by the end of this book you'll have started to write yourself a brand-new story about parenting, and gained a bit of insight about yourself, your family and your life in general. You might also know where you want to look to add more to your story.

But we never really complete that story. And being aware of that can make a huge difference. Knowing that we are works in progress, always, and that we will never know it all. To be comfortable with scribbling bits out, finding out new information, writing new passages, moving things around and sometimes writing a whole new draft.

We're going to go through it all slowly, and carefully, because it is not always easy to think about these things. I have been having these conversations for some time now, in real life with clients in therapy, online in parenting communities, and all over the place with the parents I know. And I know that with these conversations often comes a sadness that is just beneath the surface, of the wishes and longings that haven't been met, yet. The feelings of failure and disappointment. The anger that it wasn't meant to be this way. The fear that there is just so much at stake.

With these big questions and feelings, there just aren't easy answers. We can so wish there were, but often the answers involve unravelling the questions and figuring out what will work for our family. We're going to find answers, but we're going to do it gradually and step by step. It is OK to put this book down sometimes and leave it – maybe even for a few weeks – until you're ready to go a bit further. I'd like you to make notes, fold over corners, fill it with Post-its, journal about it, have conversations with your partner, co-parent, friends, parents, siblings. The slower you do it, the more likely it is that the information in these pages will lead to some meaningful changes for you and your family – whether that is a family you are considering starting, a family that is in the distant future, a family that is pottering in another room, or a family that left home a long time ago. Because it's never too late to make changes to your parenting – even when your children are parents themselves.

Here's something I've learned from the parents I've spoken to. Every parent is muddling through, hoping for the best, frequently doing things they wish they weren't. Every parent sometimes wonders how on earth they got into the mind-blowing situations that we find ourselves in as parents – from having to negotiate whether or not your toddler has to wear underpants, to heading to a police station because your grown-up child has got into some serious trouble.

Every parent sometimes looks at their child and wonders who they are and how they got here. Some parents feel more confident than others, and that's usually not because they have any special secret, it's because they already know that it's OK to muddle through, make mistakes and learn as they go. And, often, it's because they were raised by people who felt like that too and taught them that they, and their children, are good enough just as they are.

Our Story Map

We're going to start by examining the stories you've brought to this role of 'parent'. Some of them might be a bit sad in parts, others you might have imagined were chucked out and long forgotten. Then I'll take you on a bit of a journey, mapping out the different parts of you – historically and in the present. We'll be considering how other people influence you in your parenting, and your child too, of course. Then we'll bring your child into the story.

Before we start this journey together, I'd like to introduce you to two core ideas. If there are only two things you remember I'd like it to be these:

1. We cannot fully enjoy parenting our children until we understand ourselves. That includes our relationship with ourselves and our relationships with others, and how we feel about not only love and connection but power and control too.

2. Our role as parents is not to mould our children but to hold them – to support them in discovering their magical selves and their own unique way of being and to offer a solid foundation they can rest on when they need to, whether they are 5 months or 50 years old.

I said we'd be going on a journey and, as we all know, before a journey we need some safety announcements.

Please don't skip Parts 1 and 2, which are about you. I know you might be tempted to, and that it might feel uncomfortable looking at yourself. But the final two parts don't really work unless you've read the sections about you first. Just like in parenting really. When you understand yourself better, you'll find parenting simpler.

Throughout the book you'll find lots of opportunity to pause, reflect, check in with yourself and see how this is all landing with you. Please don't skip those bits either, even though I know it's tempting and you might feel it's a waste of time. When we're hoping to understand things better and make changes, we often come to it only with our heads. But we will be talking about the key relationships of your lifetime. We need to bring our bodies and souls into that too, and the pauses will allow you to do that and for me to be alongside you, making sure we're doing this as safely as we can. Bringing your head might bring understanding, bringing your heart will bring change.

I've shared examples and insights from my clinical work and my conversations with parents. While every parent and family is different, there are common themes that I see frequently. Any examples are based on amalgamations of these common issues rather than based on the experience of any one individual.

There will be things that I say in this book that give you a twinge, for whatever reason. It might be something that comes out of the blue and makes you feel a bit heart-sore, whether that's because of guilt, shame, sadness or frustration. There might be an unexpected twist in the tale. It might be about you, or your child, your partner, your family, the society that we live in, the situations that you find yourself in. Please do use all of the tools I outline in Chapter 3 to support you in those moments. We don't like difficult feelings, but they often bring us useful information. So, try to look at those moments as messages that there is something there to explore.

One thing I often find tricky when I read parenting information is the suggestion that the writer has it sorted. But I am in a process of learning too, and always will be. Knowing this stuff doesn't make the doing of it any less challenging and writing this book made me reflect on *just* how many things I wish I'd done differently. I'm here in the capacity of sharing my professional knowledge with you. My real-life, actual children think it's hilarious that I'm writing a book about parenting.

A word on who this book is for. If I'd written this book ten years ago, it undoubtedly would have been aimed at mothers – or mamas. When I started my career – built on theories that were created in times where the assumption was that mothers raised children and fathers financially provided – my view was that women needed to feel more valued in their maternal role to improve their experience of parenting. While I still believe that mothers – and all parents – should feel more valued and know how important their parenting role is, in the last 20 years my views on how we get there have changed. I've seen a phenomenal rise in pressure on women, and many fathers and partners feeling unsure about their role in the family. Mothers are given ever more complicated goals to aspire to, while feeling increasingly burdened and resentful. And fathers, partners and other caregivers are excluded from discussions about parenting and children, and from services to support them as parents, so end up falling into roles they hoped to defy. Many parents are pushing against the traditional family stories they were raised with, yet finding that society pushes back. If we are to create new stories about family, we need the whole family to be involved and included. So, this is a book for all parents and caregivers, and future parents and caregivers, and everyone who knows a parent and caregiver. We need a seismic shift in the way we treat and speak about families, and that has to start with who we are talking to and about when we say the word 'parent'.

On a similar note, throughout the book I have aimed to include the many different incarnations of 'family', including the additional pressures on families from marginalised and under-represented groups. Although I have tried to be inclusive and intentional in the language I use, without a doubt I will have made mistakes and omissions, and my apologies if this affects you at all. Plus, many of the psychological models I was trained in are themselves excluding and limited in their scope. While I am drawn to critical approaches, which is reflected in this book, as psychology itself goes through a process of decolonisation and expansion our understanding will also change. I hope you can bear with me and the errors that my future self will be astonished by.

Throughout this book I explain psychological concepts in a visual way. This is because visualisation can really help us to remember things – and if you read it, visualise it and then talk or write about it too, you are laying down lots of associations in your memory to help you recall this later. Visualisation also takes our experiences, feelings and beliefs out of our own bodies (which brings with it all the shame and blame too) and turns them into something we can look at more objectively.

However, visualisation can sometimes make people feel a bit uncomfortable, and there is huge variation in how vividly people describe visual images in their mind. Don't get too focused on what you can or can't see. If you find it difficult to imagine, you can either just go with a loose sense of what you're reading, or you could even draw or write it out for yourself. There is no right way to do this.

One last thing. Don't hold tightly to anything that I say. Nothing that I say is an absolute, and it is in bringing nuance that you will be able to apply it to your own life. You might notice that there's something missing (there is a LOT missing!). You might disagree with some things; maybe I'll talk a bit too much about a topic or I'll say something that is so unrelated to your experience that it sounds ridiculous. And that's OK, and not just OK but brilliant, because we are complex and messy humans and we have different opinions and desires and not everything that I say will relate to every one of you. But try not to throw it all out if something I say doesn't fit for you. Hold it loosely. Take what you need, and leave the rest. So much parenting information is presented in simplistic terms, giving us this impression that there is only one way of doing things. But every single person will read this book differently.

My hope is that this book can help you find a way that is uniquely yours. So, my fellow explorer, are you ready?

PART 1

The Myths and Legends of Parenting

CHAPTER 1

Unravelling Stories

'Everything's got a moral, if only you can find it.'

Lewis Carroll, *Alice's Adventures in Wonderland*

D o you remember when you believed in magic? So much of childhood involves creating not just stories but whole, mythical worlds. In the baby and toddler years, reality and fantasy often collide. And in later childhood, play can involve the creation of intricate lands with characters, histories and rituals.

We might think that, as we get older, we become more rational and reasonable. We stop believing in magic. Creating fantasies gives way to controlling finances, and getting lost in daydreams gets replaced by doomscrolling on social media. Yet our fantasies remain and influence our daily lives. We just don't always realise they are there.

In this book, I'd like to introduce a little bit of magic back into your life. We're going to go on a journey together, we'll explore different landscapes and meet some characters. We're even going to go back in time. And to start with, I'm going to tell you a story. Because stories are such a fundamental part of childhood, one that we so often lose as we become adults. But it is in stories that, throughout history and across the world, we learn about how to be humans in the world that we live in.

Are you sitting comfortably? Then we'll begin.

The Parenting Fairy Tale

Once upon a time there was a child, who imagined that one day they would have a child of their own. And as that child grew up, a little seed of an idea grew about the kind of parent they would be, and the kind of child they would have. And, without realising, that child held on to that story. It was added to through their own experiences, and a medley of books, adverts and overheard conversations. And when that child had a child of their own, they realised that the story may have been a fairy tale. Oversimplified, and idealised. And containing characters that the child no longer recognised. Perhaps even casting themselves as a character that they no longer wanted to be.

If you pause for a minute and think about what kind of parent you were going to be, or even what kind of parent you're aiming for now, what comes up for you? For many people, this ideal can be based on the parent they would love to have had but didn't. Commonly, it might take elements from your own parents or caregivers and mix them together with other images of parenting. This ideal is the fantasy parent who instinctively knows what their child needs. The one who can pop a child into bed, kiss them on the forehead and they drift off to sleep. The one who never loses their temper and always home-cooks what their children would like to eat and has a bowl of shiny fruit on the kitchen counter. The one whose children somehow go on pause when there is something else to be done – like work, or chores, or a shower, or date nights.

I can picture my fantasy parent quite clearly. I can see her in my mind's eye, lips slightly pursed with a smile playing at the corners. Clair Huxtable from *The Cosby Show* (a show tainted in the years since). Mrs Huxtable was kind, warm, funny but could stop a child in their tracks with one raise of her eyebrows. Just the right mixture of compassionate and firm. A mother, wife and a successful lawyer, sometimes stern, totally unflappable. Raising five very different children to be strong and caring. The queen of the household. And brown-skinned like me, too.

There were other mothering ideals for me as well, many of which I swallowed without realising I was being fed. The women in my life, including my own mum of course, who carried their own stories about family, relationships, work, duty, care. TV shows from the 90s where women had babies and then got on with their 'real' lives. All in heterosexual relationships, with husbands who were presented as add-ons – working outside the home, financial providers, offering the light relief.

And the babies and children? They were just cute, weren't they? And if they cried they could be soothed, if they were tired they would go to sleep, if they spoke rudely they were sent to their room. All of these mixing together into an idea of who I would be as a parent, who my partner would be and what our children would be like. There might have been a Manhattan apartment in there at some point too, thanks to *Sex and the City*.

- What about you? What influenced your stories about parents and children?
- And when did those stories start to look a little ragged around the edges?

Maybe the ideal always felt out of reach for you – because of your own experiences. Perhaps the idea of becoming a parent was even frightening because you couldn't imagine how to be a good parent, having never experienced that yourself. And that fear, of facing the gap between your ideal and your reality, might have delayed you having your own children – or stopped you completely.

Or maybe it was when you first saw a friend, or your

sibling, pregnant. And they talked about exhaustion and constipation – not quite the glowing recommendation you'd imagined.

Or maybe it was soon after you met your real-life, actual baby – when they were a bit more like a little piglet than you'd hoped and everyone left you alone with them even though you clearly didn't have the faintest idea what you were doing.

Perhaps it was before they were conceived, when becoming pregnant turned out to be so much more difficult than you'd been led to believe. Or was it during birth when things started to go wrong and you suddenly let go of what felt like a hundred different fantasies all at once – ideas not only of babies and parents, but of bodies, of safety, of trust? Maybe it was that first night with them at home when, no matter what you did, you just could not console them. Or was it later, when you stood at the window and watched your partner leave for work and the images you'd held of long walks in the park and coffee with friends were shattered by the sheer terror of being responsible for this tiny life?

Yet, so often, we don't question the story. We just think we're doing it wrong.

The Parenting Myth

There are a few fundamental ideas that underpin our parenting stories, no matter where they come from. One of them is a model – which we could think of as a commonly held myth – that looks a bit like this:

No matter your ideal, the parents are in control, and children need to be moulded. Maybe the parenting happens a little differently, maybe the children are treated in different ways, but ultimately this myth tells us that children should and will listen to their parents and tend to think that they

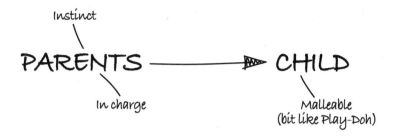

know best. And, if this happens as it should, then child-rearing is a doddle and we all live happily ever after.

Believing this myth means that, if parenting is hard, then it's because *we* are failing. We are getting something wrong, we're missing something. Or maybe it's that we got a kid who was broken, because they're not responding how they should be to our brilliant techniques.

If it's hard then it's because WE are wrong and/or OUR CHILDREN are wrong.

In recent years, this part of the story has got even stronger. It's not surprising really. We have been parenting in isolation, and increasingly our information about children comes from books, blogs and social media. We often come to parenting having been taught that our purpose in life is to achieve – at school, college, uni, at work. So we take that same framework and we apply it to our parenting. We see it as something to *do*, not someone to *be*. Somewhere along the line (around 1958, to be more precise) parenting became a verb and *we* were going to do it right. The job was 'to parent' and the outcome was . . . our child. The difference between expectations and reality got ever greater. In that gap, anxiety grew.

That myth is not just because of you, and the fairy tales that you carried. It's because of the many things that you've also experienced in your life that fed into these stories. From the earliest days of playing 'mummies and daddies', there are so many ways in which that myth is compounded. Just take the fairy tale of boy meets girl, which tends to end at the point when they get married. You don't read any fairy tales about a prince and a princess who struggled to conceive, or a new baby who just wouldn't go to sleep, or a prince and a prince who found a princess to co-parent with, or a toddler who had a special line in dropping F-bombs.

Those fairy tales and myths start to fall apart pretty quickly, don't they?

The Story vs Reality

If someone had said to you that parenting was going to be a life-changing, epic tale of both comedy and tragedy, would you still have become a parent?

If someone had said that your baby would not want to be put down and would only have long stretches of sleep if they were attached to your body, would you have still had that baby? (Not all babies do this, but we don't hear a lot about the diverse realities of baby sleep, do we?)

That your toddler would not only 'tantrum', but that these could include scratching and biting, breaking your treasured possessions, screaming at the top of their lungs in public. Would you still have had that toddler?

That your child would tell you, in graphic detail, that not only did they hate you but they also wished your best friend was their parent . . . Would you still have become a parent?

That your teenager would stay out all night without telling you, and, when challenged with your sleep-deprived, tear-stained face, would shout at you and then leave again? Would you still have become a parent?

If someone had told you that you might never experience pure relaxation again, that you'd always have one ear pricked up for them needing you . . . would you still have become a parent?

Maybe your story is different. And it may be that no matter

how hard things are, you haven't questioned becoming a parent. But all parents, at some point, feel blindsided by the challenges of parenting. Many parents feel cheated at the reality of their family life, and some parents regret having children at all. These are not the realities that we speak about.

How does it feel to reflect on this? It can be hard to acknowledge feelings of ambivalence, anger, resentment or even hatred towards our children. Partly due to one of those myths – that good parents love their children all the time, no matter what. But when we don't look at our more uncomfortable feelings about parenting, they affect us in other ways. We release them full force at someone in the supermarket or we numb them with a glass of something. It's hard to talk about them, though. Finding parenting hard and disliking aspects of our parenting life or even our children are still taboo.

So, as much as we might joke about kids being 'arseholes' or read books trying to get them to 'Go the F*ck to Sleep', we still smile and say everything's great when actually at 5am we felt a bit like we wanted to give them away just to spend some time in bed with nobody touching us.

The Magnitude of Parenting

So often when we talk about parenting we don't talk about the magnitude of it, unless we're being told in sensational headlines how our parenting can shape a child's brain irreversibly, or the ways in which poor parenting is the cause of society's ills. We talk about what's at stake, with the implication that it's ALL on our shoulders (and usually a mother's shoulders). But somehow we don't really talk about how becoming a parent turns us inside out, and leaves us raw and shattered – all while having to function as well as we can for a very vulnerable human being. And often at a time when we are at our most financially unstable, far from family (whether we want to be near them is another matter) and dealing with the most physical, psychological and social changes we have had to deal with since we were adolescents.

It's massive, isn't it? And even when we talk about how big it is, we tend to sugar-coat or talk around it. It's rare for someone to say, 'Becoming a parent is life-changing, in every way. It makes you question who you are, what you are here for and the meaning of life.' Instead we talk about the processes of being a parent. The sleep deprivation, the birth experiences, the behaviour challenges. The nitty-gritty instead of the whole shebang. And we talk about the short-term solutions we find to deal with the nitty-gritty: 'wine o'clock' and 'time out' and 'locking myself in the bathroom for a silent scream' (um, OK, maybe that's not such a common one that we talk about).

Maybe that's because it is just too massive to fully comprehend. There's so much to it. But if we don't know what we're really dealing with, how can we find useful solutions?

What if we thought of parenting a bit more like this:

It's a bit messier, isn't it? Not so much a beginning, middle and end, but a tale with many twists and turns and quite a few cliffhangers. Is there anything you'd add?

Over the coming pages, we're going to explore these stories together. We're going to get to know all the characters – properly, the ones behind the scenes, not the ones we present to the world. And then we're going to figure out what real-life story we want in its place.

And, of course, let's put some magic and joy in there, too.

The thing is, when we let go of some of those fantasies, we also find that we lose the weight of our own expectations, the pressure that those stories can place on us without us even realising. But it can feel a bit scary to let go of those ideals. You might even be noticing that you're holding on to them a little more tightly now that I'm inviting you to loosen your grip on them.

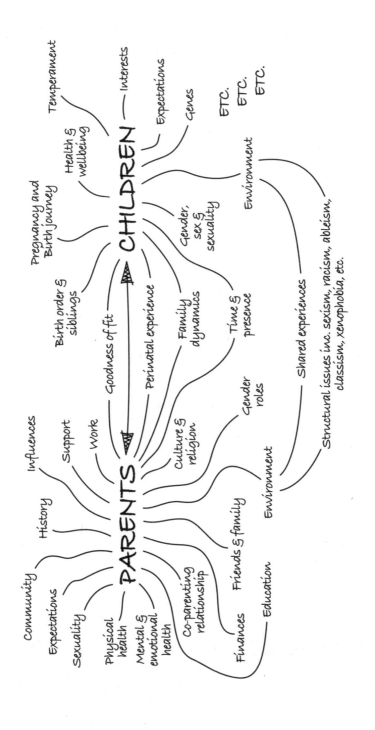

The Reality Gap

Why do we so often paint a picture of parenthood as blissful, when the reality is that it can be blissful and horrendous often in the very same moment? Even though the story is that parenthood brings fulfilment, the reality is that – on average – children simply *don't* make us happy. The rewards of having children are counterbalanced by the financial, time, psychological and social pressures.

Well, one reason for the disparity is another of those stories that we hear, from our earliest years. The story about how having children is an inevitable part of becoming a grown-up; and not only that but the most enjoyable aspect of it. So anything that deviates from that can feel so unexpected. And, because we've believed those stories for our entire lives, we assume any deviation is in some way because of us and what we're doing, rather than perhaps that the story wasn't true. It can feel so well-trodden that we don't pause to question whether it is a path that fits our own experience. But the path is often one of ideals, not reality.

Consider this. What if this story isn't true right from its very beginnings? What if it's all just a fable?

Exploring the Stories

We'll talk in the next part about your own story, but let's begin to tease apart some of the stories you are likely to have brought to your choice (whether active or not) to have a child. We've already identified some common stories, but how about those that may be more unique to you? Because we are just as affected by the environment we're in as by our individual experiences.

In the UK, where I am, we are a pro-natalist society. People are generally expected to have children and political policies are supportive of this. In a country like Greece, with a 'baby bonus' offering €2,000 on the birth of a child, people may feel even more of an expectation to have a child. Although we don't tend to think about society as part of planning for a child, it can impact on how baby-friendly our community feels and, without us even realising, influence our decisions.

This becomes more apparent when we speak to those who live outside of this expected story. Those who are childfree by choice often describe being treated with pity or criticised (despite often having given much more thought to their decision than those with children). So, whether we realise it or not, we live in a society that expects us to procreate, and most of us act accordingly. Many people don't stop to question whether becoming a parent is something they actively 'want'. And we perpetuate this story by telling people what will fit with their expectations. That we can't wait to be parents, or that we're nervous but excited. Discomfort at physical changes, fertility struggles, fear of the changes to our life, resentment at our child for causing them – these are rarely topics of conversation. So that story – that having a child is a welcome, inevitable part of our adult life – remains unchallenged.

Our stories are heteronormative too. Certainly they don't tend to include a prince or princess who didn't identify with that girl/boy binary, or whose journey to parenthood included assisted reproduction or fertility preservation, or who needed a court order to be recognised as a child's legal parent.

We carry stories and ideas about monogamy – often via religious beliefs that made their way into social norms – that a child will be born to two parents, who will stay together, so that those raising children alone (either through choice or after a separation) or in blended families may not find themselves represented in discussions about parenting.

There are huge assumptions in our stories about fertility too. We're generally brought up to believe that we'll create a baby by even thinking about sex; much of sex education focuses on not getting pregnant rather than information such as the process of pregnancy, physiology of birth and infant development.

Nowhere in that story are ideas of what happens if your body doesn't act in the way you expected it to, or if your parenting fantasy is shattered by grief and loss.

And what about money? Often the only stories we hear about raising children in poverty focus on 'don't do it', yet 3 in 10 children in the UK are growing up in poverty, alongside 1 in 6 children globally who live in extreme poverty, and this number is on the rise. Yet in the media as well as politically, low-income parents are often demonised and blamed for the ills of society.

Our economic and political context has an impact, too. It's likely you are raising a child in a mixed economy, such as the UK and the USA, where much of the means of production is privately owned for profit, but the state runs some public services. This can have a direct influence on families. Not only because we are socialised to be economically productive, in that school prepares us to join the workforce and we're encouraged to keep the economy moving through consumerism, all of which influences our family life. But also because the majority of families now rely on income from both parents (with single-parent households more likely to live in poverty) and as the cost of living has increased, there is more pressure to work, which has a knock-on impact on how we raise children. The minimum cost in the UK to raise a child up to 18 years was in 2021 estimated at £76,167 if you're in a couple, and £103,100 if you are a lone parent (this difference is due to the cost-saving that occurs when you are in a couple, in things like sharing of household bills and transport). The cost of a child once you factor in childcare and household costs rises to £160,692 for a couple and £193,801 for a lone parent. This is the highest it has been since records began in 2012. In the UK, full-time childcare before the age of three is usually privately owned, and our childcare system is the most expensive in the world, with even part-time childcare often costing more than a monthly mortgage or rent payment.

This means that while many parents (usually mothers) give up work, the majority suffer financial loss to ensure some employment continuity and are usually penalised for doing so in lack of career progression, leading to significant pay gaps. For the many parents who work full time, this too has an obvious impact on their role in the family. Until very recently, UK fathers worked some of the longest hours in Europe, and they tend to feel that flexible working policies are not accessible to them (often due to their employers' assumption that they are the main earner in the household). At the moment, even though for most families it may be financially difficult to do so, our economic and political policies encourage one parent (usually a mother) to stay at home or work limited hours for the first three years of a child's life. And in the USA, where there are 'childcare deserts', with three or more children to each approved childcare space, many families are pushed into either using unregulated childcare providers or leaving work. All of this inevitably influences our decisions about having or growing a family.

A devastating statistic from a 2022 survey by Pregnant Then Screwed found that, of 1,630 women who have had an abortion in the last five years, 60.5 per cent say that the cost of childcare influenced their decision to have an abortion and 17.4 per cent of women said that childcare costs were the main reason they chose to have an abortion.

In other surveys, 10 per cent of Brits and 17 per cent of Americans who state they don't have children or plan to have them in the future placed cost as one of the reasons. Compare this to Sweden, where generous paid parental leave and low-cost, high-quality childcare is explicitly organised to ensure parents can combine work and studying with family life.

It wasn't part of the fairy tale, was it? Having to figure out a spreadsheet as part of family planning.

Our stories are also culturally influenced. Many of the images we see of parenthood involve a buggy and a cot – rather than a woven wrap and a family bed. We buy new parents toys and muslins rather than coming over to clean their home and look after older children. And parenting tends to be done in isolation, rather than by wider family or community. While parenting styles emphasising physical closeness have become increasingly popular in the West, the predominant story in the UK is still one of independence not interdependence. Children are encouraged to separate from their parents at an early age – sometimes through choice, sometimes because of a need for a rapid return to work. Initial physical closeness quickly gives way to routines, a separate bedroom and a blankie. But perhaps your story differed from this? Often it is in parenting that our cultural differences most starkly show up, with parenting values and ideas strongly rooted in our heritage. Or perhaps your experience led you to question the ease with which such separation was meant to occur?

I'm pretty sure your parenting story is also a woman-centred one. Where Mum is paramount, and Dad, partner or co-parent is a helper. Unless you are part of the Aka tribe of Central Africa, where mums' and dads' roles are pretty much interchangeable. Or you live in Finland, where all parents are entitled to (and encouraged to take) a full year of parental leave, which can be taken in full by one parent or split between a couple. Quite a difference from the UK, whose shared parental leave policy has been an 'inequitable and failed policy', taken up by 3.6 per cent of eligible parents and excluding many.

And, especially when it comes to the tasks of parenting, we carry all sorts of mixed-up stories that are patriarchal and matriarchal all at once, with a bit of heteronormativity, capitalism and individualism thrown in. We hold within us Darwinian stories of maternal instinct – created in Victorian Britain to support male dominance – ignoring the many examples in human and animal societies where females are the dominant sex or men and women raise children together in groups. The story prevails that women stay to nurture and rear children and men go out to hunt and protect.

This has expanded over time, with women now trying to raise children who are physically and mentally healthy, feel loved and secure, emotionally attuned and academically excellent, while those women are successful at work, look attractive, have interior-design-worthy homes and are confident but not too confident. And men are faced with conflicting messages that they should be tough providers who can cope with anything that the world throws at them, while being sensitive and in tune with their own feelings and those of others, and somehow be present for their child while also rising up the ranks at work. And they end up either re-enacting patterns that feel more traditional (while wondering why their partners are always talking through gritted teeth) or trying their utmost to share parenting and be an active parent but without much in the way of a model to follow or systems to support that. In couples who are parenting outside the hetero norm, who already find themselves writing new stories of family life, these conflicts are less present.

Oh, and pregnancy, birth and parenthood should be a story of love and joy too, of course! Unambiguous, unbridled affection and devotion beginning from the first time you feel a tiny kick, developing when you meet each other's gaze for the first time and then just carrying on that way ad infinitum, even when you're woken at 2am by someone prising your eyelids open with a plastic astronaut. With no space for exhaustion or fear or annoyance or depression or confusion or any of that stuff. This despite the high prevalence of difficult feelings in the postnatal period – such as the common experience of intrusive, unwanted and distressing thoughts of causing harm to your own baby, or the 50 per cent of new mothers who experience hypervigilance in the weeks after birth (rising to 75 per cent in new mothers who have birth-related PTSD), or the approximately 10 per cent of new fathers who experience postnatal depression. When the most common experience of new parenthood is one of mixed emotion, why does this story of bliss prevail?

There's one last story I'd like us to address – the idea that becoming a parent will be our redemption. It's easy to see why we might form this story – even in our unconscious mind – because usually the images that we see of parents and families show happy people doing sensible things. So we might assume, somewhere and somehow, that we will become those happy, sensible people when we become parents. There might have been other times in your life when you've had that experience. That hope that something will shift because you've done the thing – passed the exam, or got the job, or married the person, or moved into the home – but then you wake up the next day and you're still the same person. We carry ourselves into our parenting too – our whole, human selves. We're still the same people we've always been, and our children won't bring us redemption. In fact, often they bring us face to face with our darkest parts.

I could go on, but I think you get my point.

Can we agree that the story has become really quite complicated? That *your* story of becoming a parent is incredibly complex and multilayered, influenced by your background, culture, religion, financial situation, relationships, community, work, sexuality, gender, race, fertility, your experience of pregnancy and birth, and so much more?

Could we also agree that not examining these stories and their influences on us can create confusion, discomfort and even harm? That holding on to the oversimplified stories we are so often told can make us feel different, or isolated, or somehow just wrong?

What do you think? Shall we let them go?

Blimey, we're only in Chapter 1 and we've thrown out the whole story of parenting so far. Don't worry, we're going to start replacing it soon.

Your Story

This might be a point where you want to pause and think about some of the ideas we've talked about so far. You might want to jot some ideas down in a journal, or on your phone, or use the following questions as a discussion point with a partner, co-parent, friend or member of your family.

- Where did you get your ideas about parenting from?
- When did you decide you wanted to be a parent?
- Was it an active decision or a more passive one?
- What influences have you brought to your parenting journey? Individually – both in your body and your mind – in your family, your community or from the wider society?
- How have those influences affected your decision making and feelings about being a parent?

And maybe a little deeper – now that you're starting to think about this: do you have any questions about why?

- Why did you internalise some of those stories, often without question?
- Did you come up against obstacles created by those stories because of your personal situation, choices or feelings?
- Do aspects of that story still hold true for you?

Is there anything else you might want to find out about now that you're asking these questions? For example:

- That idea that you think you got from your religious or cultural background – do you want to go and find out if it's true? (Just a note – cultural background refers to the customs and behaviours of the group you grew up in, regardless of where that was or how similar or different it was to others around you.)

- That idea about the role you play in your family – does that still fit for you?
- The missing chapters about what happens after you get married, are there any other narratives you want to explore?
- Do you have other questions or thoughts related to what you're reading? Write them all down.

And let's widen it out a bit to include some others too:

- Who might you ask these questions to?
- Where might you explore some of these ideas a little further?
- Do you want anyone else to join you on this journey, who can expand on some of your answers? Siblings who you might talk to about their memories of childhood, parents or caregivers who can give you insight into your heritage, friends who might remember your earlier values?

Head spinning a bit after all that? You can go down multiple paths and it might feel a bit overwhelming at times. I could spend the rest of my life trying to understand the nuance of my racial and cultural heritage and how that has influenced me and how that, in turn, influences my parenting. You could too. People devote entire careers to understanding just one of those areas.

So, if you are feeling a bit overwhelmed by the story of parenting opening up for you, then take a pause and let things settle again. We're going to start writing a new story soon. The unravelling is the hardest bit. But as we do clear away some of those old stories, you might also notice a little bit of space opening up, to create new ideas. It might all be a bit uncomfortable, and that's to be expected. We humans don't like change, in fact we often fight really hard against it. And we like the world to feel simple, so breaking apart some of the foundations you've been built upon might make you feel a bit wobbly. You might want to put this away and never come back to it. But I'd encourage you to stay with me.

As we say goodbye to some of those myths and fairy tales, take a long slow breath through your nose and a big loud sigh out through an open mouth. Scrunch your face up tight and then let it all relax. Give your jaw a wiggle. You could put your feet onto a cold tiled floor, or close your eyes for a few moments. Go on a wander for a little while, and come back to me when you're ready. I'm not going anywhere.

CHAPTER 2

What Is a 'Parent'?

'It's not so much what you do, as what you mean.'

E. Nesbit, *The Railway Children*

Hi. How are you doing?
If you had to describe yourself as the main character or characters in this story, where would you start? What does it mean, to you, to be a 'Parent'?

Perhaps you've wedded yourself to one of the many, media-generated parenting 'genres' . . . a gentle parent, stay-at-home parent, ethical parent. Or maybe you even follow a particular parenting approach or expert, and you're a Montessori parent, an attachment parent, a Gina Ford parent. Often, in the early years of parenting, we look for a group to fit into when we are drowning in an ocean of novelty. This idea that we have to choose a strategy has become so deeply embedded in our thinking that the National Childbirth Trust (the UK's largest parents' charity) even has an article helping you choose your camp.

Or maybe you think about your qualities, your characteristics. Perhaps calm and kind, gentle, shouty, fun, critical, creative, loving, bored, chaotic (I bet you started with one of the negative ones).

What else?

Who are you? Other than the influences that we talked about in the previous chapter, who is the complex, multifaceted human holding this book in their hands?

For example, do you have any paid employment? What's that like? What do you do? How do you do it? Why did you choose to do it, if you had a choice? How does your employment impact on you as a parent? Or maybe you don't have a job that brings you an income at the moment and your main job is to raise children. How do you feel about your role? How did you make that choice, if it was a choice? What did you do before you had children? What did that teach you?

Or even, what music are you into? What does that say about you? How does music influence you as a parent, if at all?

Or maybe you're really into mountain biking and you've struggled to figure out how you can be a 'mountain biker' and a parent. Maybe you've had to let it go, or maybe you've worked out a way that you can get some mountain bike time in without it seeming to affect family life too much, or maybe you end up having arguments about mountain biking with your partner.

These seemingly small day-to-day things make up so much of who we are and the countless small decisions we might make in our parenting.

- What happened to the you that you were before you became a parent?
- Who is the 'old you' that you sometimes consider returning to, but can never quite figure out how?
- Do you miss that 'old you'? What were they into? What did they value?
- What have you brought from that pre-parent self into the 'you' that you are today?

This is the thing that I love most about my job. We can often think of ourselves as solid objects, right? Like, here I am. I. Am.

Emma. This is me. This is how I present myself to the world. But then as soon as you dig in a little, you realise there are layers upon layers upon layers. Even how we present to the world. To some people I'm Emma, to others I'm Mum (or, most accurately, 'Muuuuuuuuum'), to others I'm Dr Svanberg, to a few people I'm Spamburger, Emski and Spanners (don't ask). How I am when I'm alone in my home is different from how I am with my school friends, and with my children, and with my partner, and with my parents, and with my sibling, and with my work colleagues. When people come to me for therapy they may come with a quite specific problem, but over time we might end up talking about their schooldays, or their political beliefs, or their nightmares. Because we are not simple. And we shouldn't be treated as such.

In fact, we're not solid objects at all. Often we wear many masks and costumes. There might be versions that the rest of the world sees, but when you shut the front door a different character might emerge, and when you get into bed at night perhaps there's another version of you. And sometimes we can wonder who we are behind these masks, and wish that someone would help us take them off.

Behind the Mask

It can feel difficult to imagine ourselves as performing, but of course we all do. And it is in getting to know what's behind our masks that we can begin to understand how we come to our parenting.

As you read this, what are you bringing? How does your body feel, right now? What experiences of other parenting information are you carrying in the reading of this book? What concerns about what you'll read?

Where else is your mind at the moment? Are you fully here or are you also thinking about the food you are eating as you read, the deadline you really should be working towards, the task you need to do later, or when your own children might need you next? Or perhaps it's hard to focus because the need for things to change, now, makes it hard to do so.

And underneath that? How does it feel to talk about how you are feeling? What happens to you and your body when you start to pay attention to it? Is it something you're well practised at, or does it make you feel uncomfortable?

What do you hold in your body about the topic of parenting? What comes to your mind when I start to ask you about parenting? What guilt are you bringing to the pages of this book – the mistakes made, the words shouted.

Pause.

How does that feel now?

What I don't want to do is give you a load of information without encouraging you to think about how it might fit for you. Because anyone can follow parenting advice when they don't have anything else to do but parent. It's easy to be attuned when all you have to do is be attuned to one child, and you don't have to work, or do household chores, or wash yourself, or sleep, or look after their siblings, or phone your friend back, or figure out how to pay the gas bill. And if I don't talk about how complicated parenting can really be, I run the risk of creating yet another one of those stories, and writing yet another parenting book that leaves you feeling you're missing some trick that makes it all easier.

Because the point of all this is – it's not easy. But that doesn't mean you're doing it wrong. Maybe the one story we need to let go of the most is the idea that parenting is supposed to be easy. Relationships are hard, and our relationships with our children are often the hardest of all, because they matter so much to us.

You might be feeling a little raw after being unmasked, but I want to reassure you that I have no intention of stripping you down and leaving you feeling unprotected. Sometimes we hold on to some of these stories because they can feel like armour to us. So, if we hold on to a story like 'a good parent always gives their children a kiss before bed', then we can feel proud of ourselves even on the worst of days because we managed to uphold that story. We can ignore the bits that didn't make us feel like such a good parent. And, often, one of the stories we hold is 'good parents cope with everything'. So you might feel a bit worried about looking at this all more closely because what happens if it is painful, or difficult, and what happens then if you suddenly feel like you can't cope? If you find something you weren't expecting? We can be so scared of opening up these ideas, examining these stories, because we have depended on them for so long.

So, just a word of reassurance again that we're going to take it slowly. That we'll keep checking in with each other, and that it's OK for you to pace yourself if you need to. And, even if you find out things about yourself you weren't expecting, there will be a part of you that has always known they were there and will be relieved that you're finally looking at them.

Let's just check in to see how this has all landed.

- Is there a part of you that has perked up, pleased to be noticed?
- Have cogs started turning somewhere else as you realise that something influenced you that you'd never even considered? You might be feeling excited to find out more, or perhaps a little wary of what else is going to be uncovered.

As I'll do at the end of each part, I'm now going to ask you three questions. I'd encourage you to take some time to think them through, write about them or talk about them with someone you trust.

1. How are you feeling? (How is your heart rate, your energy levels, how do you feel in your body? And how are your emotions? Are you feeling anxious, sad, excited, curious, something else?)
2. What has reading Part I raised for you? (In terms of information, ideas, memories, feelings?)
3. What one thing would you like to remember from these chapters?

And, before we say goodbye to this section, take a long breath in through your nose and then a slow breath out through pursed lips like you're breathing through a straw. Try that five times, slowing it down each time if you can.

PART II

Mapping Out Your Story

CHAPTER 3

Your Parenting Map

'Not all those who wander are lost.'

J.R.R. Tolkien, *The Fellowship of the Ring*

W e've got to know some of the myths and legends that you've carried into your parenting. In stories, as well as in children's play, legends often cover whole fantasy worlds. And there's often a bit at the beginning where our hero finds a map, which will lead to something special. Treasure, a sleeping princess, a new kingdom.

We've already established that our hero is a flawed one, our map is made up of psychological concepts, our treasure is a better understanding of ourselves and our children, and that this map will get altered many times along your journey. Let's start to figure out the parenting map you've been given and how you might want to redraw it.

We're going to roll out that soft parchment and start planning this adventure that we are going to take together, starting with looking at some of the areas on your map from your early childhood.

Before we take a look, though, we might have to address the door that you may have just slammed in my face.

I'm not sure what that might look like for you. Maybe you started to get a bit distracted, or fidgety, or maybe you felt confused or irritated, maybe started flicking forward to the next chapters impatient to get to the point. Because, as much as we might want to understand ourselves, it can also feel like a scary thing to do. We keep those doors closed, because we're working pretty well without looking at the skeletons behind them. This is why people don't come to therapy even when it could be transformative (well, that and it's often very hard to find good therapy that suits you and is affordable). It's why we talk about *The Real Housewives* or football in the pub instead of the things that keep us awake at night. Because we don't live in a culture where we really look at each other, and allow ourselves to be seen. We put lots of masks in the way, in fact, to stop people (including ourselves) from being able to truly see us.

So let's address some of the fears that might have come up for you already. It might not feel like fear, it might feel like distraction or irritation, but if you just breathe for a moment and let some thoughts come floating up, what's there?

They might look like . . .

- Am I going to find out my childhood wasn't as good as I think it was?
- Is this going to impact on my relationship with my own parents/caregivers?
- What if she confirms that I really am a terrible parent?
- What if I read this and I have to work harder and I just don't have the resources to do that?
- What if I get really emotional and then I stop being able to cope?
- This makes me feel uncomfortable, and I just want to feel happy.

Or they might look a bit different to that. Maybe you've read this and you're feeling like this doesn't resonate at all. All of your feelings are welcome here and maybe later on it will resonate in a different way. Just stick with me a bit longer.

We'll get to some of those fears in a while but first I'm going to remind you why we're doing this, so we can continue with a sense of purpose.

Why are we here? Because, in knowing yourself – in stripping away some of those layers and facing some of those fears – you can connect with yourself. And when you have connected with yourself, you will find it so much easier to connect with your child. And when you connect with your child, parenting them feels much more straightforward. And when they grow up and have children, and read this paragraph, it won't make sense to them because they already feel connected to themselves and others. And that's what we're aiming for.

Let's think that through a little more. Because in many ways what we're going to be creating together is a love story. Even though parenting is a story with many twists and turns, at its core (which we so often forget) is the greatest love story of our lives. Not a Hollywood romance, and one that we don't ever fully see outside of our own homes, but a very different love story to those we were raised with. So let's figure out why we're doing this – probably it's for some little humans.

You can scribble here or (if you haven't already) you can start jotting notes down in a notebook to look back over later on. Having an intention – a 'why' – will help you keep going if it feels uncomfortable reading at any point and you want to walk away from it.

Why are you reading this book?
What is your hope?
Who are you reading it for?
Why does it feel important now?

You might want to ask yourself those 'why' questions a few more times (this is called the downward arrow technique and it can really help us get to the heart of our beliefs and ideas). For example:

47

Why do you hope that?
For what reason?
What does that suggest?
Why?

Ask yourself these questions until you get to something that feels true for you.

Perhaps it's 'because I want to really enjoy the time I have with my children', or 'I deserve to know myself better', or 'I want the beauty of seeing and being seen', or 'I don't want to live with such regret', or 'I feel determined to break cycles that have been in my family', or simply 'I want more love in my home'. Or perhaps it's completely different to all of those – whatever you've written is right for you.

Looking at Your Map

You might already feel you have a parenting map that you're happy to follow; maybe you just want to know if there are some landmarks you've missed or paths to explore. Or you might be hoping to clearly change direction, redrafting whole sections of the map because of new discoveries you've made. Or maybe you want to shred the map you were given, rip it into tiny pieces, burn those pieces and start completely from scratch. Whether you're in familiar lands or entering uncharted territories, let's be adventurers for a little while.

To make sure we do this safely, I'd like to bring two things along with us. Your guide, and your resting place.

Your Guide

When you're exploring, it can really help to have a guide. Someone who isn't afraid to get lost, who can help steer you back to the path, and pull you back up again if you fall.

Obviously, I'm going to be a guide of sorts. I'll direct you in exploring your map and creating a new one. A co-cartographer, so to speak. But we need someone to hold your hand too.

In Chapter 1 I mentioned parenting ideals. And I said that your ideal might be based on the kind of parent you would have loved to have had but didn't . . . or maybe an amalgamation of some of the elements of your parents or caregivers, and other people who cared for you – teachers, neighbours, family members, characters from books, TV or films. Can we flesh them out a little?

By the way, there's a reason you're not choosing your real parent or caregiver here and I'd rather you choose someone who isn't actually real. That's because real people are flawed, and make mistakes, and sometimes you get irritated with them, and sometimes they can hurt you badly. So if you choose someone you know, even someone you usually get on with, and you need to bring them to mind for comfort but you've just had a weird conversation with them, you won't find them as supportive as they need to be. So we're going to create an imaginary guide, someone who is just purely here to help you navigate this journey and look after you when you need it.

Do you have someone in mind? Or a sense of a someone? It may not be an actual person, it might be a mythical creature, or an object, or just a sort of feeling. What sort of qualities does this person or thing have?

Often when I do this exercise with clients in therapy, they choose someone kind and caring but also firm and boundaried, who gives them that sense that they are in a safe pair of hands. The kind of person who you could call with a burst tyre and they would not only know what to do but would also get you home and give you a cup of tea and put their arm around your shoulders.

Have a read through this next passage but then close your eyes at the end and see if you can get an image of them in your mind. I know you might be tempted to rush through this bit but really

49

try to slow down here and feel this person or character beside you. Think about how you would feel in their presence.
Write those words down somewhere, so that as we go through this book you can come back to them. Maybe even on the inside cover so they are always close by.

> Is this the kind of person you would choose?
> What qualities feel really important to you in this guide?

Some people find that this exercise brings them comfort, but for others the idea of bringing to mind a safe and caring person can be incredibly difficult. This might be because you just haven't ever had that experience and it's really hard to imagine what it's like. It might be that you've learned

> Would they have a particular smell? If they gave you a hug or soothed you in some way, how would it feel? What might they wear? What would their voice sound like? How would you feel when you heard their voice?
>   If you were angry, how would this ideal caregiver react?
>   If you were sad, how would they respond?
>   If you felt uncertain, or unsettled – what might they do?
>   What soothing and comforting words might they say to you?

to harden yourself to soothing, because it wasn't available to you or because you were mocked when you needed comfort, so you've learned to feel a bit cynical about it. It might also be because you had a parent or caregiver who could be soothing sometimes but absent, critical or frightening at other times.

When these things happen to us as children, soothing can get tied up in something that feels a bit scary. So, if this is you, I'm sorry that you experienced that and that it is hard to access something comforting as a result. We will be exploring that a bit more as we continue, and you might find that you can come back to this exercise later on and find it a little easier.

But, for now, that doesn't mean that you don't have a guide. You might have learned to depend on yourself and only on yourself. And you've kept yourself safe all this time, and done a fine job of it. So you can be your own guide here, too, if you need to.

If you'd like to, you might want to picture an object that you associate with this guide. If something springs to mind, then see if you can find a real-life object that you might be able to carry in your pocket, hang around your neck or leave beside your bed. Something that you can take out and hold in your hand as you're reading, or in moments when you're in need of a bit of parenting yourself.

TESTING OUT YOUR GUIDE

One of the things we do sometimes to test out the above exercise in therapy is to try out a small irritation to see whether there are any tweaks that might need to be made to your guide. It means that we can make sure they are right for you before anything comes up where you might be calling upon them.

So, can you call to mind something that you have found a bit annoying lately? Something just a bit niggly – maybe a phone call that made your blood pressure rise, someone cutting you up in traffic, a pushy WhatsApp message from someone . . . Now, still holding that incident in your mind, will you bring up your guide? Think about what they might say to you. Sit in the glow of their care for a short time – what does that do to your body, your thoughts and your feelings?

Having done that, is there anything you'd like to change about that guide? Maybe you need to make their voice a little deeper? Or their hug a little tighter? Or make them a little taller?

By now, hopefully you have a guide who feels right for you, to accompany you on this journey.

How does it feel in your body when you remember this?

What do you notice, in your heart rate, in your limbs, in your head, in your fingers and toes?

What sort of thoughts come into your mind as you remember this event?

To really set this in stone, you might want to spend a bit more time with your guide before you move on – writing about them, drawing or painting a picture, whatever you would like to do to strengthen the idea of them. You might want to bring your guide with you as you go about your day. Just imagine them alongside you, a companion to offer a little support when you need it.

Your Resting Place

When we go on a journey we also need somewhere to rest. Somewhere that feels safe, cosy and calm. This might be a place that you found comforting in your early childhood, it might be a place you have good memories of, or it could be a totally made-up place. This is based on an exercise that is used in both trauma-focused Cognitive Behavioural Therapy and another trauma therapy called Eye Movement Desensitisation Reprogramming (we psychologists LOVE a fancy name).

Just be aware that it should be a place that feels non-threatening. For some people, what comes to mind first might be a place where you felt safe because you were hiding. But if this is at all associated with a sense of threat in your body then notice that, because it won't be as soothing as we'd like. Sometimes our calmest places are those that we imagine, especially if we've had a lot of difficult experiences. So it's totally fine if your place is lying on a cloud, or on a tropical island you've never been to. As long as it's somewhere – real or imaginary – you feel safe and content.

Got somewhere in mind? Again, it doesn't have to be super clear, just a vague idea.

Read through the next passage and then see if you feel able to close your eyes and go off on this journey.

If this is a place that you have a photo of, or can download a photo of from the internet, then I'd suggest that you do that. You can even put it up somewhere in your home, or save it as your screensaver.

Now, remember that irritating incident we talked about before? Will you just bring that back up to the front of your mind. How does that feel? Ugh, a bit annoying isn't it? Hold that feeling in your body but then get ready to go back to that resting place. Close your eyes, and off you go – remembering to use all of your senses to really land there. Spend a bit of time there and come back when you're ready.

Back? How did that feel? What did that do to your body, when you arrived at your resting place? Was there anything that you needed to change? Any colours that needed to be turned up? Or sounds that could have the volume raised? Make any little tweaks you might need so that your resting place feels like sinking into a hot bath at the end of a long walk.

Put down any baggage you're carrying and sink down onto the nearest surface. Where are you? What's going on around you? Is there anyone there with you?

How does it feel being here, in this place?

What are you sitting on? What does that feel like in your body? Settle a little deeper into the surface beneath you. What are your feet on? Just focus on them for a moment.

What's the temperature like? What does it feel like against your skin?

What can you hear? Tune in to those sounds.

Can you smell anything? Anything else?

And if you reach around, what can you touch? How does that feel? Anything else nearby you'd like to touch?

Do you have a taste in your mouth?

Have a good look around you, really notice what you see. Turn up all the colours in this image so that it becomes even more vivid and vibrant.

How does it feel in your body to be here? Where do you feel that, in your body? Really tune in to that feeling and let it expand in your body.

Sit here for as long as you like, enjoying being in this place. And remember that you can come back at any time. Then say goodbye, knowing that you can come back whenever you like.

The Quick Version

Did you do either of those exercises? Or just skim through them?

When we're in a state of stress – which we often are – even the idea of pausing and reflecting can feel like too much. You might want to ask yourself why you're speeding through this, and whether you might allow yourself a little more space when reading. But, if not, here's another quick exercise to bring you a sense of safety and comfort in your body if you find that anything that you read makes you feel upset or uncomfortable.

The Blame Game

One last thing before we look at your map. As you're getting to know about what's on there, you might be tempted to do three things.

Take a quick look around the room that you're in and look for circles. How many circles do you see?

And how about squares? Can you see any squares? Where? How many?

Perhaps you'd prefer to look around and spot things in your favourite colour.

Or simply say to yourself the day, date and time.

That's it. Just bringing us back into the here and now. You, as a whole person, sitting here reading, not lost in the past or lost in your thoughts.

If anything that you read makes you feel like putting the book down and forgetting about it - look for circles and squares and then see how you feel.

Firstly, blame your parents or caregivers for mistakes that they made, or things that they did or didn't do that are having an impact on how you feel today.

Secondly, avoid looking too deeply into this because you don't want to think badly of your parents and caregivers and are worried that you could end up blaming them, which would make you feel super guilty.

Thirdly, blame yourself for not knowing this stuff before now, and making mistakes with your own kids.

One thing I'd like you to keep in your mind is that people, as a general rule, do their best with the cards they are dealt. Blame can feel helpful, because it gets discomfort out of our own body and places it in someone else's. This can make us feel absolved, for a moment, but it doesn't help us make changes. Shame might make us more likely to make up for things, but we can also get stuck in a spiral of self-criticism. So, sure, be angry you didn't always get what you needed, feel sad that you did things you regret. Then thank yourself for being here and reading this so you can work some of that stuff out. You could even use your guide to tell you some lovely words to help you do that if you need to.

Another thing to remember is that we can reflect on the impact that circumstances and relationships had on us – we might even be angry for a little while about this – but that once we have found a way to resolve this for ourselves we can find that our relationships actually improve. With our parents and caregivers, this often looks like letting go of the more childish parts of our relationship with them and meeting them as fellow adults.

Often blame (for ourselves and others) also comes because we have that feeling that they, or we, should have known better. But this is a journey, one that never really ends, with a map that might change throughout our lives. Everyone worked with the maps they had at the time. And you're the one who is choosing to redraw the lines. Sometimes we redraw maps not just for us and our children, but our parents and ancestors too. And that's a brilliant thing.

The next few chapters are going to take you through some of the key ideas about what makes you who you are as a person and as a parent. Some of what comes up for you might feel difficult. We're doing this because we're examining what you're bringing to your parenting journey from your own history – because without knowing yourself it's very hard to really know your child.

As always, take your time with it and remember you can return to your resting place, or look for your favourite colour around you, or put the book down and grab a glass of cold water. And please don't just struggle through; pause if you need to. The slower we take this, the more meaningful it will be. Feelings of guilt, shame, hurt and sadness might come up, so let them be here. If you can treat them as visitors coming to bring us messages about your experiences, rather than unwelcome guests you need to push away, it might feel a little easier.

CHAPTER 4

Stories from Your History

'I can only note that the past is beautiful because one never realises an emotion at the time. It expands later, and thus we don't have complete emotion about the present, only about the past.'

Virginia Woolf, *The Diary of Virginia Woolf*

Right. I know people don't really like looking into their childhood, and it's a bit of a therapy cliché that everything comes back to your parents. But, really, how could it be any other way?

You're not an adult who just became an adult one day and let go of everything that went before. You're a whole human who has lived for years, and each one of those years and the experiences you had during them and the people you met have all got you here today.

There are parts of us, and parts of our past, that we might have tried really hard to forget about or ignore. But they're there, whether we like it or not, and they sneak up on you when you're least expecting it. One of the things I love about clinical psychology is that our understanding is grounded in lifespan development – from cradle to grave and everything in between. Because it all matters, and shapes who we are.

What can be so unsettling about pregnancy and early

parenting is that we can suddenly find ourselves face to face with some of those earlier parts of us. We might have felt we've left those bits behind, but then something is reignited in us.

Why is this?

The Swamp of Ghosts

In the corner, hidden behind a fence, you might notice a no-go zone that is hard to see. Here lie your ghosts and – because these are the bits we generally stay away from – we're going to start with them.

As we saw in Chapter 2, often we have an idea of who we'll be when we become a parent. Perhaps we'll magically let go of the bits of us that don't fit with our idea of what a good parent is. We won't carry forward the things our parents did that we don't want to repeat. We often don't have a plan for how we will *actually* do that – as we've established, a lot of this is based on fantasy stories – but we often know what we *don't* want to be.

But then, at some point, we just . . . are. We become the parent we thought we wouldn't be. A phrase slips out as an echo of our mother's voice. Or maybe we just feel a feeling we don't want to feel towards our child, or ourselves.

And then we can feel so ashamed that we even had that feeling. Disappointed in ourselves, and angry. We want so much to do things well, and then something slips in unnoticed and takes us over for a moment.

Or maybe we work so hard to be that ideal parent that we are aspiring to be – and we feel like we've got it all sorted . . . and then we step on a wooden train or the baby poos all over the bed or the kids are playing ninjas instead of getting dressed and . . . the façade falls down.

It might not even feel as clear as that – maybe more that you slipped out of yourself for a moment, or that you reacted in ways that you didn't quite expect but you're not exactly sure why. Or feeling sudden fear, or helplessness, at a time when you're 'meant' to know what you're doing.

These are your ghosts. The ghosts that creep into your body and sometimes fly out of your mouth, saying phrases you thought you'd never say, feeling feelings you'd hoped you'd never feel, your face falling into an expression that made your heart stop as a child, your hand gripping a wrist in a way that you remember feeling on your own skin.

Sometimes ghosts show up more in our babies or children than in our own actions. Like when they're asleep and you're thinking about them, perhaps you think of them as a sweet little creature doing their best to navigate this difficult world. But, when they don't do as you expect, suddenly you find yourself thinking thoughts about them that you don't really want to have – that they are manipulating you, or just need to be taught a lesson, or that they are difficult, or that they are spoilt, or trying it on . . . or the myriad other things we think and say about our children when the chips are down.

You might not have noticed this for yourself, but maybe a partner has pointed it out to you? That they can't bear it when you sound like your dad? Or that sometimes you remind them so much of your gran? Or that thing that you did – that wasn't quite what you'd talked about when you discussed having children. Sometimes we are so determined that we won't be haunted that we don't see our own ghosts.

For many people, these ghosts intrude for a moment and we might just notice them and let them slip on by. We might even meet them with humour – 'Oh man, my mum used to say just that!'

But in some families, it can feel like the ghosts have taken over completely, that we're possessed by the patterns of generations past. We might simultaneously recognise that we are acting in a way that we don't want to, while feeling unable to do it any other way. We might know on one level that our child simply needs us, while raging at them for asking something of us. Like an internal battle where we are trying to exorcise a ghost from our past. And while we battle away, it can feel almost impossible to see that there is an actual baby or child or children in front of us – instead we are blinded by the ghosts that live inside us.

Whether they show up every day, or just on occasion, let's bring those ghosts into the light.

Is it OK to dredge this swamp, and make it all a little clearer? You might want to call upon your guide to help you to do this exercise, and remind yourself that you are an adult now, and have control over your own life.

- What are the things about your own experience of being parented that you don't wish to repeat? (There might be many, there might be few.)
- Why not? Why don't you wish to repeat them?
- How do you remember feeling when these things happened to you as a child?
- In your parenting journey so far, have there been moments when you have repeated these patterns (where you have been haunted by these ghosts)?
- How do you think your child/ren felt in these moments. (Hi, guilt! Do you mind just stepping to one side for now?)
- If so, what have you done when this has happened? How have you felt? How have you responded to your feelings? (Ignoring them also counts as a response.)

Pause. Breathe. Welcome back.

The Ghosts We Feel but Can't See

Sometimes our ghosts are really hard to see, because they are not experiences that we remember but more experiences that we hold in our bodies. Resmaa Menakem described this beautifully in his book about transgenerational racial trauma, *My Grandmother's Hands*, writing:

> Our bodies have a form of knowledge that is different from our cognitive brains. This knowledge is typically experienced as a felt sense of constriction or expansion, pain or ease, energy or numbness. Often this knowledge is stored in our bodies as wordless stories about what is safe and what is dangerous.

Our ghosts might come from experiences that we had before we had language to be able to understand them; they might be experiences we had in the womb. They might even be experiences that happened long before we were born but that have been encoded in our bodies through our genes and then laid down even stronger through our experiences. While we know our experiences growing up can shape our later life, we also know that even our experiences from conception to birth can affect us through the information we receive at this time and what this information tells us about the world we are entering into. More so, we are now aware that the experiences of our ancestors can impact on us through the information that is passed down through our very DNA. This research – such as Rachel Yehuda's suggestion that descendants of Holocaust survivors carry a higher sensitivity to stress and anxiety disorders – demonstrates the way that trauma and oppression can ripple through a family for generations. Even where parenting influences (such as parental stress) are accounted for, we find that these ghosts are passed on through our bodies too, until someone pauses to bring them into the light.

One of the mechanisms that could explain this is the discovery that the HPA axis – the connections in our brain that are linked to our body's response to stress – is extremely responsive to our experiences. So if our great-grandparents experienced high stress, this might pass on a heightened response to stress in our grandparents, and if their own environment leads to this being 'switched on', this sensitivity can then be passed on to our parents and then on to us. And if we figure that out, we can take steps to lower the stress in our own bodies and begin to reverse that cycle for the generations that follow us.

We humans are primed for survival. Our ancestors' experiences leave 'markers' in our own bodies so that we can keep ourselves safe. The trouble is that our vigilance to threat might remain even when the environment around us is a safe one, and this might cause us problems in our present situation. If we are wired to scan for danger, we tend to see it everywhere.

- How do you think that the experiences of your parents, grandparents and ancestors may have influenced you?
- Do you have a history of traumatic experiences in your family story? This may be objectively traumatic, such as war, displacement or natural disaster, or more personally traumatic, such as abuse, neglect or violence. How do you think this might have influenced you today?
- Do you see any ways that this has been passed on to your own children (for example, a preoccupation with their safety, parts of your own heritage that you feel have been silenced, worries about them that are based on your own experiences of the world)?
- How do you feel about this? Has this been part of your parenting journey so far? In what way?
- Do these experiences and ancestral stories have an impact on your daily life as a parent now? Perhaps through continued relationships with your family of origin, or through the impact in your own body?

Carrying Our Angels

If you look a little closer, you'll also see what look like fireflies around that swamp. These are your angels. They exist in the positive relationships we experienced and our caregivers experienced too – the things that we want to repeat and want our own children to feel. Those moments where we felt deeply cared for, understood and secure. Where we felt filled up, whole and held in someone's mind – whether or not that person was a parent or caregiver. We might have many memories of these times, or only one or two. Do any of these moments spring to your mind?

- Can you remember a time you felt really cared for? Even just a moment. This might be someone giving you a kiss on the forehead, or a memory of a soft jumper you were pulled into for a hug, or the kind, concerned expression of a neighbour.
- How does that feel for you to remember that? How does it feel in your body? What thoughts come up for you?

This might be an easy exercise for you; you might have lots of lovely warm memories of times when you felt loved. These might be associated with particular people. Perhaps a smell comes to mind – of your auntie's perfume or the smoke on your father's clothes as he came in from work. Or perhaps you notice touch, the feel of your mother's cool hand on your forehead, the warmth as a blanket was tucked around your shoulders, the pleasure as someone gently ran a brush through your hair.

You might find the exercise difficult – maybe because the memories feel few and far between and that brings up negative emotions of sadness or anger. Or perhaps you don't remember anything at all. You might find it easier in that case just to remember a feeling. All of us, at some point, have had even fleeting moments of feeling close and connected to someone. This might be a kind teacher, or the lady in the local shop who slipped you sweets. See if you can feel that in your body, notice how it feels and see if that jolts any more details about that memory – like who was there, where you were, how old you were, how did you feel, what did you smell, see, touch, hear, taste. And if it's too hard to remember, perhaps think about experiences that you witnessed, family relationships that you aspired to.

- What are the 'angels' you would like to pass on in your own family?
- Are there any experiences that you really enjoyed as a child that you want to replicate in your family? These might be reading a particular book, watching TV on a Saturday night as a family, baking a cake together before a birthday – something that you remember helping you feel loved and safe as a child.
- How do you remember feeling during those times?
- Where does that sit in your body, that feeling?
- Do you think there are moments that your child has that feeling too? What was happening? What stops that from happening more often?
- As you remember these angels, do others come to mind?

Even by identifying those ghosts and angels, you might have a clearer sense of what you want to let go of, and what you want to replace it with.

Our ghosts tend to come from the people who cared for us when we were growing up, and they can feel really painful to look at. Like all scary things, we don't always want to look at them directly – often we want to close our eyes, bury ourselves under the blanket and stick our fingers in our ears. But if you're able to look at them, what do you see? Where do you think those ghosts came from, for your own caregivers? And where might they have come from before that?

Ghosts pass down through generations, unnoticed, until someone decides to pull the blanket down and see what's actually there. It's a hard thing to do, and you could take a moment to notice that this is exactly what you're doing right now. Well done, ghostbuster.

CHAPTER 5

Stories from Your Childhood

'It takes courage to grow up and become who you really are.'

ee cummings

We've explored that swamp and talked about the ghosts and angels from your past, those experiences that you and your ancestors had that you might be carrying into your current parenting. So let's tune in a bit more to how that actually feels for you, what it means to you. And I'm not talking about the you that you are now, in your conscious adult mind, reading this book. I'm talking about the little you who experienced those things, who still exists in your body, fully formed just as they were then.

The Pathways

Just like any good map, this one has pathways criss-crossing all over it. Let's have a look at some of them and how they lead back to little you.

Memory is a tricky thing and we still don't completely understand it and how complex it is. In fact, the more we learn, the more our old understandings crumble. We've tended to see memory as like papers being filed away in a filing cabinet, but actually it's way more complex than that. It's more like pathways. There may be hundreds and thousands of pathways on your map. Some of them are well-trodden and signposted, they have smooth gravel underfoot and lampposts all along them – you can go down them with zero effort. Those are ones labelled things like 'where I go to buy milk' and 'the place I put my dirty clothes'. Others have got a bit overgrown but with a bit of effort and a pair of sturdy boots you can trample down them and get to where you want to be. Those might have signposts for 'holidays by the sea' or 'favourite childhood songs'. With some, you start going down one pathway and, in doing so, a whole set of other pathways get lit up, ready to explore!

Then there are some pathways that you can't even call pathways any more. They've disappeared under brambles and, even though you may have a vague feeling there used to be a path there, it's become pretty impossible to access. That one leading to the things you learned for your school exams, for instance. There might even be a few pathways that we've built walls around, and put up big 'no entry' signs to, because they're a bit dark and we're worried there are wolves down them. Some are covered over, but become lit up all of a sudden when we're reminded of them, even when we're not looking for them (and actually would rather forget they were there). Do you have any like that? Just notice them; we don't need to go down there just yet, but we'll be taking a look a little later on.

To understand who we are, we often look back at our earlier memories, of who we have always been. It's even a cliché, isn't it, that therapists will ask you about your earliest memory. But actually, most people don't remember anything before three to four years of age. Considering all the research telling us that the first 1001 days of a person's life are foundational to their later mental health, that means there's a lot there that we don't understand about ourselves.

There's a good reason for this. We find it hard to articulate memories from our early years because being able to recall memory depends on so many factors – not just the strength of the memory itself and how often that path has been walked down, but also how able we were to use language at that time, and our cognitive abilities when we created that memory.

Yet in early parenting we can sometimes find that memories of our own childhood come flooding back – or that old feelings re-emerge that we thought were long past. There might be moments when all of a sudden – when we are holding our new little baby, or toddler, or faced with our child, teenager or even our adult child or grandchild – we are transported back to the way we felt when we were their age almost as if we were right back there. We might not recognise that this is happening; instead we might feel floored by a whole-body feeling, or surprised at our level of distress, or full of rage that we don't understand.

This can often come, too, when we see our own parents or caregivers interacting with our children. In witnessing them, or experiencing their absence, we begin to access how we ourselves felt when we were cared for by them. Sometimes, when angels are present, this can be a bonding experience, helping us understand our caregivers in a new light.

Sometimes, this brings haunting ghosts and questions of 'How could they have treated me that way?' Those little kids we carry within us can come out longing to be parented again themselves. It can also be super confusing if our caregivers are able to care for our own children with more tenderness than they showed us, leaving us in the very peculiar position of being a bit envious of our own children.

Why is it that suddenly these little kid memories and feelings become so present when we become parents?

I'm no neuroscientist, so my understanding of the ways in which the brain changes during pregnancy and in the postnatal period – for all parents, not just birth mothers – is limited. But this is a period in which our brains dramatically reorganise, due to hormones, new experiences, sleep deprivation and our interactions with our children. Just becoming a parent can 'switch on' the brain changes that need to happen to make us respond to our children, although this happens in different ways for different people depending on a whole host of factors (and can also leave us particularly vulnerable to mental health problems during this time).

When this happens, it's a little bit like lots of pathways that had long grown over suddenly get lit up with big, flashing arrows saying, 'This way!' This may be because just being with a child at the same age as we were when we formed that memory makes it easier to access (something called context-dependent memory recall, where just the close association with a child may open up a pathway to our own childhood memories). It may be because of changes in the hippocampus, an area of the brain linked to memory, in the perinatal period. It may also be that we are more invested in paying attention to memories that previously didn't feel quite so significant.

When I say 'memory', I'm not just talking about those TV scenes we sometimes have playing out in our brains. Sometimes, and especially with those preverbal under-four type memories, they are more like feelings. We might feel suddenly filled with fear when our baby cries, or we might shout out of the blue – having a tantrum to rival our toddler. Or in more complicated ways, we might suddenly be convinced that our baby hates us, or act to resolve a problem we see in our child that is actually more pertinent to an experience we had ourselves. Sometimes memories come as feelings in the body, or a sense, or a phrase being repeated, thanks to those ghosts we talked about already.

Do you mind if we wander down one of those pathways, to find out a bit more about what's at the end of it? To talk to little you? Let's head back to your early childhood.

The Early Childhood Pathway

What does this pathway look like for you? Is it one you've explored many times before? Perhaps you walk it often with your family, reminiscing about past events. It might be well-trodden because you've explored it yourself, with a friend, partner or in therapy. It might feel a little overgrown, because you're an adult now and it's not so relevant to you any more. There might be a huge gate there, padlocked, and guard dogs. Or you might find it hard to spot, in which case just imagine that it's there.

Whatever it looks like for you, I'd like you to imagine it for a moment. Notice what comes up for you, in your body. Use grounding exercises – like breathing, or focusing on the here and now – if you need to, and remember you can go to your resting place whenever you like (see page 53).

We're going to ask your guide to come here too, so just take a moment to get them firmly fixed in your mind, and picture them reaching out a hand to you. They will walk this whole pathway by your side.

If you had a safe, calm childhood you might be feeling a bit impatient at this point, and wondering why we need all of this preparation. For some people, looking back at childhood is a pleasant, everyday experience. There are also many people whose bodies go into a threat response at the very mention of the word 'childhood'. And there are many more sitting on the spectrum in between. I don't know where you lie on that spectrum and it's my job to make sure you stay feeling safe while you're reading this. So, if you are reading this and starting to feel panicky, please listen to your feelings – that's a sign you might need someone real to walk this path with you, not an imaginary guide. You're welcome to keep going if you feel OK doing so, but take it slowly and do a quick skim through of all of the chapters so you know what is coming.

Let's go.

OUR HOME

At the end of this pathway is a home, and it can look however you want it to look. It might be a childhood home, or it might be something imagined. This house represents your early childhood experiences.

You and your guide are going to look at your home together, so have a good look now from the outside.

- Is it warm and welcoming? Or a bit shabby and run-down?
- Are the lights on or off? Is the door open?
- How does it feel to be looking at it? How are you feeling about going in?

Just notice those feelings; they are all welcome.

As you walk through the front door, do any childhood memories come back to you? They may not, but if they do just pause to pay them a little bit of attention. What sort of memories are coming up? How old are you in these memories? Who is in them? How do you feel in them? You might want to stay here a little while before we continue.

THE KITCHEN - THE HEART OF THE HOME

The first room we're going to explore – taking our guide with us – is the kitchen. The kitchen is the heart of the home, the place in which we may gather as a family, a room of good smells, homework done at the table, laughter sharing a meal. It's also a place of tension, where our relationship with food (and often our bodies) is defined, where arguments may have blown up; or it may be a place you remember as empty.

For us, the kitchen is going to represent the feelings that you remember from your earliest experiences, which is going to help us understand what the atmosphere was like at home. I'd like you to sit down in the kitchen – perhaps at a table, or a breakfast bar, or at the counter – and see how it feels to be there.

Just start by noticing what your kitchen looks like, whether there is anyone in it, and how it feels for you to be in it. Is it messy with clutter on the surfaces? Or pristine and clean? Or somewhere in the middle? Is it daytime or evening? What's the temperature like in there? Anything cooking that you can smell?

And what do you notice in your body when you start to think about how you felt as a child? Feelings of warmth, perhaps in your tummy? Or is there a bit of trepidation? Maybe you're starting to feel anxious, in which case take a long slow breath and then sigh out through your mouth and remind yourself that you're an adult, reading a book, and that you get to decide what happens next.

As you start to tune in to the emotional experience of being a child, I'd like to share a bit of research that you may have heard of which helps us to bring a framework to these experiences. I'm just going to remind you that we are reflecting on your own childhood here but this may also resonate with how you parent now. Notice the feelings that come up, and remember that you're here to learn and possibly do some unlearning too.

THE ~~THREE~~ FIVE BEARS OF PARENTING

Back in the 1960s, clinical psychologist Diana Baumrind outlined three parenting styles, all centred around the way that power and responsiveness appear in parenting. They are still used to understand parenting today, although they have since been expanded to five.

I think of these a little bit like the story of Goldilocks and the Three Bears. Seeing as we're in the kitchen, let's imagine there are bowls of porridge on the table. I'll use the word 'parent' here but this may be another caregiver, one who parented

73

but was not your parent. And, while these may not have been how we always experienced our parents, usually a parent will have a predominant style.

First we have the authoritarian parent. This porridge is a bit too salty. The authoritarian parent holds all of the power in the parent–child relationship and is not responsive to the needs of their unique child.

This would be a typically strict parent, who is fond of phrases like 'don't speak until you're spoken to, and 'while you're living under my roof, you follow my rules'. There may be warmth, but this is also a parent who expects a high level of discipline in the home, who demands that the child is a responsible contributor to chores, and may use parenting strategies like a naughty step, sending a child to their room or spanking in order to achieve compliance. At the more extreme end, this can become abuse.

Indulgent or permissive parents are the sweet porridge. The first taste can be delicious but it soon becomes apparent that this isn't going to feel great in the long run. This parent is usually very loving and responsive, and allows the child to hold all the power in their relationship. You might hear them say things like 'oh she's just learning to express her anger' while their kid whacks your toddler on the head with a tennis racket. They don't have many rules, structure or routine and generally allow their children to decide the state of play. When, inevitably, they need to encourage a child to moderate their behaviour they will use strategies that continue to give the child control, for example, through reasoning, pleading or a little bit of emotional manipulation, such as 'Oh you don't want to make Mummy feel sad do you?' – hoping to achieve compliance through cooperation not control. Permissive parents may consciously want their child to feel independent but they may also feel afraid of their own potential power as a parent.

For both these parenting styles, conflict or disagreement is not welcomed. For the former, disagreement is suppressed – the parent's word is law. But in the latter, too, disagreement is discouraged through indulging the child.

Authoritative parents are the 'just right' of the porridge world. They try to tune in to what their child needs and respond to it, and power is shared in the relationship. Children are aware of what is expected of them but are supported to meet those expectations, and any demands are negotiated with recognition of the interests of the child and the adult. Authoritative parents might be heard saying things like 'Let's talk it over together,' 'What do you think?' and 'The answer is no, let me tell you why.' Warmth, understanding and acceptance but within clear boundaries are the USP of this parenting style.

Our fourth bowl of porridge is empty, representing the rejecting or neglectful parent. This is a parent who, for a multitude of different reasons, doesn't engage with their child. In this relationship, no one holds the power; instead it is as if the child is simply not there. This is particularly common for parents who may have been neglected themselves, those who are overwhelmed with other demands or those who use substances that leave them disconnected from the world and the people in it.

More recent research has suggested other types of parenting style, most of which still fall into the four bowls we've already discussed. But there is one other that is worth a mention, that of the helicopter parent (aka overparenting or intensive parenting). We're going to come back to this in Chapter 10 but it might also have influenced how you were parented. This has become increasingly popular over the last four decades, particularly during a time of economic prosperity when parents became less concerned about getting food on the table and focused more on the success and achievement of their children. It is reflected in the activities children do – with playing outdoors independently being replaced by a parent-scheduled play date – as well as in the amount of time parents spend with their children, which in the USA translates as an increase of 1 hour and 45 minutes each day between 1975 and 2005.

The helicopter parent is one who is both involved and responsive but, unlike the authoritative parent, continues to stay highly involved when – developmentally – children begin to need more independence. This is the parent who hovers over the porridge bowl, then ends up spoon-feeding the porridge into their child's mouth even when they become an adult and – crucially – never allows them to experience hunger. Helicopter parenting comes from a positive place of wanting a child to succeed and be happy, but doesn't allow emerging independence or the experience of learning from their own mistakes.

As we start to get a laser focus here on the parent–child relationship I just want to widen our view outside of the kitchen and remember the world outside that house. Often research is presented in all-or-nothing ways – that you as parent are x, and this is creating y outcome for your child. It's all about the parent–child duo (usually mother–child). However, Baumrind herself emphasised the role of society in raising children: both in terms of the norms of a community but also in how involved the state is in supporting parents. Newer research has emphasised the two-way relationship of parenting styles, suggesting that parents may change their approach according to the needs of their child. And what about the cultural context we live in? Parenting styles relate to cultural expectations, not just individual needs or responsibilities. The impact of parenting style on children is moderated by what the child deems normal in the community in which they live and by different goals for parents (e.g. in one area the goal might be teaching a child how to avoid danger, whereas in another, even only a few miles away, the goal might be going to a prestigious university).

I wonder how you feel reading this, and whether you recognise echoes of your own childhood as we examine these bowls of porridge. You might feel like you take from different bowls in your own parenting. While we might change our parenting behaviours day to day and even moment to moment, generally we will have one bowl that we were given regularly – and one that we serve up to our own children.

One of the key ideas when learning about parenting styles is the idea of power – who is in control and why? Control can be defined as both behavioural control (defining rules and encouraging a child to stick to them) and psychological control (intruding on a child's thoughts, and using strategies like manipulation to influence behaviour). As you can see, there is a sweet spot where control is shared between the child and parent but, in different ways, children are often up against a defined image of who they are meant to be and how they are meant to behave.

- Who held the power in your home growing up, and what impact did that have on you?
- Was there warmth in your home? How do you know?
- How do you think you were usually responded to? For example, with curiosity, concern, impatience, withdrawal?
- Do you think your individual needs – you, as a person – were taken into account by the people who raised you? What did that leave you with?
- Was your experience similar or different to that of other children in your area? In what ways? What did this mean to you?
- Let's bring your own children in for a moment. What's the power balance like with your own child/children?
- How does this feel for you?

Don't forget, if this is bringing up things that are leaving you unsettled, about your past or present, you can either go to your resting place for a few moments to reset yourself again, or perhaps you could ask your guide to share some supportive and reassuring words. If you're feeling heavy, you might want to close your eyes, put your hand on your heart and repeat those words out loud. Or you could reach out your arms and lean your head and shoulders back a little, opening up your chest and breathing into it, then sighing out as you straighten up.

WASHING UP

Let's clear those porridge bowls off the table and scrape them out. Give those bowls a slow wash in some warm, soapy water and let yourself stand there for a moment. We're in the kitchen, so imagine you can feel cold tiles against your feet. Lift up your toes, and slowly set them back down again. Take a long breath in, and a longer breath out.

We're going to head a little further into your childhood home. Ready?

CHAPTER 6

Stories from Your Babyhood

'We carry accumulation of years in our bodies and on our faces, but generally our real selves, the children inside, are still innocent and shy as magnolias.'

Maya Angelou, *Letter to My Daughter*

As we leave the kitchen, we're heading into the nursery. This might not have been an actual nursery for you, it might have been a shared bedroom or other sleeping area. You might not remember it, but you can imagine you do.

What's it like in here? How does it feel to be in this room? What feelings do you notice coming up in your body?

The Nursery – Where Relationships Are Formed

What happens in the nursery is the backbone of an enormous amount of psychological understanding. Many theories and therapeutic models are based on the premise that our earliest relationships form their own map of relationships in general, which we carry through with us into our adult life.

It's why the therapeutic relationship is so important – because what gets enacted in the therapy room is a reflection of what happens in your other relationships; it becomes a safe place for you to experiment with different ways of relating to others.

If we have had safe, consistent relationships with others we carry this into our relationships throughout our life – with our friends, work colleagues, romantic partners and children. And when our caregivers have been inconsistent, absent, preoccupied, intrusive or frightening we carry this into our relationships too. These early experiences are not just the map but also the paper the map is written on. If we are handed a map full of warm, close and caring experiences, then it is easy for us to recreate the nursery we had. If we have been handed a map full of difficult or even dangerous experiences, we may find ourselves recreating them too. And, as is the case for many people, we spend a lifetime trying to create something different.

The T Word: Childhood Trauma

We're now talking about trauma in our early relationships, and trauma can be a tricky word. How much of our current experiences can we attribute to childhood trauma (aka 'shouldn't I be over that by now?').

If I'd written this even two years ago, I would now have written something about how it can feel like a stretch to imagine that our earliest experiences can have such a profound impact on our later feelings and relationships. But social media, filled with both therapists and those recovering from their experiences, has done a huge amount to normalise discussions about childhood trauma. Simultaneously, this has been met with derision – with suggestions that this pathologises normal experiences, and leads to a lack of resilience.

Only you know where you stand on this, whether you embrace the increased discussion of mental health and the normalisation of terms like 'trauma response' and 'triggered' or whether it feels uncomfortable to you. But whether or not mental health discussions feel acceptable, they are happening at a time of incredible global distress and lack of access to person-centred mental health support. We still, individually, find it very difficult to label what happened to us as 'trauma' and survivors of childhood trauma often do not seek support. This is due to the ways in which children are often blamed for their experiences by those perpetrating them (to the extent that unworthiness, shame and guilt can become part of their developing identity e.g. being 'bad'), the added shame as children grow up and realise that what happened to them may have been societally 'unacceptable' (which creates a further obstacle to disclosing their experiences; the invalidating responses survivors often hear when they do finally seek support – like being mocked for talking about it on social media, for example! – just strengthen this).

More than just a buzzword on TikTok, childhood trauma is more prevalent than we might imagine (or be able to bear), with more than two-thirds of children reporting their experience of at least one traumatic event before they reach age 16, such as abuse, neglect or witnessing violence in their home. Emotional abuse is a common experience too, with over a third of people self-reporting this, as well as around 18 per cent of people experiencing emotional neglect. So it's not unlikely that the increased discussions about childhood trauma are, in fact, highlighting a common experience that has existed unspoken for far too long. Even more so, by breaking the silence that so often compounds traumatic experiences, the way that social media enables us to read about and share stories might support people in processing their traumatic experiences.

We don't always think of our experiences as traumatic, especially when we haven't experienced specific traumatic incidents such as abuse, and especially when our experiences may have been seen as 'normal' in the environment we were raised in. But many people have experiences of relationships that have left them feeling less psychologically safe in some way. It can be helpful to think about trauma in the way we would a physical injury – we might experience a broken bone that is clearly in need of treatment. But we might also experience multiple small injuries that leave us bruised and protecting our body from further harm. Sometimes we hide these injuries well, and they are dismissed as little bumps, but they can do lasting damage.

That might have been a tough paragraph to read, so take a breath. Even if you haven't experienced such incidents yourself, being a parent heightens your sense of threat and it is hard to face the experiences children can go through. And if you have experienced such incidents, or been through them with your own children, these can shift our perspective of the world. But right now, sitting here, are there any threats around you? Are you safe in your home? Bring in that resting place if you need to remind your body that nothing is happening right now. Trauma can build up in us through repeated difficult experiences, and it can feel impossible to imagine that we can change the way it has taught us to see the world and other people. But over time, and repeated new experiences, we can absolutely create change.

And if reading that has highlighted the lack of safety you currently feel, please consider looking at local sources of support to help you find safety in your life. These might be through your health or welfare public services, charities and voluntary organisations, workplace support or online help.

Let's focus back on the nursery. How do you feel about looking back at your earliest experiences, and wondering how they have influenced how you feel now about yourself, about your child, and about others in your life? We can find it really difficult to see patterns in our own life, but often as soon as we begin to reflect we find that we are repeating the same pattern over and over again. Or, perhaps, having the same argument but in different ways and with different people. This can feel frustrating enough when it's with a parent, romantic partner or friend but it can feel so difficult when this starts playing out with your baby, child or teenager.

Shall we get to know those patterns a little bit?

OUR BABY SELF

As we look around the nursery, I'd like you to imagine what this place was like for you in your earliest days. It might feel impossible, so just see what comes to mind. But probably you have a sense of you as a very little person – a baby or toddler. Where are you in this nursery? And is there anyone with you?

Let's start just with you.

The idea of connecting with our littlest selves can feel so unimaginable, but these really early experiences shape us in so many ways that come up when we become parents. When we are faced with our own actual little baby – or even just the idea of that little baby – our own earliest longings come back to us.

As you'll know if you have spent any time with them, infants are little bundles of extreme feeling. They can go from peaceful, sunny, smiling and babbling to a red ball of rage in ten seconds flat. And, of course, in these earliest days they have no way of explaining what they are feeling, so hunger and satiety, cold and warmth, comfort and discomfort, contentment and dissatisfaction – all are experienced as enormous, full-body feelings.

They can feel so hard to interpret – which is possibly why they have been such a huge topic to study. And to really understand infants, and how we feel as infants, we must turn to psychoanalysis.

If you are a psychoanalyst, my apologies for what comes next. Because I'm going to boil down over a hundred years of rich exploration into a paragraph.

As babies, we are intensely vulnerable and we depend on tuned-in care from those around us in order to survive. We frequently feel like we are falling apart, and we need adults to hold us together. If we get tuned-in care some (please note *some* not *all*) of the time as we grow up, we internalise that care and feel able to support ourselves. Especially in times of stress, we have a sense in ourselves that we can be OK. If we haven't received this tuned-in care, as a baby we don't attribute this to our caregiver, but to ourselves. *We* must be to blame otherwise the consequence (that our caregiver is flawed and therefore unsafe) is too great. So, we do whatever we can to be able to feel safe – whether that's silencing our cries, or learning that to smile in that particular way gets the best response from our caregiver, or staying very still, or whatever else will help. Many of us have these wordless experiences that can feel quite terrifying, stored deep in our minds. And becoming a parent brings them all to the surface.

Psychoanalyst Joan Raphael-Leff calls these our 'wild things' – 'the "formless" things without names, the untamed, unprocessed, passionate, chaotic things that seethe deep below the civilised surface and erupt at times of greater permeability'. One of those times is becoming a parent, when, by holding our newborn in our arms (and later, our toddler, our child, our teenager, our adult child), we come face to face with how we felt at the same age. It is, perhaps, the hardest part of being a parent. At every stage, we have to re-experience some of the messy feelings and experiences we had ourselves at that time while trying our hardest to support our child through them.

I don't know about you, but I quite like the idea that there is still a little baby me curled up inside my body. The only thing is that, when that baby wakes up, it does so with pure, unbridled emotion. Have you ever had the experience of an 'unreasonable' reaction? Feeling abandoned by a friend, or murderous at a work colleague, or heart-rendingly grief-stricken by a partner . . . this is your little baby self popping out. And the things that trigger its awakening are those moments as a baby that left you feeling that way.

- How does this land with you? When you think of those deep, sometimes baffling emotional experiences that you've had, can you imagine that this says something about your infantile needs and longings?
- What do you think that little baby went through?
- If you imagine that you have a little baby curled up inside you now, how would you like to look after it? What does it need from you to feel safe and content?
- Can you think of ways that this has come up in your own experience of becoming a parent or planning to be a parent?
- How has your little baby, or toddler, or child self shown up in your parenting experiences so far?

OUR INTERNALISED PARENTS

When we first walked into this nursery, I asked you to notice who else was there with you. I'd like you to tune back in to that, if you can. You might wish to invite your guide to come in too, perhaps to stand by your side and place a loving hand on your shoulder.

As you probably gathered from getting to know that little baby in you, most models of psychological development emphasise that we develop through our relationships with others. Psychoanalyst and paediatrician Donald Winnicott went so far as to say, 'there is no such thing as a baby', outlining that a person only develops *with* someone else. The primary target for this attention has historically been the mother. But as I outlined in Chapter 1, there are also many different influences on how we develop as humans – our parents, caregivers, siblings, wider family, teachers, peers and communities – so that increasingly research looks at attachment 'networks', not just that parent–child couple.

Can you imagine that there is a rocking chair in this nursery, and that you as a little baby are being held by someone, or someone is in that rocking chair? Who would they be? How do you imagine they may have held you? What is their face doing? If you were crying, what do you suppose they would do? Would they have held you close, looked at you with confusion, popped you in your cot to get over it on your own? How do you imagine it felt to be held by them? How might they have held you? How did they speak to you, and what kind of words do you imagine they said?

If you spent your early life separated from your parents or caregivers then it is likely that this experience was very different for you. These relationships are built over a lifetime but you might hold, in your little baby self, some residue of this. You might have some feelings about not being held for some time, or being held in ways that were difficult for your little body to experience. You might wonder what this experience was like for you, and I'd encourage you to also think about other caring adults in your life who may have fulfilled some of this parent role for you.

It can be tricky to imagine what these earliest of relationships were like, because of course this is absolutely a non-verbal experience for us. So notice what happens in your body as you're reading. What do you feel inside your body? Where do you feel it? Are there any emotions attached? Don't question them, we're not looking for objective truths here, we're looking for *your* truths. You might be noticing a block in there – that you're not feeling much at all. If that's the case, just go with it; that's telling you either that you don't want to go there or that for some reason it's hard to remember – we'll talk about that a bit more in a moment.

If you do get a feeling, I just want to put a little marker in here. Might this also be a feeling you experience at times with your own child? When does that happen? How does it feel to you when that happens? How do you think it might feel to your child in those moments? Just notice it for now; we're going to come back to this.

Is there anyone else around the rocking chair? Your other parent, or perhaps other members of the family? Maybe a sibling helped to look after you, or an auntie or uncle, grandparents. There might be others there, perhaps someone outside of your family such as a family friend, a teacher, care worker or foster parent.

The main theory that explains why these relationships are so important – one that now has over 70 years of cross-cultural, robust research to back it up – is attachment theory (which is fundamentally different to, and not to be confused with, attachment parenting). That is, that we build our sense of self and others through our early relationship with a primary caregiver (whether or not this is a parent) – although newer research is emphasising that attachment develops not just with one person, but in our interactions with all of those who care for us. This happens because we need closeness to a caregiver or caregivers in order to survive, and depending on our caregiver we will adjust our behaviour (even as young babies) to stay close to them. Our experiences influence: how we feel about ourselves, how much we are able to understand, tolerate and regulate our own emotions and the emotions of others, how we show up in our relationships with others and even how much room we have in our minds to think and learn.

Key to this is the 'sensitive responsiveness' (or lack thereof) of our caregivers – how in tune they are with our needs and how responsive they are to acting upon them appropriately. This creates patterns of familiar expectations in our relationships, unless something happens to change those expectations – which might be a tragedy such as the loss of a parent, or it might be a positive shift, which can happen by building a secure attachment relationship with someone else (such as a partner, friend or therapist).

What's beautiful about attachment theory is that it shows

how much our relationships mean to us. We don't develop an attachment style on our own – attachment is a strategy that we use to try to get the best out of the caregivers we have. They are the sanctuaries we return to. Even if they aren't always safe or consistent, they are familiar. The difficulty is that, as we develop in our lives, we assume other people will treat us the same way that they did. The father of attachment theory, John Bowlby, called this our 'internal working model' of relationships – this is our blueprint.

I think of it a bit like a dance that we learn with a particular set of partners. The key to the dance is that it keeps us close to our caregivers – locked in a dance even if it's a difficult one. The problem with this dance is that we tend to look for part-ners who will dance the same dance our caregivers taught us . . . and when they won't, we often force them to dance it any-way and ignore any attempts at other steps because it's what we are familiar with.

The Family Room

Let's step out of your nursery and bring your caregivers into the family room (or the living room, sitting room, lounge, or whatever you called it in your home). We've pushed any sofas out and there's a record player, playing some music. Thinking of that baby you, and the people who cared for you as you grew up, let's try to figure out the dance that you learned together. It may be hard to think about this as a baby, but you will also find some clues in the relationships you found your-self in as a child, and also later with friends and partners. Over the years this has been explored as four key dances, although other researchers have expanded on this to demonstrate how complex our dances can become. Just as with the porridge bowls, we might not dance this dance absolutely all the time but these are the steps we most often fall into.

The Waltz: Secure Attachment

First up is the waltz – a dance with a steady rhythm and flow. The parent or caregiver is in the lead but takes cues from their child. Each dancer is in their own space, but connected to each other. The child can have some distance but be welcomed back in for closeness when in need of security. This has been called secure attachment, and is the attachment pattern of the majority of people worldwide. When we have been waltzed with as babies and children, we see everyone around us as being capable of a waltz too. We see other people on the dance floor and invite them to waltz with us. We acknowledge that not everyone is able to waltz, but we don't feel that we have to join them in their dance.

What does this waltz look like in reality? A baby who cries and knows that most of the time they will be responded to by a caregiver who will try to figure out why they are crying and soothe their distress or fix the problem. A child who loses their temper and is met with curiosity, acceptance and care. A teenager who slams a door and hears their parent call through it, 'I'm here, if you want to talk to me when you're ready.' An adult who is self-sufficient but can ask for help when needed and expects an empathic response (and, even, doesn't take it personally if one isn't received but instead looks for an empathic response from an alternative person).

The Irish Dance: Avoidant Attachment

The next dance is the traditional Irish dance – avoidant attachment. What are we avoiding? Connection, dependency, emotions. This has historically been the next most common dance in countries where individualism is valued – such as the UK, Germany and the United States. Dancing next to each other, not touching. On the top half (or on the surface) things are controlled, straight and steady. Under the waist (or inside the body) there might be frantic movement but you won't see it unless you look down (or inwards).

In reality, what this looks like is a baby who cries and – whether purposefully or due to their caregiver having competing demands – consistently is not comforted or may be actively rejected. Parents may be present and even protective, but not soothing. So the baby learns to swallow their cries (there are good survival reasons for this). This is a preschooler who will busy themselves playing quietly, or put on a bright smile while internally feeling upset. A teenager who slams their door knowing no one will come to check on them, and finds other ways to manage their strong feelings. An adult who cuts off their feelings in order to understand the world in more cerebral ways – or even who cuts off their feelings in order to look after everyone else's. An adult who walks away from difficult conversations, or responds by minimising or dismissing the emotion behind them.

The Argentine Tango: Anxious Attachment

Next up is the dramatic and often beautiful Argentine tango. A dance of high emotion, passion and conflict, where partners may be clinging tightly to each other, cheeks pressed together, and then the next moment be on opposite sides of the dance floor. This is ambivalent/resistant/anxious attachment (ironic that this unpredictable pattern has so many different names) and is the next most common attachment pattern after secure in countries that are seen as more 'collectivist', with tight social ties, such as Japan and Israel.

What does this Argentine tango look like in reality? A baby who cries and sometimes is responded to with love, sometimes with annoyance, sometimes with rejection, sometimes with distress and sometimes ignored. The child, instead of swallowing their feelings as in the Irish dance, ups the ante because they don't know what they're going to receive. They cry louder, cling to their parent while simultaneously pulling away. They may hit them, shouting, 'I hate you' but silently they are asking, 'do you love me? Are you there for me?' Or they may find complicated ways to try to get positive responses from their caregiver, and be described as 'manipulative'. As a teenager, this might look like frequently falling deeply in love, while terrified of being alone. In adulthood, the Argentine tango may mean we need frequent reassurance of our worth and importance from those around us while being utterly convinced we will be rejected at any moment (and sometimes pushing them away in the process).

The Dance That Isn't a Dance: Disorganised Attachment

Last of all, we have the dance that isn't really a dance – it's a combination of many different dances and it is confusing, and ugly, and people get hurt. It is impossible to predict what your partner is going to do, so you have to prepare to be spun, flipped and knocked flat on your back. This attachment pattern has been called disorganised attachment, but research psychologist Patricia Crittenden has pointed out how very, very organised it often is because the baby or child has to navigate themselves in complicated ways to keep themselves safe in the context of physical, emotional or societal danger. This might be due to emotional or physical abuse, but it may also be that they are growing up witnessing violence, or have a caregiver who is consumed with their own previous trauma. This can show up in such a variety of ways – a baby who looks frozen, a child who calls their parent but is fearful when they come, a teenager who turns their fear and anger on to their own body with self-harm, an adult who longs for intense closeness, then pushes you away hard or suddenly withdraws.

It's important to remember that these dances develop because they keep us close to our caregivers (even when they are frightening ones). Where we run into problems is when we go out into the world and the dances we learned in our nurseries don't always fit with the dances of others. The dances that kept us safe as children may come to cause us injuries.

The questions that follow are big ones. Take them slowly, pause as you need to and use the tools we discussed in Chapter 3 to support you (see pages 49–57).

- What has this brought up for you? Do you recognise some of your patterns in the dances I've described above?
- If you had more than one parent or caregiver present in your early life, did you dance the same dance with them or different dances? If they were different, how did you dance between them? How do you think this has influenced you?
- Have you had the experience of trying to dance your dance with someone and finding your metaphorical feet getting twisted up and falling flat on your face? Like someone finding your closeness intrusive, or someone wanting more emotional response from you than you felt comfortable with?
- Has anyone ever managed to teach you a different way of dancing?
- If you have a partner, what dance do they have to dance? How does that fit with your dance (more on this in Chapter 8)?
- Why do you think your parents or caregivers danced the dance they did?
- What dance do you think you might be in at the moment with your own child? Sometimes we can repeat these dances, very unconsciously, because they are so familiar to us – if we have been taught an

Irish dance, then we might find a waltz just feels too up close and personal, so we'll naturally dance at a little distance from our babies and children.

· Or, you might notice that you are trying something different with your own child – many people who were taught an Irish dance actually end up in an Argentine tango with their own child, and vice versa. This is a sort of pendulum swing we do to offer something we didn't have, but we often go a little too far the other way. Does this apply to you?

There is a lot that we still don't know about attachment. Our family rooms are very linked to our kitchens – those who have been raised to dance a waltz are likely to provide a 'just right' bowl of porridge too. Research has historically focused on the mother–child relationship or looked at attachment only between two people. Although we know that different caregivers (both within and outside of the family) may influence how a child and adult grows up, we don't yet really know how this happens and whether we should be looking at how we're taught to dance by all of the people we are raised with. It could be that dancing a waltz with both parents offers us additional stability, it could also be that dancing a waltz with one parent might buffer us from a more difficult dance with another parent. And that dancing a waltz with one parent who primarily cares for us will have a greater impact on us than if it is danced with the other parent who is less involved. We don't yet fully understand how other caregivers, such as nursery keyworkers, teachers or other members of the family, contribute to these dances.

It's useful to remember that the majority of people do dance a waltz – and that even those who have experienced mistreatment as children may go on to still dance a waltz. One study found that, of children who had been raised in institutions where they suffered from 'structural neglect',

17 per cent still managed to have a secure attachment relationship with their favoured caregiver. There are many complex reasons for this – to do with our genetic predispositions, our own characteristics like temperament and personality, our environment, other people in our life, how much or little additional stress we experience. Having even one warm and supportive adult in our lives can help us learn to waltz against all the odds.

And we can change our dances at any point, although this might take time, and is easier with a good teacher.

Where Are You Now?

It's not an easy thing to look back on our childhoods, even if we feel like they were happy. We might notice things that we hadn't noticed before. We might wish we hadn't noticed them and try to shove them away again.

There's an often-used metaphor in trauma therapy about cupboards.

At the moment, you're standing in your family room. If you step out, into a hallway perhaps, imagine there's a cupboard there – maybe one of those old-fashioned linen cupboards full of towels or sheets. What we tend to do (because, like we've said, it's hard to look at this stuff) is shove all our bad memories, difficult experiences, unresolved feelings, challenging thoughts into that cupboard, and slam the door shut. And whenever something else comes up that makes us feel a bit uneasy, we shove it in there too. If you've had traumatic experiences, sometimes that cupboard door comes bursting open in the form of nightmares, intrusive thoughts and flashbacks. But for all of us, if we've been shoving stuff in that cupboard for a long time, we can find that it's all got very cluttered. And then when something happens – like having a child – the cupboard gets opened and all those scrunched-up towels land on our head.

Over these past few chapters we've opened up that cupboard door and, bit by bit, looked at some of the linen. Perhaps that might be picking up a pillowcase that represents getting shouted at by a parent as a little kid, and in picking that up it's helped you make a link between that authoritarian porridge bowl and the times you suddenly find yourself shouting at your own child out of the blue. Or maybe there was a bedsheet there about how sometimes your caregiver could be super warm and loving but at other times suddenly cold, and that's helped you to make a link about how much pressure you're now putting on yourself to make sure you show up *every single time* for your own child, which is leaving you exhausted and more likely to need to retreat.

Before we leave your childhood home, let's just take a pause to see where all of this has left you now.

- Have you learned anything surprising about your own childhood experiences?
- Is there anything that you wish to explore further – perhaps by talking to a parent, caregiver, sibling or another family member, family friend, neighbour – to help you understand your own experiences?
- What are the key feelings that you're left with after reading these chapters? Do you need to do anything to support yourself at this time? (Don't forget about your guide and your resting place.)
- Did you notice any resistance or avoidance in looking at these things? A part of you saying, 'Don't go there, Emma!' Why do you think that is? (There's no shame in this; often we need to do this exploring a little bit at a time.)
- What do you think you have been repeating from your own childhood without realising?

- Is there anything you've been working really hard not to repeat, so you've done a pendulum swing the other way?
- Knowing what you know now, are there any changes you'd like to make in your home right now?
- What might you need (support, conversations with others, buy-in from your partner . . .) to be able to do this?

Every time you do this, and think about what your childhood and past experiences left you with and consider the impact of this (positive and less so) in your adult life, you neatly fold up another piece of linen so that cupboard becomes much simpler to look in. This means that your everyday parenting comes from a place of conscious awareness, rather than as a reaction to something from the back of the cupboard.

And this also means that, when you have discussions or conflicts with or about your own children, you can easily open that cupboard and pull out the right pillowcase to understand it better and even share it with them. Maybe the one that says, 'You might say that I'm being overprotective, but when I was little I had a few dangerous experiences that left me wanting to really make sure that doesn't happen to you. We can talk about how to get that balance right.' Or the one that says, 'When my baby shouts with glee I want to put my fingers in my ears because stress at home meant I'm sensitive to loud noise. I'd like to explore ways to make this more bearable for me.' And, in understanding where these things come from for us, we not only stop them inadvertently affecting our daily parenting but we may also accept them with less judgement, and even allow our children as they grow to see us as humans who have whole histories behind us.

They'll still inherit a few pairs of dirty socks that have been shoved right at the back, because we all do, but they might have a clearer idea of how to deal with them.

Leaving Our Childhood Home

We're going to step out of the front door, but let's do something first. I'd like you to imagine that your guide is still right there next to you, with a hand on your shoulder. Perhaps you're standing at the door, looking in. Take a look at what is there now. Who is in that home now? How are you feeling – perhaps you're still looking at a baby you in that nursery, or maybe you're a toddler, or a child. Perhaps memories have come back to you in reading this. Maybe new people have entered the home too, and some people may have left.

I'd like you to invite whoever is there in that home – the little baby and child parts of you, any family members or caregivers there too – to just take a look at you, standing in that doorway, supported by your guide. Allow them to see you as you are now – an adult. Maybe even a parent, with a child or children of your own. Someone who is able to decide the dance they want to dance.

Let's step out of the front door. And let's take a little look at this map again, and see what else we can explore.

CHAPTER 7

Stories from Your Adulthood

*'We can never go back. I know that now. We can
go forward. We can find the love our hearts long
for, but not until we let go grief about the love
we lost long ago, when we were little and had
no voice to speak the heart's longing.'*

bell hooks, *All About Love*

I'd like to lead you down another path. This time we're going to your current home. Where you live now, whatever that looks like. Bring it up in your mind, and let's step through the front door together. Your guide can come with you if you want them to – we're moving into the here and now, and it's up to you whether you want to leave them sitting close by or whether you'd like them to come along.

I don't know what your home looks like, but can we imagine that, as we enter through the front door, there is a full-length mirror in front of you? Pause here and have a look at yourself as you are now. See it all, the bits you like and the bits you like a bit less.

We can forget this so easily, can't we? That we are adults. When we're taken over by younger parts of ourselves, or find ourselves stuck in familiar patterns that take us back to earlier life, we forget. Sometimes it's mind-blowing that we are expected to look after children, and pay bills, and show up every single day to our work tasks (in and outside the home). Sometimes we might even feel like toddlers ourselves.

It's so bittersweet that these younger parts come up so powerfully when we become parents. Because to be the parents we want to be, we need to feel at home in our adult selves. Grounded in who we are, confident in our responses and flexible in our attitudes.

But what does being an adult really mean?

- What is an adult to you?
- Where did you get those ideas from?
- Do you still believe in those ideas?
- Is there anything you'd replace them with? What kind of adult do you want to be now?
- What stops you from feeling like an adult?

An Image of You

The thing is, often when we feel we are being most 'adult' is actually when we are living up to an ideal, one that is not sustainable. Does that resonate with you? The ideal might be based on an adult you knew or know, or the comparison you make to other people. Maybe that feeling when you're 'smashing it' – working efficiently, answering your emails, ticking stuff off the to-do list, remembering to pick up the dry cleaning, eating your five a day, getting the kids to bed on time, being attentive to your partner, remembering to call your family. And then the next day, or the next moment, you spill your coffee all over your pyjamas and realise you've run out of toilet paper and the cat throws up on the floor and you don't feel like a grown-up at all, and actually you'd quite like an adult to come and take over.

Because the problem with ideals is that they tend to be

unrealistic, and built on some of those stories we mentioned in Chapter 1, so they're hard to sustain. And, often, it's not really ourselves we're working from, but an image of ourselves.

Why do we create them? These idealised images of ourselves? Often it's in direct response to some of the messages we received – from our parents, families, communities, school, media, culture, society. We form an idea of how we are 'meant' to be – the version of us that seems most acceptable to other people – and we strive to meet it. And when we don't, we can feel like failures (rather than question whether the ideal is something we really want to aspire to or can even achieve).

So much of our adult life is lived in reaction to those little baby and child parts of us we got to know in the previous chapters. Moving away from the times that we felt shame or vulnerability, protecting ourselves with hard armour or clever emotional shenanigans, so that we will never ever feel that way again. And so that no one will ever know that, deep down, we don't really know what the hell we are doing. But these protections can get in the way of really getting to know ourselves and really getting to know our children (as well as other people in our lives). They stop us from truly moving into adulthood. And do we want to live life waiting to be found out?

Can I invite you to sit down for a moment? In your favourite chair, or maybe you want to get into your bed (the one in this imaginary house – but if you're home now and want to really do it, feel free). We've talked about who you were, and what from the past you might be carrying. We're going to talk about what you want for your own children. Let's talk first about what stops you from getting to know who you are now.

Hiding Ourselves

We can be our own worst enemies. We might know ourselves well, and accept all of the different parts of us. But usually there are parts of ourselves that we cut off and try not to look at too closely. One of the reasons it's important that we look at all of them, aside from our own well-being, is because our babies and children see them ALL. All that stuff shoved in the cupboard we saw in the last chapter? Our children may not understand what it is or where it came from, but they absolutely know it is there.

As we discussed when we got to know your dance, children need to stay close to us to keep themselves safe, and will learn how to get the best out of us. Part of that involves using all of their senses to *feel* what is emanating from us. Little antennae picking up on our nervous systems and emotions so they know how to approach us. You might have hidden things from yourself, and your friends, colleagues and partner. But your children see through it all. And any mismatch between what they see and what you say is just confusing. So you may as well embrace it all and see whether there's anything you want to tweak. Because chances are they'll be pointing it out to you anyway.

Often the protections we build up are like little walls around the baby-and-child feelings that we have carried with us – worry about abandonment, criticism and rejection, fear of anger or aggression (our own or other people's), anxiety that we are forgotten or invisible. Sometimes they are walls we've built because of messages we've received from others – that we need to ask for less, or toughen up. Sometimes they come from society – that we need to sculpt ourselves to conform. We need to break down some of those walls in order to see that our fears will not be realised. And sometimes, if our fears *are* realised we need to find ways to manage them instead of building the walls again.

This is often the hardest part of therapy because we think that it is the walls that are keeping us safe. But the walls leave us disconnected. And we might find, when we look behind them, that we no longer fear what they have been holding back.

Our Walls

Across many different psychological models is the concept that we develop strategies in order to feel as safe as we can going out there into the world and dealing with other people. Some of these are really healthy, and of course we all do it. We might become a bit of a joker when we're feeling uncomfortable, to disarm the person we're with and keep a conversation flowing. We might put our own needs to one side and become a helper to connect with someone who needs us. When we are doing this in healthy ways, we're still able to see a problem we're facing in its entirety, and also acknowledge our own limitations.

When things get a bit trickier is when, especially in times of stress, we turn to particular strategies that actually make us or the people around us feel a bit worse. Perhaps as adrenaline rises in our body, we shout at our nearest and dearest, which helps us release the pressure but leaves us feeling guilty and them withdrawn or angry in return. Or we just knuckle down and go through the motions, switching off our feelings. These strategies, and others like them, don't resolve the stress in front of us, and can leave us feeling upset, disconnected and sometimes frustrated with ourselves or others. But they work (because they keep those walls up, protect us from feeling vulnerable, and they feel familiar) so we keep doing them.

We choose our strategies based on many different factors – the dance we talked about in the previous chapter, how much we are repeating our caregivers' actions and how much we are reacting against them, other messages we've received from people around us, our communities, faith, favourite films, who we are dealing with in the moment. It can be really helpful to think of these as characters who exist inside us all the time and pop out when they are required of us. Sometimes we can feel really exasperated with some of these characters, but they have all been developed, by us, to ensure that we are safe.

So shall we bring some of yours in to join you where you are sitting? And welcome them? Bring your guide in here too if you want to – chances are they might be a character that you're aspiring to, so we might as well invite them along.

The Cast of Characters

I'm going to outline here some of the common characters that have shown up in my therapy room and some of the reasons we develop them. Again, hold these loosely. Some of them you might relate to closely, others might be unfamiliar to you – although you might recognise them in other people. Maybe you won't relate to any of these characters; if so, consider your own instead. Many of them have positive, helpful traits that we find useful in navigating our everyday life. But when they take us over completely, or dominate our thinking, they can lead to us losing touch with the other parts of us and alternative visions of the world.

THE CRITIC

One of the most common characters I hear about is the Critic. I'm guessing you're going to be familiar with this one. What does yours look like? Whose voice do they have? What sort of messages do they bring with them?

In psychology, the idea of an inner critic, or internal moral guide, goes back to Freud and the superego. Sometimes our Critic can be relatively benign, pushing us forwards to achieve more, do better, strive harder. This might be an eerie feeling of not quite 'good enough'. But it might also be a voice that spits insults at us, sneers, 'who do you think you are?', points out the myriad nasty opinions others may hold of us. The Critic collects yardsticks to measure ourselves against – and we tend to come up short. Its mantra would be 'Must Try Harder'.

Often this character has come in response to a feeling of inadequacy, perhaps feeling that expectations have been set that were not being lived up to. We fear if the Critic were to relax, then maybe our worst fears would come true. That we are, in fact, useless, lazy and worthless.

There is a part of the Critic that we don't always like to admit to ourselves – that we can be harsh Critics of other people because we also measure them with the same yardstick.

THE LOVER

Aka the Caregiver, the Nurturer, Earth Mother/Father. This is the character who deals with stress, distress and conflict by pulling people in close and looking after them. Sometimes to the extent that their own needs are subsumed by the needs of other people.

Is this a character you're familiar with? What does the Lover look like to you? What does their voice sound like? What do they encourage you to do?

For some people, this loving character can bring up feelings of disdain or even fear. So if this comes up for you, just notice that. It isn't unlikely that you have a Lover in your life who might be fulfilling some of this caring role on your behalf.

This is a character who encourages peace and love at all times. Difficult behaviour in others must be met with a gentle smile, and a compassionate touch on the arm. Other tasks are dropped the moment someone expresses a need for us. This character says out loud, 'Of course,' 'I would be delighted to,' 'It's never too much trouble.' And, it whispers to us, 'Don't complain,' 'You should be grateful' and 'Others have it so much worse.' Anger is firmly not allowed (which means that other people might be roped in unconsciously to express anger on our behalf).

This character may come from a feeling of invisibility and unworthiness – where others' needs have been so much greater than our own, we have learned to push our own away. That might have been a parent who needed us to care for them (physically or emotionally), or growing up in a family where our siblings' needs consumed our own. Our need for love is met by giving others what we wish we could receive ourselves. Our sense of worth comes from how much others are satisfied with what we are providing for them. Asserting our needs is equated with asking too much.

For some people there can be some feelings of omnipotence attached to the Lover – a sense that no one else can offer quite what we do. This can bring feelings of satisfaction and pride, but also frustration, resentment and rage when we (inevitably) need a little love for ourselves.

THE FRETTER

What's that moving over there? The Fretter is constantly scanning for threat, ready to act at a moment's notice. They don't have much time to sit next to you and hold your hand; they are on to solutions, and fast. Sometimes a good problem-solver, sometimes a busy bee with an endless to-do list, sometimes a whirlwind who creates problems as fast as they can fix them. This is related to your 'flight' response, a character who is on high alert at all times, preventing catastrophes (even the imaginary ones) and ready to get you to safety.

If you've had the kind of experiences where your body became primed for survival – whether from before your own birth, from your experiences up to now or the environments that you've lived in – it's likely your Fretter is very present. They may be a constant source of anxiety in your life. Or they may take the form of a troubleshooter who prevents disaster.

What does your Fretter look like? How are they standing? What does their voice sound like to you? The Fretter loves to say things like 'disaster is just around the corner!', 'we need a plan' and 'how could I have let that happen?'

The Fretter doesn't like feeling out of control; in fact, any situation they can't control will cause them to go into overdrive. The Fretter doesn't always understand that other people may not want to go along with their ideas and plans, or might even see them as overly anxious. Sometimes they are very apologetic when their plan hasn't got them the desired outcome, feeling to blame even for things outside of their control. Sometimes our Fretter can stop us from relaxing, but this character is also heavily rewarded by a society that loves a planner.

This character arises from anxiety – feeling out of control and helpless. It works so hard to avoid anxiety but, in doing so, creates new things to feel anxious about.

THE STOIC

Related to the Fretter, but with a coat of armour, is the Stoic. This character has zero time for feelings – and finds them rather unnecessary, actually.

Is this a character that you know? What do they sound like to you? What facial expressions might they make? How would they sound? What do they look like?

The Stoic loves to say things like, 'Don't waste your time worrying,' 'Pull your socks up' and 'At least . . .' or 'It could be worse.' This is a character very linked to the Irish dance of the last chapter (see page 90), who deals with the messy bits of life by largely ignoring them and sometimes silencing them. In some cultures, this character is highly praised for its pragmatism and independence. A whole school of philosophy has devoted itself to this ethical doctrine. For the Stoic, the goal is to live according to rationality and reason. Our more primitive appetites and urges should be tightly managed.

This character often develops from a lack of validation of our own feelings, such that feelings become a hindrance. For some, this goes even further and the Stoic puts up a hard coat of armour. Our feelings can't get out – but others' feelings also can't get in. Conflict is responded to with withdrawal, and maybe even disapproval, a 'get a grip' attitude.

Of course, the downside of the Stoic is that, no matter how hard we try to ignore them, those pesky emotions have a way of getting out somehow. So we may have to try harder to keep a lid on the Pandora's box of our own feelings – and in refusing to see them in others, we lose out on seeing the whole person we could get to know.

THE WARRIOR

The Warrior can take on different forms. Sometimes a fighter for injustices, sometimes a fighter for our own needs to be met and sometimes an actual fighter.

Do you have a warrior in you? Or recognise this in someone else you know well? What does your Warrior look like? Do they remind you of anyone?

Children are full of Warrior spirit, striving for fairness and justice in the world; sometimes we hone these characters in our later life or sometimes we hide them away.

The Warrior says, 'That's not fair!' and their mantra is 'Be the change you wish to see in the world.' But the Warrior can also be a bit controlling, with a fixed idea of the world *they* wish to see and how people within it should act. When this is challenged, the Warrior may fight harder, or feel defeated. Warriors may protect those they perceive as weaker, or in need, and may show a determination to change things for the better.

Often Warriors arise from powerlessness. Some children who have been mistreated in their earlier years may polish their inner Warrior to make sure that they, and others like them, will not go through this same experience. You can look for Warriors working in charities, campaigning, in politics and in the caring professions.

THE OGRE

Perhaps linked to the Warrior, but when that fighting instinct becomes verbally or physically aggressive. Some people show their anger throughout their lives; for others their Ogre lies dormant until something pokes it and then it comes bursting out. Like, for example, having children.

What does your Ogre look like? It's likely that you have one in there even if you keep it very well controlled and it doesn't come out often. It is our natural 'fight' response to stress. How does your Ogre sound? Does it have any phrases? Perhaps 'Listen to me!' or 'Do as I say!' or maybe just a guttural yell. Or perhaps it expresses itself in more subtle ways.

In parenting, the Ogre often shows up in that salty authoritarian porridge (see page 74). But, especially if we have been raised by caregivers who were frightening, we might be terrified of our Ogre. We might suppress any sign of anger, and idealise our nurturing capacities as a parent (the Lover may keep the Ogre in firm check). But, in times of stress or when we might see our child, partner or someone else as potentially overpowering, the Ogre might come storming out to protect our own vulnerable parts. This anger can come out as shouting, or even physical aggression, which might feel like it comes out of the blue and appears especially when we are faced with the aggressive impulses or surges of independence of our growing children. The more we have idealised the role of parent – and thus not allowed valid feelings of resentment or anger, and forgotten about our basic human needs – the more the Ogre might be stoked. Essentially, if we are in a submissive role as a parent, at some point we may feel we need to dominate to reassert our sense of ourself as a whole person. This can be difficult to experience for our children, but also for us, if we are invested in not repeating the anger we experienced ourselves.

I am not talking about verbal or physical abuse here, where there is a sustained power imbalance and controlling behaviour between partners or between parent and child. I am describing unwanted and unwelcome expressions of anger and aggression – a roar out of the blue, a shattered glass, a forceful hand on an arm, picking up a child more roughly than intended – which often shock us as much as our children. However, there is a spectrum. Many thoughtful and reflective parents can tip over into acts of emotional and physical abuse when under extreme stress or pressure. The difference is if someone views this as an urgent catalyst for change or as their entitlement as a parent. Abusive cycles in families can be difficult to change without specialist support and guidance – but it is possible to do so. If the Ogre is showing up more than you would like, it might be time to speak to a professional about getting to know this Ogre in safe ways.

The Ogre can shut out other people, and frighten them (and also frighten other characters in us). But if we can befriend it, often we find it is bringing us useful messages about how we feel about power in our relationships, and our own natural feelings of aggression – and it can lead us to discover how we can accept and channel our anger in healthy ways.

Often the Ogre can hide much more powerless parts of us, and has a deep fear of vulnerability. Which leads us on to . . .

THE WOUNDED SOUL

Some people might be very familiar with a defensive character who appears, always, deeply wounded and maybe victimised. This character is fond of saying, 'It's all awful,' 'What's the point?' and, perhaps more quietly, 'I give up.'

Is this a character you recognise? What would the Wounded

Soul look like to you? What might they sound like? What sort of clothes might they wear? What colours do you associate with them?

The Wounded Soul can live in stark contrast to the Fretter and the Stoic, who may find it sincerely frustrating even if they all live within the same body. It can often be a counterpart to the Ogre – when the Ogre is moved past, the Wounded Soul might be hiding behind it. Yet, this is often still hiding the more vulnerable parts of us who feel sadness and grief rather than a defeated hopelessness.

The Wounded Soul is often a character we develop because we've run out of other options. In a situation of acute threat, this would look like a 'collapse', where we just lie down because we don't have anywhere else to run and fighting won't help. We may look like we're functioning, but we are just going through the motions and may withdraw.

As with the Ogre, the Wounded Soul may develop in the face of helplessness and powerlessness – which might come from a parent but may also develop in response to societal inequality. For example, experiences of childhood poverty have been linked to more helpless behaviours in adolescence and adulthood as the sheer quantity of social and physical stressors that may be faced by disadvantaged children impact upon their sense of mastery and control.

THE FLOATER

A final common character is the Floater. Not to be confused with the Lover, who may be permissive but present, the Floater comes into play when we need to escape. This might be linked to the freeze response, and seen as a form of dissociating or cutting off from the world (as well as ourselves).

Dissociation has been most commonly linked to experiencing acute trauma – as a survival mechanism to horrific experiences, we might just go elsewhere in our mind. We may also learn to dissociate in order to cope with difficult relational experiences in our early life – whether that is as clear as a traumatic experience at the hands of a caregiver (what is known as 'betrayal trauma'), or the 'quieter' experiences of not being consistently responded to in an appropriate way by a caregiver. We don't always know when we are working from our Floater; especially if we have been raised to be compliant, we might be Floating a lot. In essence, if we have not been fully known by our caregivers, we may find it difficult to stay fully knowing of ourselves. We might tune out for other reasons too – such as being sensitive to sensory stimulation, growing up in crowded conditions that meant getting a break meant going into your head, or because we get very little respite in our current life so need to drift away to recover.

We all float sometimes – we might daydream when we're stuck doing a boring task, or zone out on our phones when we're tired. But when the Floater becomes a character that you often use to cope with daily life, your usual processing can be disrupted – so that our sense of ourselves in the world, our expression of thoughts, our memories can feel fragmented. It's like that feeling when you daydream on a long car journey – when you suddenly realise you've travelled some distance without noticing – happening frequently throughout your day.

Do you have a Floater? What might your Floater look like? Or maybe they don't really look like anything at all, but feel like more of a fog descending. What do they sound like, in your mind?

In parenting, we can often find ourselves floating – as a means to cope with the more mundane parenting tasks, because we are sleep-deprived, because we don't want to play a Disney or Marvel character for the millionth time. Especially in early parenting, floating can be essential to tune in to that dreamy baby state. But if we are doing this regularly, and as a result may miss our child's bids for our attention, it can cause problems both for us and for our children.

Bringing the Characters Together

Perhaps there are many other characters that this makes you think of, joining you now where you are sitting or lying. Maybe you as a sibling might come up, or you as a person in a new country, or you at work, or you as a Japanese person, or you as an autistic person, or you as a wheelchair user. There may be an important character based on your faith, health, culture, community, race, physical form.

And we have your guide too, who might be a sort of idealised parent figure who fits into one of the above or might be a mixture of other characters too.

- How do you feel having read through those character descriptions? Are there any you recognise clearly? Others who you realise exist in you that you hadn't noticed before? Any others that we haven't talked about?
- Where do these characters show up for you?
- Where do you feel them in your body?
- At different times do you utilise different characters?
- Are there any characters you try to push away or avoid?
- Do they know about each other?
- Do they know about YOU?

The important thing to remember about these characters is that they are not WHOLE humans. Each of them may be a part of you but they are not all of you, even if sometimes it might feel that way. Some of them you may wish weren't there, some of them you may wish you could act from all the time. But actually we are made up of all of them, working together in different ways, plus the more vulnerable little-kid parts that we met in the earlier chapters, plus so many other factors – our relationships now, other ways we've shown up in the past, our current needs.

What might it feel like to allow all of these characters to have a voice? To speak about what is important to them and why they feel they need to be there? And, also, to see each other and recognise the benefits that these different characters bring? Often, they don't know about each other's existence. At other times, they might tag-team and work closely together, like the Lover and Critic, who might discover gentle parenting practices and push us to achieve perfect parenting status, or the Fretter and the Warrior, who might work together to try to create more safety for our children.

One of our main aims in therapy is to bring together all of these different characters, so that we can feel more integrated – more whole. Then we can know more clearly why we are acting as we do, and even who we are being influenced by.

Bringing In Our Children

Of course, as in all our relationships, these characters will come out with our children. The Floater might come in when you've been asked to read a favourite book for the ten-millionth time that day, the Warrior might come bursting out when another child runs off with your toddler's favourite toy.

But one of the trickiest things about these characters is that sometimes we can *give* them to our children. This might be because we don't like those characters, such as the Ogre. Maybe we want to be a perfect, unflustered parent so when our child doesn't allow this somehow (for example, by telling us that they hate the food we've so lovingly prepared or, even, by telling us they hate *us*) and we feel a flare of anger, we 'push' this into them so that *they* become the Ogre – a horrible, ungrateful little pest. Or, conversely, we are so invested in having a perfect child that we 'push' the Lover into them and only really see their loving, pure, gorgeous parts and ignore the more complicated, irritating and challenging parts.

When we understand all of these characters in ourselves

– what we are bringing, in our entirety – we stop needing to do that. And then we have the opportunity to see our child as they truly are – and understand their characters too.

- Does this resonate with you? Have there been times your child has 'taken on' one of these characters, in your eyes?
- What did that feel like for you?
- What does that feel like now, noticing that?
- Are there particular characters you tend to look for in your child?
- Are there characters your child brings out in you?
- If you have more than one child, do you notice that they bring out different characters? Why do you think that is?
- Are there characters in yourself that your child notices, that you wish were not there? How does it feel to have these noticed? Why do you think this character is there? What do you feel about them? What do they offer you?
- If you are talking this over as a couple or as co-parents, do you notice this happening between your partner/ co-parent and child or children? You could discuss these questions together to consider how this plays out in your family.

Where Are You Now?

So, we've met all of you, now. Well, gosh, really not nearly all of you – but some of the key components. It's been quite a ride.

How are you feeling? It's complicated, I know, and your head might be spinning a bit. But if we can get all of these different parts of you to help us in understanding your parenting journey, your daily experience of it might just get a whole lot simpler. If you show your own, actual real-life child some understanding, and your Wounded Soul comes out reminding you that you never received understanding yourself, you can listen to what they might need *right now*. Perhaps that's understanding what you experienced in your own past, and offering yourself some compassion for what you missed out on as well as pride in trying to give something different to your own child or children.

If your parenting experiences aren't going as you'd hoped, and your Critic comes in comparing you to other people, calling you names, berating you, then perhaps you can notice what that leads you to do, think and feel. How does that critical voice affect you? Perhaps then you can pause and ask, 'Why do I believe the Critic this time? What stories do they hold that they are telling me? Do I believe those stories? What is this costing me? What does the Critic worry would happen if I were to speak with more kindness?'

When we act from these different characters, we can lose our sense of wholeness and find it harder to see others as whole people too. But even just knowing they are there, and that we can be curious about what they are bringing with them, helps us to update some of the stories they hold.

How Change Happens – Without Us Noticing

Often, in my therapeutic work, this is a process that happens organically. In getting to know these different characters, initially we might only notice after the event that they showed up. Then we might get a bit frustrated, feeling that they pop up when we don't want them to. But, if we can continue that sense of curiosity, compassion and acceptance about why they are there in the first place, we find that they start to shift and that we learn more about who we are behind those walls. What often happens next is that we notice them arrive in the moment, and we realise that we are in a more observing position and able to make more conscious choices about how we want to respond. And then, all of a sudden, we realise that these characters are starting to merge together a little and we are letting go of some of those walls as we develop a more solid sense of who we are when we're not acting these different roles.

It can be a frustrating process and often people experience a 'who the hell am I?' moment. As we said earlier on, we can think that a character is 'us' and aspire to be acting in that part all of the time, and we might have strong feelings about that and why we felt the need to do that! As we start to untangle ourselves we realise that these characters might have been hiding other parts of us too, which we might now want to get to know better. To make things even more complicated, we might realise that other people relate to these characters and might not have seen behind those walls at all! This can affect our relationships at home, in friendship groups, at work. It's a lot.

So, what do we do with that?

MOURNING

First of all, if you haven't already, could you take a really big sigh in and a huge long sigh out from your open mouth? Let's do that again. And one more time, and even one more time after that, until you feel a sense of calm in your body. Give yourself a little shake, yawn and stretch if you want to. You have done a LOT of work.

You might be feeling a bit lighter, liberated, clearer in your mind about what you are bringing to . . . well, yourself. You might have lowered a few walls. But you might also be feeling pretty churned up about all of this. Maybe it's brought out some difficult memories. It can be so hard to face the ways in which we've learned to protect ourselves, because it means we might come face to face with what we've been protecting.

If you're feeling sad, please allow that to be there. If you're angry, allow that too. A reminder that we're not blaming or shaming here, we're working from the understanding that everyone has done their best with what they had. Sometimes 'best' wasn't enough for you.

There might be grief coming up for you – for the parts of you that you've kept hidden, for the love you wish you'd had, the opportunities you've lost, the family legacies that you inherited that you didn't choose. Sometimes we need to grieve for those parts of us that didn't get what they needed, in order to really step into the present. If that's where you are, how can you give some room to that? Spend some time thinking about how you feel, talk to others about it if you need to.

Allow yourself to mourn for what could have been, so you can look ahead to what will come.

If you're tired, give yourself a breather and let this all settle. You might find in the coming days that you notice more of these characters and how they show up in your life. You might feel a little confused, and that's OK. It's been full-on. So take your time, write about what you're noticing, talk to someone, talk to lots of someones. And just keep remembering that you're doing something pretty amazing by walking these paths with me.

Let's just check in before we move on.

1. How are you feeling? (How is your heart rate, your energy levels; how do you feel in your body? And how are your emotions? Are you feeling anxious, sad, excited, curious, something else?)
2. What has reading Part II raised for you? (In terms of information, ideas, memories, feelings?)
3. What one thing would you like to remember from these chapters?

PART III

The Other Humans
in Your Story

CHAPTER 8

Partners Who Parent

'The greatest lie ever told about love is that it sets you free.'

Zadie Smith

Although sometimes we may feel that we do, we don't exist in a vacuum. We are influenced not only by our histories but also by the people we are connected to and the environments we live in. These might be things that affect us directly – like state-led postnatal care, or the head teacher at your children's school, or the accessibility of playgrounds in your area. But they go all the way up to the attitudes in your society and historical changes that you live through such as, for example, a global pandemic, #MeToo, Brexit, #BlackLives-Matter, the repudiation of Roe v. Wade, global recessions, the climate crisis. All of these interact with each other, and shift over the course of a lifetime. And, just as all of these things will influence our parenting, they will also influence our children.

This is what we so often miss when we talk about parenting. We focus on the role of the parent in a child's life, but less on the ways that children are born into whole networks of other people. Part of development is figuring out how to exist as part of these networks. And we focus on what parents are doing, and hardly at all on what is happening in their lives and how this influences their feelings, their parenting capacity and their decisions.

One of the most important influences on our parenting journey is who you are raising your child or children with. It's obvious really, isn't it, but where in all the stories about love is the one about how love can be stretched to its limits at 4am when you're both looking at each other over screaming children, with your eyes pleading 'DO SOMETHING!' Or, stretched to breaking point when you're looking at a partner who is fast asleep despite those screaming children . . .

When we talk about parenting, we tend to focus on a mother and a child. We rarely discuss parenting as a couple, the role of fathers, partners and co-parents, or the impact of parenting solo. But, here in the UK, the majority of people parent in an opposite or same-sex couple. And while the number of lone parents is increasing, with one study finding that a third of families they studied had experienced single parenthood, blended families are also increasing due to those lone parents finding new partners. Families shift and change over time, so a child might be raised by parents, grandparents and step-parents in their lifetime. And we as parents might have to negotiate our parenting decisions with all those people too.

Somehow, we have to join our maps together with the maps of numerous different people – some of whom want to go in a very different direction to us.

And *that* can be fraught with tension.

If you are currently parenting or planning to parent with someone else, you might want to consider getting them involved in this book if you haven't already. What I tend to find in my clinical practice and conversations with parents – especially where they are parenting as a couple – is that one parent has spread their map out, examined it, got some tour guides involved to help them navigate the uncharted territories, and then invited their partner to spread their map out too. And the partner's response is tantamount to 'I don't need a map,

I know the way.' Or perhaps 'I have my own map, you should definitely follow me.' Or sometimes 'What map? I don't have a map.' Sometimes behind those responses are 'What will happen if I get out my map?' and 'What will you think of me if I admit I don't know the way?'

And of course we end up wandering down different paths. And then issues start to appear in the form of resentment, frustration and disconnection.

Then that can make it a bit more confusing for everyone – because the parents and caregivers can become more invested in proving their way is the 'right' way than they are in connecting as a family and going on this journey together.

Some of us have a few more barriers to let down before we can even consider this sort of reflection – so it may be that you know already that inviting your partner or co-parent to read this book together might create a problem you don't have the energy to resolve right now. But if you think they might be up for doing this together, it might be an idea to chat about that now so that you can discuss the rest of it together. They can read the first few chapters on their own (and it is SUPER useful for you as a couple to understand these things about each other) and you could then work through the rest together.

I know how tricky these conversations can be, so feel free to show them this:

Hi – I'm Dr Emma Svanberg and I'm a clinical psychologist who works with parents-to-be, parents and caregivers, and I'd love for you to read this book.

We tend to think of parenting as something that comes naturally to us (especially to mothers). But actually parenting is a skill that we learn just like any other. Some people do have many of those skills handed down to them from their own parents – but many others need to learn them (and sometimes need to unlearn a lot too). Add to that, all children are unique and they may need you to learn about *them*, to be able to offer them what they need. Often, learning about ourselves and how we work can really help us see how our children operate.

When we learn this, we can find that parenting becomes much easier. Easier for us as parents, easier for us as people outside of our parenting, easier for our children. Which can lead to a bit more harmony at home. And what gets us there most quickly is doing that learning together as a parenting unit, so that you're on the same page and don't end up arguing about it when your child is mid-meltdown. Think of it like building blocks. The more aligned you are in your parenting aims and values, the more skills you feel you have up your sleeve, the more connected you are as a parenting team – the more solid the foundation is beneath your child's feet. Which means they will find it easier to flourish, and you will enjoy parenting more. And maybe your other relationships too (including your relationship with yourself).

If you are parenting on your own, or you know that your partner or co-parent doesn't have the headspace to consider this at the moment, everything that follows might help you understand that a little bit more, too.

You might be reading this and thinking that there is no way you could have this conversation with your partner because you feel afraid of their response. When there is abuse – whether that is physical violence, emotional abuse, coercive control (including financial control) – these conversations may not, in fact, be safe to have. If this feels like you, then please consider connecting with a supportive professional or organisation to help you bring safety into your life.

Joining Your Maps Together

We're going to spend the next few pages figuring out what can make it really hard to fit your maps together as a couple. Of course this is different in all couples, but there are themes that I hear about every day that I hope will shed some light on what happens within your four walls too. We can so often feel that we are the only ones to experience couple conflict, and often we are so invested in presenting a picture-perfect family life that we don't share these conflicts with those around us. If we did, we'd know just how common they are.

Imagine that you've spread your maps out together, but there's a gap between them.

If you take a look between your maps you'll find that gap is labelled 'imagined family life vs reality', and it may be as wide as the Grand Canyon. Let's call it Couple Canyon, if that's not too cheesy. There are bridges that can be built, but if you look a bit closer you might find a troll waiting underneath ready to jump out and shout at you if you try to cross over. This troll shouts things like 'But this just isn't FAIR' and 'You can't be tired, I'm tired' and 'You sound just like your mother/father' and 'You have no idea' and 'Your commute to work is basically a holiday compared to what I'm dealing with at home' and 'I just don't understand how the place is such a mess when you've been home all day' and 'If you talk to our child like that then you'll scar them for LIFE' and 'Oh God I'll just do it'. Sometimes it doesn't shout anything, it just glares so hard you run away.

When we're having problems as a couple we can often look over at our partner and wish that they could be different. If only they were calmer, more tolerant, less naggy, more understanding, put less pressure on us, stopped micromanaging us, spoke to us in more caring ways, shared their feelings, etc. then everything would be fine. It can really help to imagine that it's not that either one of you is the problem. It's the troll that's the problem. If you can team up to build a strong bridge then your relationship can be a bit more troll-proof.

Yet what can make it even harder to build those bridges is that you might start to figure out a way back to each other but then the land shifts and the canyon widens. The imagined family life changes as the world changes and things like gendered roles and expectations, childcare and work shift too. As a parenting couple, it is easy to feel like we've just reached solid ground and then find that it's suddenly shaking beneath our feet.

Becoming Parents

So, I'd like you to imagine that you're standing on one side of the canyon, on the edge of your map. And your partner is on the other side, on the edge of theirs. You'll know how far apart you are at the moment, and also some of the sections of bridge that you have already built together.

First let's think about why that gap opened up in the first place. It might, in fact, have always been there.

One of the trickiest things about becoming parents together is that it can highlight all of the parts of a couple relationship that might have felt acceptable until the relationship came under pressure. For most parent couples, once that first year or so of parenthood has passed, they find that they have weathered the storm and perhaps even come out stronger. But if our journey to parenthood or becoming parents has exacerbated previous problems, or created new ones, we can get stuck in conflict that feels very difficult to resolve.

Becoming parents together isn't just about having a child – it involves bringing together two possibly very different value systems and trying to create a shared set of family values. This is difficult enough – and even more so if we have to build other bridges to cross too due to different racial, ethnic, socioeconomic, political, class, cultural or other backgrounds.

Becoming parents also changes us as individuals, and in raising our children we may come face to face with all of the things we talked about in Part I. We often find that what we want from our partnership has changed. And what we want to offer to our actual, real-life children (not the ones that we imagined together) might be different too.

Let's start at the beginning. Where you started from as a couple. What you wanted for yourselves. If you take a look on your individual maps, you might be able to see a little Cupid in the corner, raining arrows down. They'll be labelled different things depending on what led you to develop your ideas about being a couple and your ideas about love. Perhaps they are labelled things like 'Happy couples love everything about each other' or 'I must not repeat my parent's relationship' or '90s romcoms' or 'Dating and relationship rules that I read in my teens and twenties that have seeped their way into my unconscious' (that's a common one).

And, just as we did in understanding you as an individual, the more we understand how you work as a parenting unit, the stronger that bridge will be for you and for the children who will happily skip across it without fear of trolls.

The Broken Bridge

Thanks to Cupid – and the sorts of ideas and stories we see and hear about as we grow – often we enter our couple relationships with clear ideas about what they will be like. These might relate to the dances we learned about in Chapter 6, alongside all those other arrows. And, because love is a powerful thing, we can even convince ourselves that we are living out these ideas. We see our partner through a lens, determined to see the love story that we think is written for us. And we act in ways that match that story too (even if there are others in our cast of characters who might feel silenced, feel a bit worried about how that story will end or jump in to defend us).

These are some of the stories that built the bridge between us before children came along. On that bridge is written, maybe in invisible ink because often these things are unspoken, the agreements that you have with each other and the expectations that you hold of each other.

Perhaps those words read something like . . .

'As we create our life together, I feel like I really want to look after you. We both feel that our relationship is important and we will prioritise that by, for example, making sure that Friday night is always for us. We'll get home, put comfy clothes on, get a takeaway and watch a film together. We care about our families and want them to be involved in our lives, so we understand that if a parent calls when we are together, that is a call that needs to be answered. We have an expectation that I/you will give up work to raise our children when we have them.'

Or maybe:

'We both work full time and we care about our jobs, so we will support each other in achieving our ambitions. Freedom and independence are priorities for us, so we will not complain when the other one cancels plans or spends a lot of the week with friends or other people. We agree not to feel a sense of duty over each other's friends and families. We hope having children won't change our lives too much.'

Or perhaps:

'We want to create a relationship that works on our unique terms, and we talk a lot about what we both want. It's important to us that we have an equal partnership - our responsibilities at home and to each other are shared and openly discussed. We will bring this openness and wish for equity into our parenting.'

These are the briefest of examples and of course there are multiple nuances to these expectations that we negotiate over time, without even realising. From small things like who takes the bins out and which side of the bed we sleep on, to the bigger things like how we relate to each other's families and friends and how we distribute our money. And the unspoken things like whose opinion gets listened to the most and how prepared we are to do what society thinks we should.

What happens when we have a child – often even from when we first start talking about having a child – is that the bridge starts to wobble, and maybe even break. We realise that there were lots of things unspoken that we no longer can or want to do. Or other things cause cracks to appear. So we need to strengthen it, rebuild the broken bits by reassessing what is written on them.

Except, we don't tend to do that. Because we're tired, and because we feel like we 'should' just be able to navigate this stuff without discussing it (because of those romcoms, maybe) or because we don't want things to change. Sometimes the bridge crashes to the ground completely, and we forge on our separate sides of the Couple Canyon without knowing what our expectations of each other are at all and feeling angry and resentful that they're not being met.

Try answering these next questions together. Sometimes we might disagree on what our bridge was built on – or feel that we had or have a role that hasn't been recognised. Often we are in positions that we feel trapped in and can't imagine what a bridge might look like. If you can, just hear each other out without judgement or correcting each other's perspective. You could even take it in turns to talk without interruption while the other commits to deeply listening and trying to understand your view even if they don't agree. Or write out some notes separately about what you both think of these questions, then discuss them together. Sometimes the differences between these ideas can help us understand where our disagreements come from. And in working together to build a new bridge based on life as it is now, we might get a step closer to joining those maps together.

1. What do you think your bridge was built on before you had children or started talking about children? This might cover household responsibilities, money, friendships, family, sex, roles, and much more.

2. How clear were the words on that bridge? Did you talk openly about your expectations of each other and the relationship? If yes, what helped you do that? If no, what stopped you? And if no, how do you feel about talking explicitly about your expectations of each other? (Are there any stories getting in the way here, like that it's not very sexy or romantic to talk about this stuff? What do those stories cost you?)

3. How do you think the bridge has changed, or broken, since becoming parents or talking about having children?

4. What do you think needs to be spoken about in order to build a new bridge or strengthen the one you have already? (For example, household chores, the bits of yourself that you're feeling vulnerable about, emotional exhaustion, work pressures, wider family difficulties.) In bringing those assumptions, expectations and resentments to the surface you may find solutions that work for you, as you are now. It's important to note here that parenting and household chores are two separate topics. They are often linked together (and that's worth a discussion in itself), but separating them out can resolve a lot of confusion.

5. What makes it harder to fulfil these expectations and assumptions? What do you think your partner needs to

know about your life as it is now that could cause that troll to emerge? (E.g. that the expectation that you'll be home every night at bath time might be too hard to fulfil because of work pressures, even though you really wish this wasn't the case. Or the assumption that you'll have a chat after dinner feels impossible because you're so drained by the end of the day, but could we connect in another way, or just tolerate that for a little while? Or even the expectation that you'll complete this book together feels overwhelming because actually reading is a challenge for you but you'd love to hear a summary if that's OK?)

Come Together

Alongside those pressures on couples, we also face expectations about what it means to be a parent in our individual roles. Couples often assume that one partner will be the primary parent and the other partner will be in a supporting role. This is often amplified by the way complex child development research has been reduced down to the importance of one primary caregiver. How this plays out in many families – because of an intricate mixture of gender expectations, work, money, social assumptions, emotional awareness and so much more – is that one partner ends up feeling overburdened by their unseen caring responsibilities and everything that comes along with that, while the other might feel excluded and unsure of their position in the family. Inevitably this can widen that canyon, and can come with an unspoken assumption that the other parent's map doesn't really matter that much.

Yet the reality for children is that both parents – and the other people in their lives – influence them. They read all of those maps whether we know it or not – and whether we're familiar with them ourselves or not.

We talked in Chapter 6 about how attachment is not only a dance between two people, but encompasses a whole network of dancers – so a child might learn different dances with different people and also learn to dance together in much more complex relationships. Let's consider how the dances that you learned about back in Chapter 6 might help you to do some bridge-building as a partnership.

Family Dances

We can imagine that a couple start dancing together as a duo. At its best, even when we may not have been taught that steady waltz by our own parents, with time and understanding we might be able to learn to waltz together. And this helps us to practise the warmth, reciprocity and intimacy that help us in our parenting. As we become parents, ideally our waltz will expand so that we become a family dancing together, feet in sync, with each individual contributing to that steady rhythm.

But what can happen in many families is that both parents (or more than two parents or caregivers) are dancing their own steps, out of sync with each other. And the more this happens, the more the bridge cracks.

We might find that one partner is trying to pull the other in close, and the other is constantly running back to their own side of the canyon. Or that both partners are tightly clasped, cheek to cheek and unable to step away without one of them falling over the bridge. Both partners may be dancing alone at the opposite ends of the bridge, or even far into their own maps out of sight. There might be complicated steps involving other people too. We may have been attracted to partners who offered something different to the dances we were raised with, or we might find that we have repeated familiar dances without realising.

When we bring a child or children into these dances, we are forced to look at the steps we have been taking together and figure out how to welcome them on to the bridge with us. The love we have for a child, and our eagerness to dance steadily with them, can make us acutely aware of the anxiety, avoidance, criticism, withdrawal, rejection and even denigration that might have been part of our dance before their arrival.

We also have to figure out how to bring someone else into these steps. Sometimes, even when we're dancing different dances, we learn steps so that they can have a steady rhythm. For example, if one parent is dancing an Irish dance of avoidance, and the other has a bit more of an Argentine tango of anxious attachment in their repertoire, when a child joins we might find that we compensate for each other so that our child has a consistent tempo. But, often, we battle over the steps that we think our child should learn.

As a result, children may have to carefully figure out how to dance all these different steps to stay on that bridge with us. Sometimes there isn't room for a child to come into the dance at all. Or sometimes a partner is cast aside and the child is the only dancing partner – someone who might finally dance the steps you've always wanted to dance. Sometimes, a child is swung in a rhythmic tug-of-war between their parents, who are both convinced that the child has to dance their steps with them. Where parents are involved in a conflict, a child might feel a conflict in their own loyalty too. This can be confusing for a child, who has to ally themselves with one parent in order to feel safe – a process called triangulation.

Let's pause here for a moment, because this might have brought up some difficult feelings for you. We tend to focus on our parenting and much less on our couple relationship, even though it can feel difficult. We might have considered the impact on our child or children but often we find it hard to go there. Parenting often brings huge frustrations into our relationship and, in the whirlwind of family life, it can be hard to figure out where to even begin to make things feel better. But once we notice the steps we're dancing and look at how our children are getting led around, we can begin to make changes if we need to. If possible, see if you can discuss these next questions with your partner or co-parent. Otherwise, have a think about them on your own.

- Going back to Chapter 6, what dances do you think you both learned – and how do these dances work together?
- Are there times you have struggled to follow each other's steps? How has this shown up in your relationship?
- Is this sometimes a source of conflict?
- What sort of dances do you think are happening between you (individually) and your baby/child/ children?
- How do you think your children are involved in your dance as a couple?
- Is there anything you'd like to change about those dances? How can you do that?

Sometimes we need to get a professional dance teacher involved to help us get back in sync as a couple who are parenting together. Often people assume that couples therapy is for when couples are on the verge of separation, or when there are high levels of conflict. In fact, couples therapy can be a brilliant way of supporting you through life transitions and giving you the space to consider how you want to move forward as a team with a skilled, objective third party.

Let's pause again, and take a few breaths here, for a moment.

This is big stuff we're talking about – we're discussing attachment relationships between you as a couple, you individually, you with your children and you as a family. We're only on Chapter 8 and if we were in a therapeutic relationship together, it could well have taken us months to get to this point. So just check in with yourself, call up that guide if you need to, take yourself off to your resting place, or just put this down for a few minutes and take some long slow sighs. If your head is spinning for any reason, go and do something else for a while and let this settle before you come back to it.

Bringing In Our Children

This is a tricky bit, something that even when we know it deep down we can find really hard to bring to our awareness. How our couple conflicts impact our children and the way they relate to us. What happens to our children when that bridge is broken. As you read on just remember the intention you set in Chapter 3 – why you're reading this book and your hopes for your family (see page 47). This is stuff that we've often shoved right to the back of the cupboard, but let's bring it out and take a good look at it, so we can fold it neatly away.

When couples feel content (most of the time, because we're never content all the time) in their relationships, it's not hard to see that this has a positive impact on their parenting. Satisfaction in a relationship is, of course, associated with more cooperative parenting – parents support one another and resolve parenting differences more amicably. And shared involvement in childcare from the adults in their lives not only benefits children but also improves relationship satisfaction, leading to more allied parenting practices. This creates a cycle where everyone benefits.

But tension in a relationship not only affects how joined up parents are in their parenting, it also spills over into individual relationships with a child. When we are arguing with our partners or co-parents, we are more likely to argue with our children too. Or, we might compensate for the lack of intimacy or affection in our couple relationship by pouring this into our children.

It's not just triangles that can develop but spiders' webs of sticky relationship dynamics – where parents can end up 'gate-keeping' each other's relationship with their children and acting out their conflict through their children – and children can express their unease through their mood and behaviour.

It gets complicated pretty quickly doesn't it, which explains why conversations about your relationship and parenting once you have had children can feel so very difficult. We're not just talking about how you deal with bedtime – we're talking about two different, individual histories coming together around unique (often demanding) children in complex social circumstances.

- Does this resonate with you in your own couple or co-parenting relationship?
- Where does this leave you?
- Is there anything you'd like to change in the way that you respond to your partner/co-parent? Especially now you might know a little more about their map?
- What stops this from happening?
- What needs to change in order to make progress together?

Parent ≠ Mother

That Couple Canyon is often so wide because what we thought we'd want when we first imagined our family life might be very different to what we wanted when we met our partner, and might be different again when we have an actual real-life child. Part of that difference comes from the shifting ground of gender roles in our couple relationship.

I'm focusing more here on families who find themselves in heteronormative set-ups. I say 'find themselves' because that is so often the experience of parents I work with – that they seem to have landed in a traditional family set-up without having actively wanted this to happen. Couples and families who are parenting outside of heteronormative expectations have often figured out how to join their maps up before children come along. Without the fairy tales of family life that heterosexual couples have been raised with, LGBTQI+ couples and non-traditional family set-ups (such as friends choosing to parent together or a parent who chooses to have a child solo) are more likely to create maps based on the roles that suit their unique circumstances. That's not to say that conflict doesn't arise, or that there aren't additional difficulties such as stigma, but just that gender roles may not be as central to them. And, of course, there are many couples who do actively choose to parent according to more traditional gender roles, but find that their maps join up because this has been a conscious choice with open discussion around shared values.

As ideas about masculinity and femininity evolve, as well as the very concepts of gender, family, parenthood, we can feel that we're trying to build bridges on constantly shifting sands.

Of course, this is not how we have these conversations in our homes. We don't tend to say, 'I don't want to do your laundry because I resent the patriarchal structures that have meant both that I considered how to fit parenting into my life before I even started my career and also that my work was less financially rewarding than yours, so I've ended up juggling part-time work/staying at home with our children and I resent how little that is recognised by you and by wider society, so you can wash your own flippin' underpants.' Nor do we tend to say, 'I have no idea what you're talking about when you say I need to validate our children's emotions because from about the age of five if I even considered that I might have an emotion other than joy or anger I would have been ridiculed by everyone, so I don't actually quite know what my own emotions feel like let alone our child's and I wish I could talk to you about this but

I don't know how without feeling really exposed and you're so frustrated with me that I don't know how you'd take it.'

And we don't tend to sit down when we start talking about having a child together and chat about what we learned about mothering and fathering from seeing our own parents, and how that impacted on us, and what we might want to do differently in the context we are currently living in.

Maybe now we might see more chats about mental load, or the unequal ways that childcare and household labour is divided up between couples. This is certainly a topic that comes up regularly – and heatedly – in the conversations I have with parents. And this is a reality – that our gender revolution stalled with our parents' generation, with cross-national trends showing that women still do twice as much household labour and childcare as men. This is despite global trends towards more egalitarian family set-ups, and often despite our very best intentions. Trying to figure this out for our own families tends to bring out the troll from under the bridge and lead to a battle about who has it the hardest.

What we can more easily talk about as couples is feeling stuck. We might be at a point where we know the canyon is there, but we don't know how to build the bridge because we haven't quite established what we want it to look like yet. And it can be so hard to talk about for these very reasons – because we're not just talking about laundry, or tantrums. We're talking about hugely complex societal stories about power and inequality that have influenced our lives and are so hard to untangle that we don't know where to begin.

This is something that I see a lot in the parents I speak to. Dads who wish to be different to their own fathers or models of fathering they may have seen as normal, but who do not know how to and still feel the pressure of wanting to be a 'provider'. Being more involved, but finding it hard to step out of a traditional, authoritarian role. Wanting to feel more emotionally connected to their families and build strong bridges, but not speaking the language that can cross that canyon. Mums who feel torn between the mothering role that has been held up to them on a pedestal, questioning the self-sacrifice of their own mothers and dealing with the reality of juggling work, family and their own sense of self. Reluctant 'captains of the household' feeling dissatisfied, resentful and burnt out but without time to do anything about it between work deadlines, school plays and stocking the fridge, and wanting someone else to do the bridge-building.

Perhaps we can simplify it all. Because what we're aiming for is a (fairly) sturdy bridge that our child can dance on, and the foundation of that is simply love. Love that brought us together, love that provides a rhythm for our family, love that might look nothing like the arrows Cupid shot at us but which keeps us connected through adversity, and love that we want to express to our children and receive from them. But love is a really difficult concept for many people.

How can we ensure that both men and women are allowed feelings of love, and are encouraged to express love to each other and their children? Because really that's all we're talking about. How we raise our children in loving homes, and what that looks like to us. And, for bonus points, how we ensure we continue to feel loved by one another – in the way we need, not the way our partner assumes – when we're covered in snot and can only talk in grunts.

Whether or not you are reading this with a partner or co-parent, I'd really encourage you to talk over these next questions together with them. You might want to add some of your own depending on your own family arrangement. You could go through them over a few evenings, or spend an hour reading through them and using them as a conversation starter. Even if you are not in a couple, if your relationship is amicable see if you are able to talk over some of the stories that influence you in your parenting. If you are parenting solo, gendered expectations and how these show up in your life may still feel relevant even if not a source of conflict.

Again, please listen without judgement and holding a sense of curiosity about each other's experience. There are no right answers here. Each time we learn these things about each other, we understand each other better and we build that bridge a little more.

- How are you feeling about being a mum/dad?
- What are the stories that you have heard about being a dad/mum and what a dad/mum does?
- What are the expectations this created for you?
- Do you have particular role models in your parenting? Do they fit with what we're aiming for as a family?
- When you think about the gender of our children, what does this bring up for you about the ideas you've heard about your own gender? Do you want to do anything differently for them?
- How do you feel about love? And the way we show love to our children and each other? What do we need from each other to feel loved, in the stress of family life?

Even when we are clearer about how we want to build bridges in our own home, we might notice that there are other obstacles in the way. Pregnancy and birth information is women-focused, and services are centred on a mother and her infant. Expectations of parents by wider society are deep-rooted – mums and dads experience both small but important differences (like a dad being smiled at for pushing a buggy while a mum pushing that same buggy might be tutted at for taking up the pavement) and big ones (such as the 'motherhood penalty' – the gender pay gap increasing for mothers). And policies and structures that encourage more equal parenting are lagging far behind. Those few countries that support equal involvement in both work and home not only improve women's opportunities for work but also show major benefits for both the couple relationship and both parents' relationship with their children. Where policy has been put in place to allow that Couple Canyon to be bridged, life satisfaction increases – especially for women. So while we can have these conversations in our homes, we also need societal support to give families the chance to really figure out what will work for them, in their own unique circumstances.

So, if you do sometimes find in your own home that the canyon can feel uncrossable – you're not alone. And while we can find ways to make things work better for us, it can help to know that there are some really big obstacles in the way to building those bridges. If we can team up as a couple to find ways to overcome them, we might find our way together again.

Dealing with Conflict

Sometimes it's hard to think about having these conversations together because even talking about having a conversation can cause yet another argument. Just as we looked at power in our relationships with our own parents and caregivers, it's important to look at power in our couple or co-parenting relationships too. Because power struggles can really get in the way of being able to find solutions. Asserting our power offers us validation of our role in the short term but keeps us stuck in that role (which we may no longer want when we stop and think about it!) in the longer term. This feeds that troll under the bridge.

Power can be demonstrated overtly ('I'm putting my foot down! Don't undermine me!') or covertly through gatekeeping ('You're not soothing the baby like that – here, give them to me') or withdrawal ('Screw them, if they won't engage with this I'm just going to do it all by myself.'). One partner might also feel less willing to talk about change or compromise because their position allows them to hold more power – whether consciously or not – and this might lead to a rupture in the relationship that feels difficult to resolve.

But most adults who parent together, whether as a couple or not, have a wish to resolve conflicts in order to best support their child or children. And rather than get caught up in who is 'right' – who needs to change to solve problems – it can help to see that troll under the bridge as a shared problem. So what does the troll need to be able to let you pass over that bridge?

You could think about the troll as another character – one that is protecting you both in different ways from some of the injustices or conflicts that impact on your relationship or have affected you in the past. What might that troll need to hear from both of you to be able to step aside? What might you need to hear from each other?

Having the opportunity to get to know each other's maps can really help you tackle that troll too. It moves us away from blame and towards an understanding of how we operate. So we can see our differences with compassion, and build on our individual strengths. One partner might turn up excited about their hammer and nails, the other might be determined that wood is needed . . . but together you can figure out how to turn all of that into a bridge that works together.

Bridge-building

Once we bring these ideas to light we have a huge opportunity to create a revolution in our own home. We get to decide how we want to parent together and the sort of foundation we want to create for our own family. We get to decide what that bridge looks like, and even how we want to landscape that Couple Canyon.

Here's a starting point for some conversations together on how to bring all of this into a plan. You might just want to choose one or two to go through together at a time, and set aside a good hour to do so. Think about the information that you have learned from the previous chapters about your own experiences and how they might be influencing you both in your couple or co-parenting relationship and also in your own parenting. If you are parenting solo, many of these questions will also be relevant for you.

Just a few tips first. Try to listen to each other without judgement – we have all developed attitudes, beliefs and opinions based on what felt right for us and what has kept us psychologically safe. We might find some of these hard to let go of or adapt, but when we can come to compromise about this as a couple or co-parenting unit then we can create more solid foundations for our children. We all operate differently, and are often attracted to people who are very different to us. So while we might get frustrated because our partner is quiet, they might just need a bit longer to process and consider what we're saying, and feel overwhelmed by our impatience. Or while we want to go away and research different ideas, our partner might need to know that we want to find a resolution as much as they do.

You could also prepare by having a talk about talking. Make conversations easier by telling each other what works for you, what you find difficult and what you are hoping for. And as you're talking, make it OK to check in with each other (for example, 'You're really quiet now and I feel like you're tuning out' or 'You're talking about a lot of different things, would it be OK to slow things down?'). Healthy communication strategies aren't part of any romcoms but they can make for a more harmonious home and, as a bonus, if this becomes part of our family life and our children see this too, we can build a household where curiosity about and compassion for each other's experiences becomes more everyday.

If you find yourself getting annoyed or frustrated, then take a break. Bear in mind we're dancing the dances we learned a long time ago. This stuff doesn't get resolved overnight. And if trying to have these conversations proves harder than you'd hoped, it might be time to speak to a third party together to help you parent as a team.

- What do you want to model for your children? In terms of how you model communication, gender roles, stress management, work–life balance and so on?
- How would you hope that they might parent their own children in a partnership?
- What values do you both hold dear for your family life? What are the bridge-building blocks you see as essential for family? (Values are fundamental guiding principles; they might include how we relate to one another, what things are important to us, how we are in our home and work/school.)
- What do you think our parenting strengths are? What are the things we need to work on together? How can we help each other do this?
- How can we stay a team even when times are tough? How are we going to remind each other that we've made a commitment to do this?
- In light of the emphasis on imperfect alliances, and knowing there are many ways we will frustrate and annoy each other, how are we going to stay supportive? How can we give each other the time and space we need to be separate people? What do we need from each other to show that we still care even when we're irritating each other?

Set aside time every week to check in with each other – without judgement – to see how parenting is going for each of you, to keep maintaining that bridge and form an alliance against that troll.

If you are in a blended family, you might want to expand

the conversations in this chapter to include the other adults who are involved in parenting your child or children – or consider ways to ensure your family dance can stay as steady as possible.

How Change Happens – Slow and Steady

Often what happens when I'm having these discussions with parents is that one partner can really see where they'd like to get to and is frustrated that their partner doesn't seem to be on board. Particularly when we are talking about changing the balance of household labour and childcare, or the ways that we are parenting – we are never just talking about the surface-level topic, we are also speaking about something much more fundamental, which is rarely named. So – if we are the partner hoping to make changes – we might experience a push back, or reluctance to engage, or dismissal.

Change is hard, and a resistance to change isn't a sign of stubbornness or unwillingness. It's usually about fear. Fear of what it means that we are being asked to change, fear of what it means that we developed these behaviours in the first place, fear of what will happen if we do something unfamiliar. Fear of messing up. Fear that we're not good enough as we are.

We need a lot of patience to be a willing and active participant in a family, and even more patience when we are instigating change.

Here are five things that could help a little:

1. Change is incremental

Change happens slowly, over time, and often not in the way that we expect. Because we often implement change at times of crisis, we tend to set a high bar. Then we get frustrated and despondent when it's not reached.

If we can set incremental goals on the way to a larger goal, we might be able to hold on to hope while we create change. This can happen together as a team. So perhaps the end goal is sharing bedtime more equally. On the way there you might need to support each other, figure out what works and expect a few bumps in the road (from the children too, because little humans resist change just as much as big humans).

2. It's never just about the 'thing'

When we're making a change – even when we might understand what we're aiming for – our hearts might not have caught up yet. So we might agree to a change, and even want that change, but when we're faced with the reality of it in the moment our old dance gets repeated. Those little kid parts come up and say, 'Well I had it SO much worse' and the Ogre might come out and put their foot down. This can feel really complicated to untangle, but strong reactions are usually a sign that something from those stories about your or your partner's childhood and babyhood may have been touched upon. Rather than getting frustrated at what might appear to be resistance to change, get curious together about why change feels hard.

3. Clear, repeated communication supports change

It might take a while for a general principle to filter down, to figure out together what it means to us, to be tested against stressful moments, then finally be understood by the heart and absorbed into everyday life. We might need to discuss a topic or goal repeatedly before it really lands. And even then, we often behave in automatic ways, so inevitably there will be times when we slip back into something familiar even if we don't want to. One of you might feel like a broken record, but applying the same idea to many different real-life situations takes time and calm, repeated communication. A 'Hey, you know when you x, y, z to our child? That was that thing we were talking about' will bring more movement than our usual 'What are you doing? We said we weren't going to do that!'

4. Keep listening to your little kid

What makes this all so much harder, of course, is that those little kids inside us get activated both in our relationships with our partners and in watching their interactions with our own children. This can create such a sense of urgency in us that the previous three points are hard to tolerate. And we can respond from those more vulnerable baby and little child parts of us – or from some of those characters we developed to shield those vulnerable parts from further harm. We might feel personally under attack when we witness our partner acting in a way that affected us as a child. So how can we respond as calm, curious, patient adults when the little kids in us are taking over?

Knowing this about each other can help us understand why sometimes a behaviour might bring a big reaction. And knowing this about ourselves – through all of the exploration we've done so far – can help those younger parts of us feel listened to so they don't pop out quite so suddenly.

5. Forgiveness makes change easier

Most of all, which we will discuss in more depth in Part IV, when we're making changes we're going to make umpteen mistakes, and feel defeated and like things are always going to feel difficult. Just as we said at the start of this book, we are all works in progress, always. If we can forgive our partners and co-parents when they do things we wish they wouldn't, that will help us talk about the change we want to make with more compassion. And, of course, we have to forgive ourselves too.

Where Are You Now?

It may be that quite a lot shifted for you, and maybe your partner or co-parent too, over the course of this chapter. You might be left with more questions; there might be some issues that you realise you need to talk over in more depth. You might have found a bridge. Or it may have felt that the Couple Canyon grew even wider if those conversations just felt too difficult to have.

Take some time to see where this has all landed with you. Maybe you're wondering whether you feel OK about the role that you're in. Maybe you feel OK in the role itself but you need a bit more acknowledgement from your partner or other people. Maybe you would like to model something different for your children.

We've also spoken about mammoth, historical issues that influence us all. But we can build a simple, little wooden bridge between our maps just by being prepared to listen to each other. That might not result in shared parenting responsibilities, but it might mean a partner understands just why it's so important that they get up with you at night-time, or ask you about your day, or listen to you rehash the details of a tantrum.

And just by asking, 'What's really important to you?' and 'Why?', we create a structure we can build on. We might not solve these gaps overnight, or even in our lifetime, but we can help each other to stay on the bridge.

In the next chapter we're going to think about other people in your life who might influence you as parents – those who have contributed to our maps as well as the very paper they are drawn on.

CHAPTER 9

Your Supporting Cast

*'After a good dinner one can forgive
anybody, even one's own relations.'*

Oscar Wilde

I 'd like to take a look back at your map and see if there's
anyone else milling around. Because one of the things I
hear most from parents is just how very lonely parenting
can be. It can feel like a paradox, because you are so rarely
alone, but modern parenthood isolates us from others. Socially,
and emotionally.

Some of this comes from those stories we talked about earlier. Stories like 'Parenting is natural so I should be able to do
this on my own,' 'It's not OK to ask for help otherwise people
will think I'm not coping' and 'My family and friends don't
approve of how I'm parenting, so I can't let them know how
hard I'm finding this.' Some of it comes from modern life, and
how often we are parenting behind closed doors with enormous and ever-changing pressure (more on that in the next
chapter). Some of it comes from our particular circumstances,
which can leave us lonelier than others (such as if we are a new
parent with a small baby, or are parenting a child with a
chronic illness or disability, or parenting alone). Some of it
comes from how much parenting practices or our parenting

aspirations have changed since we were parented ourselves, which can make us feel we are treading new ground alone.

But we humans are social creatures, and historically and cross-culturally we have raised children in groups. And, when we are pouring out our love into our children, we need love poured back into us. We need connections with other humans. Psychoanalyst Wilfred Bion described this most accurately in his concept of containment. As parents, we are containers for our children. We absorb their raw emotions, digest them and hand them back in more palatable ways. And we need this too – in a way that works for us. We need people, our communities and society as a whole to hear our raw emotions, absorb them and let us know that they are acceptable. This frees us to move forward and think of solutions ourselves, ones that will work for us. But we so rarely receive this.

Did you consider how supported you'd feel, or not, when you became a parent? Because we don't often acknowledge just how quickly the visitors drift off (and how they sometimes don't even come for subsequent babies). Or how often visitors come when we're desperate for a shower and the use of our arms, but then sit down as we make them a cup of tea and stifle the pleas for help. Sometimes we have multiple people around us, we might even be living with extended family who are all there to hold a baby and offer a snack, but feel lonelier than ever because they keep telling us what we should do and how we should feel and their assumptions are a world away from our wishes and our reality. And sometimes when we do ask for help – from friends, family or professional services – our desperation is minimised and dismissed as a normal part of parenting when we feel like our world has collapsed.

Just as a little aside – when we are in the thick of parenting stresses we can often assume that others have (or had) it easier. That in days gone by parents were better supported, or that other cultures offer more support for families. But loneliness and isolation have long been the experience of 'homemakers', since around the nineteenth century. Even in cultures that are praised for their care for mothers (such as the many cultures that support a period of around 40 days to restore maternal well-being and health after pregnancy and birth), in our modern world many parents find that these rituals simply add pressure in the absence of wider family support. And while we might long for support from our wider family, this can be complicated too. For example, one cross-cultural study across 11 countries found that the role of the mother-in-law was often cited as a source of unhappiness for new parents . . . so those jokes do have some truth to them after all.

Parents want help that they actually find helpful (not the help that is prescribed by traditional rituals, institutional care or family and social norms). And this help might look completely different for different families in their different set-ups. And, of course, being offered help that we don't find helpful makes us less likely to ask for help again. Being shamed for needing help (which is a horribly common experience) makes it even less likely.

Although of course we need many things as parents, two things become particularly important: practical help and emotional support. And, as we discussed in Chapter 6, becoming parents can bring us back to our most primitive, infantile needs. So often the first people we think of when we are in need of both are our own parents and caregivers. And we tend to think not of our actual parents and caregivers but the idealised ones. And that in itself can leave us feeling more isolated.

Those internalised parents or caregivers who taught you the steps that you're still dancing might well be external, real-life parents or caregivers who you are still dancing with today. If you have a look on your map, where are your own parents or caregivers on there? Still in your childhood home, in your current home or on a pathway in between? Or maybe they're not on your map. Many parents are parenting without their own parents alongside them. Even when a parent has died, we can find that becoming parents brings us into a new relationship with the memories we have of them. If we have become estranged – which is more common than we often realise, affecting around 1 in 5 families in the UK and 1 in 4 in the USA – having our own child can sometimes be the catalyst either to reconnect or to create more distance.

In the next section I'm going to talk about grandparents, but these words may not fit with your experience. So please take 'grandparent' to mean an older adult who took on a caregiving role with you, whether or not they are a blood relation, who may still be part of your extended family unit.

The Role of Grandparents

Historically, parents have turned to their own parents and wider family to support them in bringing up children. But, just as ideas of what family looks like and what parenting involves have changed enormously in the past 50 years, so have our relationships with our families of origin. And our expectations of them have changed too.

Some of this might be practical. Globalisation means that our families may exist across borders. However, there has also been such a significant shift in parenting that we might feel worlds apart even when we live next door. Even when we might share parenting styles with our own caregivers, or repeat the dances that we were taught, parenting practices and values have changed to such an extent that differences in attitudes to parenting will almost inevitably arise between generations.

What stories do we hold about grandparents? Kindly old ladies who come smelling of mints and teach our children how to mend their clothes? Tweed-wearing old men who connect our technology-focused world with slower-paced joys like fishing and woodwork? Loving, warm, grey-haired people who swoop in to kiss boo-boos and fold the laundry?

Does that describe your experience? Many grandparents absolutely are engaged and supportive members of the family, with around 40 per cent of grandparents in the UK and Europe offering regular childcare that brings mutual benefits to them and their grandchildren.

But this doesn't reconcile with many of the experiences I've heard about from the parents I speak to. These may be stories about grandparents who are absent for a host of reasons – from estrangement to simply making the most of retirement. Or those who are present but bring tension. Or grandparents who can't quite let go of the role of mother or father, bringing a power struggle over who is in charge. Or grandparents who they love but who, they suddenly realise, don't feel very safe for their own children. Or even just grandparents who are trying their very best but find it really hard to get their heads around how much parenting has changed and the expectations on them, and what this means about their own childhood and parenting journey.

While we might long for grandparents to ease the burden of parenthood, the reality is that the real-life, actual parents in our lives – coupled with the internalised parents we took on back in the nursery (see page 85) – can create a messy heap of mixed emotion for us. And for them too. Being challenged on the parenting choices that they made, at a time when perhaps that was the norm, can raise incredibly difficult feelings for grandparents who felt that they were doing their best with the information and capacity they had at the time.

Unsurprisingly, relationships with our parents and caregivers in our adult life often map on to the kind of dances we did with them in our childhood. There are similar cultural differences too – with, for example, detached parent relationships more common in Germany, amicable relationships more common in Norway, ambivalent (high-closeness alongside high-conflict) relationships more common in Israel, and the

USA seeing the least harmonious relationships between parents and their adult children.

- What fantasies about grandparents have you held? How has that changed?
- How has becoming a parent changed your relationship with your own parents or caregivers, if at all?
- How has becoming a parent changed how you view your own childhood, if at all?
- How can you, as an adult, grow into your parental role if you are still someone else's child? What does this mean in terms of what you might lose yourself?
- Where might conflicts arise in your parenting values or differences?
- What do you think has changed since you were a child, in parenting expectations?
- What circumstances were your parents/caregivers raising you in?

Remember when we talked about those internalised parents – and the baby self that they looked after (see page 83)? Coming face to face with our baby self as we raise our own children brings our ideas of what is acceptable parenting into stark relief. What felt OK for us may not feel OK for our children. We might look on our experiences differently. We have to move from being the kid in that relationship to being a fellow parent, and growing fully into our own adulthood, and that isn't an easy task. These relationships are often negotiated over time, with our partners too, and while some families will create close and supportive grandparental relationships many more will find whole new levels of grief and confusion and have to figure out where to draw new boundaries and create new relationships.

It's important to say here that you don't always need to have this conversation with your own parents or caregivers in order to resolve any of those hurt little kid feelings that come up for you now. Having conversations about the kind of parent you would like to be, and what this has raised for you about your own experience of being parented, can be tremendously difficult.

When caregivers are still alive, still present and are receptive to hearing our experiences, longings and hopes, this can be a step towards a healthy adult-to-adult relationship based on mutual support and acceptance of our shared (flawed) humanity. But sometimes, for a variety of reasons (not least that previous generations were often not brought up to discuss emotions openly), our parents and caregivers may simply not be able to open these doors with us. In these situations, rather than resolving past hurts, we might need to consider what we need to get resolution for ourselves and, sometimes, how to buffer ourselves.

So there might be more mourning to be done. Think back to that baby self that we met before (see page 83) and ask yourself what they might need from you right now. Do they need you to make a commitment to care for yourself? To call up your guide? Or to go and get a bear-hug from someone? Or perhaps just to read these words: 'I'm sorry that you didn't get what you needed then. This is a different time, and you can get what you need now, as an adult.'

Is there anyone else on those pathways?

Grown-up Siblings

We don't tend to talk much about these relationships in adulthood and how influential they can be for us and our children. Yet, our sibling relationships may be our most enduring. Our relationships with our siblings can vary, and change over our lifespan. They may be close, intimate relationships, actively hostile relationships and everything in between. When we feel that a parent has involved themselves in our sibling relationship, or favoured one sibling over another, we're more likely to not get on in later life. Conversely, siblings who have positive relationships with their parents are more likely to have warm relationships in adulthood. In some families, siblings may have been the ones to raise us – or we may have already had parenting experiences in caring for younger siblings. And our own experience of being a sibling can impact not only on our character (for example, firstborns are often more responsible but more likely to be stressed, while last-borns may be more rebellious!), but on how we relate to our own children and their position in the family. For example, if we see our younger child pestering their reluctant older sibling to play – as an older sibling ourselves who remembers how intrusive that could feel, we might be more likely to encourage our little one to find something else to do. But as a younger sibling who remembers that feeling of rejection, we might lean towards encouraging our bigger child to tolerate their little sibling.

If you didn't have siblings, that too can impact on how you feel about your role as a parent, how you feel about whether or not your own child has a sibling and even your tolerance for sibling battles.

- If you have a sibling, or siblings, what's your relationship like with them now?
- How involved are they in your family life?

Just as we may repeat dances we learned with our parents, in our own families we might find that we replay our own sibling relationships in the small things that we encourage and discourage between our own children. If we widen out that dance to include all the members of our wider families, we can even find that our children get pulled into the dances that we have with our siblings.

For example, siblings arguing over the level of involvement grandparents have might be an 'it's not fair' argument that has continued for decades.

Siblings can also offer support, and as aunts and uncles provide important relationships to our children. They might offer fun, be a confidant(e), even buffer the relationship between us and our children in times of conflict. And, as there are fewer fantasies and fairy tales about aunts and uncles, our siblings are often free to develop their own, unique relationship with our children.

- If you have a sibling or siblings, how was your relationship with them growing up? How about now?
- How do your siblings influence your children? And how do they support you in your parenting, if at all?
- If you have more than one child, what are you hoping for in their relationship? (Just pause to see if this feels realistic, or are there fantasies creeping in here? Where have those ideas come from?) How do you feel about supporting this relationship?
- What do you find most difficult about the relationship between your own children? Why do you think this is? Do those difficult moments remind you of anything from your own childhood?

How Change Happens – The Family Equilibrium

Becoming parents can lead to changes in our relationships with our own families, in both positive and more difficult ways. When we are trying to do something differently to how we were raised, this can feel like an implicit criticism to those who raised us or were raised with us, even when we value their presence. As our own families develop, and we form new family units, we and other members of our wider family might also experience a sense of loss of the family of origin we are leaving behind. And as we develop into our own adult, parent selves, we might also grapple with the assumptions that our families of origin make about us.

- What was your role in the family growing up?
- How has that shifted over time?
- How do you get 'pulled' back into old roles? How do you feel about that?
- How would you prefer to relate to those from your family of origin?
- How does your role in your family of origin influence how you feel about yourself now?
- What does this make you think about the family you are creating now?

It can be helpful to use an idea from family therapy to understand why this can feel like such a struggle when we become parents. If we think of a family as a system that creates its own sense of balance and order, each member contributes to that. Our families write stories that we are characters in, often over many generations. These stories make sense, but we may find as we grow and change that the role we are in no longer applies to us. However, to restore equilibrium a family will often – completely without realising – try to pull us back into our role because that is what makes sense in our family story (one of the reasons why you might end up feeling like a teenager when you're with your family for the holidays). Change occurs when one or more members of the family disrupt that equilibrium and bring about a seismic shift. This may feel uncomfortable but, hopefully, the family will then reorganise around this new narrative. We can rewrite our family stories, even those that were written a long time ago.

Remember that the map we have been exploring together might be pretty ancient. Multiple generations old, and rewritten many times over. And our siblings and other family members might have versions of this map, too. When we start to walk a different path, away from our childhood home, and say to our family, 'Hey look, let's go this way!', they might worry about us getting lost. That maybe we'll never find our way back to them.

These new paths can show up in so many ways. Maybe one new path is about asking our children what they want rather than telling them what to do. Maybe another is about sending our child to nursery when our parent stayed at home to look after us. Maybe one is about moving away from the rest of the family. Maybe another is about bringing up a child in a different religion, country or culture.

In bringing together our map with our partner's map, our own family might even join up with that troll under the bridge, saying, 'You can't do that! That's not how we do things!' The pull back to the family home might not be about our parenting at all, but the changes that have happened to us as a result of being parents. For example, perhaps we are shutting the metaphorical door to our own home and our family doesn't understand why that door isn't always open, why we're not inviting them with us.

As we develop our own family, perhaps experiment with new dance steps, change the way we cook our porridge, exorcise some ghosts, lower some walls, we are creating new pathways, and writing new stories. Sometimes those around us, from our past and present, might join us on that journey, sometimes they need to see that we're not in danger before they'll take some tentative steps, sometimes we need to show them the map we're writing, and sometimes even if we light the way they will just want to stay put. There might be a sense of loss, on both sides, as we all figure out our new roles. As we rewrite our maps, it can help to find ways to say, 'I know you're worried that I'll get lost, but I want to explore for a while. I promise I will find my way back home, but it might just be to visit.'

You might be reading this thinking about how it feels to be parenting in the absence of any support or relationships from wider family. One of the conversations that often comes up with parents I speak to is how hard it can feel, as a parent, when others make assumptions that there *is* family to call upon. Sometimes we might need others around us to create a different version of family, or find ways to look after ourselves as parents with little support from others. Which brings us on to . . .

The Village

If you take a look back on your map, over by your current home somewhere I'd like you to draw in a little group of people. Maybe it's just one or two, or maybe you have a few people in your village. You might even have a few different villages, groups of friends that you've gathered over the years. Having a parenting community – people to ask, 'Does your child do this too?', to share childcare duties or do an emergency pick-up when you're stuck elsewhere, or to offer a supportive smile when things are falling to pieces – can feel like a lifeline when you're in the parenting trenches.

I imagine this isn't a new concept to you – that parenting takes a village. Since 2015 I've run an online parenting community called The Village, which was set up specifically for parents to support one another and offer solidarity in the ups and downs of parenting.

Yet, as with so many things, friendships can be another huge transition when we become parents. Old friends might suddenly feel a world away, especially if they are at a different stage of life. It can be particularly hard on friendships if one person is going through difficulties in their parenting or their fertility that aren't shared experiences. And new friends can be so hard to find.

Part of this is because we don't quite know what we might be looking for in a parenting community, as we're just figuring out who we are as parents. Our identity changes and shifts in ways that can feel really similar to our teenage years (a concept known as 'matrescence' for mothers and 'patrescence' for fathers). Remember how awkward you could feel socialising as a teenager? Becoming a parent can bring a new sense of social discomfort, especially if you also have to try to split your attention between the needs of a new baby or an impatient child while attempting to hold a conversation with a stranger who also has to split their attention. And just as Bridget Jones had her 'smug marrieds', we may also find smug parenting pals who appear ('appear' being an important word there!) to have it all sussed, which leaves us feeling even more isolated.

As with so many things in parenthood, this is a time when we need social support more than ever but find it so hard to reach.

Just as we discussed in the last chapter, we might also discover that – even when we are trying so hard to build a parenting village – there are some obstacles blocking our path to them. A mammoth example, of course, is the Covid pandemic, which left parents completely village-less. There are subtle obstacles too, which we may not always consider. For example, many urban environments aren't built with children and families in mind, making it harder for parents to spend time together.

It might take us time to add that village to our map, and it might not look like we imagined. But just as during adolescence, as we become more assured in our parenting identity, we might find that a little community forms without us realising. Hopefully one that welcomes un-cleaned homes, overtired children – and you, just as you are.

Where Are You Now?

As we get towards the end of Part III, having explored the relationships around you from your past and present, I wonder what your map is looking like now. Perhaps you have a clearer idea of what is influencing you as a parent today. Perhaps you might also have a clearer idea of who you are as the adult that you are now. Hopefully you have a greater insight into how you want things to be in your own home, and the conversations that you might need to continue to have to keep rewriting that map in a way that makes it clear for you.

But, I want to remind you that these are difficult topics. This might have brought home to you just how isolated you are in your parenting, and how hard it has been to find solidarity. There might be questions raised for you about what you want for your own family, and how different that might be from what you experienced. Perhaps it's led you to think about who has been on these pathways with you, or even just held up a lantern to light the way.

Before we move on to talking about the little humans in your life and get to know their maps, first there is likely to be something hiding on your map that keeps you stuck in stories, making it hard to see your child for who they are. Let's take a look at some of the stories that might be influencing your daily life as a parent.

CHAPTER 10

Stories from Society

'In youth, it was a way I had,
To do my best to please.
And change, with every passing lad
To suit his theories.
But now I know the things I know
And do the things I do,
And if you do not like me so,
To hell, my love, with you.'

Dorothy Parker

There are many things that you might have expected to feel as a parent. Love. Joy. Wonder. But there's one feeling that can be quite dominant in parenting, one that definitely isn't represented in the beautiful images of parents gazing adoringly at their offspring, one that hasn't made the poems or songs about parents and their children.

The feeling of uselessness.

We've talked about how becoming parents can put us in touch with the baby and child parts of us. And how it can lead us to question what it is to be an adult, and how we can get in touch with ourselves by stripping back some of the strategies that we've used to try to make ourselves feel more adult. We haven't talked yet about how we come to terms with the huge gap that exists between what we might believe a 'good' parent is and how we, as parents, actually feel day to day.

Because being a parent can challenge everything in our being that leaves us feeling capable. Suddenly in touch with the primal parts of ourselves – and facing the most elemental parts of humanity by tuning in to these little creatures that are babies, toddlers and children – we are . . . lost. Experiencing, perhaps for the first time since our own childhood, what it is to be adrift. There is nothing that can reduce the most competent, powerful adult to a ball of anxious insecurity like a newborn baby who just cannot be soothed.

And, because we have been raised to be purposeful, capable humans, what we tend to do is find the ways that can help us feel purposeful and capable again. What can be more attractive – when faced with the ball of rage that is an inconsolable newborn, or the boneless screeching mass of a frustrated toddler, or the scowling hate-filled frown of a child, or the sullen disapproving glare of a teenager – than guidance on what to do?

If you have a look at your map you'll see two pathways there. They are beautiful pathways, they may as well be paved in gold. They are well lit, and signposts pop up all over your map reminding you that they are there and directing you to follow them. There are lots of other people wandering around those paths, and important-looking people telling you this is the right direction. If you start to walk down them you'll find phrases written along their edges, saying things like, 'We only have 18 summers with our children, make them count' and '5 mistakes to avoid when speaking to your children'. And as you wander down them, full of hope, you might notice that you're feeling a little anxious. But you keep going, and there are others on this path with you who help you feel like you're going the right way. And as you keep walking you realise that you're not just feeling a little anxious, you're feeling very anxious, and like you're getting it all wrong, and that you don't even belong on this path. But you keep going because at least you have a path and it seems like it could be the right one, and you don't know if there are any alternative paths.

And then, all of a sudden, you hit a dead end. And you realise you've lost your way.

Welcome to the dead ends – the two paths of high-pressure parenting. We tend to walk these paths at the same time, often without realising, until we hit those dead ends and don't know where to turn. Maybe the dead end is your own exhaustion. Maybe it's a child who doesn't follow that path with you. Maybe the dead end is all the stuff in your life outside of being a parent. These are paths that appear to lead you towards your child but often lead you in the opposite direction.

The First Dead End: The Pressure to Raise Perfect Children

Pathway number one is the pressure to parent children in increasingly prescriptive ways. Have you walked along this one? We think that this path will lead us to a happy child. In fact, where it often takes us is along a route littered with all the ways in which we feel we are failing them.

Intensive parenting as a trend actually began with Boomer parents – when parenting started to focus on optimal development and teaching children to succeed. Since then, with our increased knowledge of neuroscience and how early attachment experiences (those dances we discussed earlier) affect brain development, there is a familiar feeling in parenting that there is just . . . So. Much. At. Stake. It seems that every single little thing we do has a clear outcome, and the outcome is either an unblemished child or (if we get it wrong) a damaged one.

I've had many clients whose anxiety is amplified by the way that complex psychological research has entered our mainstream consciousness – from pregnant women terrified that work strain could wire their unborn baby's brain to high stress, to parents concerned that not soothing their baby instantly would leave them feeling neglected and affect their relationships for the rest of their life, to those who become increasingly concerned as their child approaches the age of three because, essentially, 'I've messed up and now it's too late, I've broken my child.'

It is true that our early relationships are influential. It is even true that our early experiences affect brain development. It is also true that our brains are plastic (your brain is changing RIGHT NOW!), that attachment is a rhythm, not a technical rule book to follow, that people and their environments change constantly, and that child development is complex. And there are zero psychological studies that determine absolute cause and effect in parenting behaviours and child outcomes, because there are so many different variables to consider. Nothing is set in stone.

Children – and all humans – are so complex, we will never really know whether they do x because of y. They are made up of many layers and influenced by many things. We won't ever understand all of them.

We can really agonise about this as parents, can't we? If I have a strict bedtime routine will my baby or child sleep better? If I had a C-section will my baby have asthma later on? If I had postnatal depression, will my child have behavioural problems at school? If I separate from my partner, will my teenager find it harder to form a romantic attachment as they grow up?

Often child development information is presented to us in this way. It starts even when we just look at advice on becoming pregnant – suddenly, even though our adult lives have been pretty nuanced up until that point, we get a list of Dos and Don'ts. Follow this path and it'll all be OK. But while there are certainly things that make it more or less likely that something will happen to someone, there is very rarely a direct cause–effect link.

So, if you follow a clear bedtime routine, your baby or child *may* be more likely to sleep – but factor in also temperament, genes, screen exposure, illness, body temperature, worries, your own separation anxiety, your own history of sleep . . .

If you had a C-section your child *might* be more prone to asthma later on, but there is a huge range of moderating factors; and we're not entirely clear why it might happen but there are a number of different theories – none of which are conclusive.

If you had postnatal depression then your child *might* exhibit behavioural problems later on . . . but people with depression might also be more likely to report their child's behaviour as problematic (because when we are low in motivation and joy an active child can be an extraordinary challenge). And there are other factors too – such as the link between poverty and postnatal depression and the link between the community-level effects of poverty and child behaviour problems. So postnatal depression might be one factor in a child's behaviour – and certainly parents with mental health problems should have access to support to counteract this – but if this is happening within a family and a community where there are multiple other stressors then community-level approaches need to be considered too.

And your teenager *might* have difficulties with romantic relationships later if you separate from your partner – although the evidence for this is mixed. But this may also be moderated by the quality of your relationship prior to divorce (young adults whose parents had high levels of conflict before separating are more likely to see divorce as a favourable outcome) or the relationship the child has with each parent – and this may also represent a more positive view of relationship break-ups so that children are less likely to stay in a difficult relationship.

There are loads of possible reasons and solutions out there to the daily problems you struggle with, with your child or children. And often parents will find what works for them through a process of trial and error – when we get off the path and figure out what works for us. We change all the time and our children change all the time, and our hoped-for outcome might change too. Often the process of change will involve experimentation, gathering information from different sources and then seeing what works. Sometimes the process of change involves acceptance that this isn't what you expected. And sometimes it might involve getting a professional involved, someone who can really get to know your family and how it operates.

So how can we step off this path? Firstly, we need to realise we're on it. Secondly – and this is a tricky one – by realising that our children might be on it with us too. Trying to optimise our parenting also means trying to optimise our children, and this creates an obstacle to actually getting to know them just as they are. And might even raise the likelihood that we'll be preoccupied with the flaws in them, and that the stress of trying to raise perfect children will spill over into how we relate to them and respond to them. If that feels tricky to read, don't forget this is a well-lit path that looks very appealing. Last of all, we need to figure out how we can reduce the pressure on ourselves to raise perfect specimens of humanity.

If this path feels familiar, see what you make of these questions:

- When you think about parenting, what do you see as its aim? There might be lots of different answers here!
- What are the 'outcomes' in your child that you might have been working towards (e.g. sleeping through the night, being an adventurous eater, being calm, being smart, etc.)?
- Where have these ideas come from?
- Do these ideas add any pressure on you?

- Are there any alternative ideas that could reduce that pressure (e.g. 'If I shout at my child I will damage them for life' might be 'If I shout at my child I can apologise, and let them know I am human')?
- And let's add something to make sure that you're being looked after a little here too. What do you need to help you ease the pressure even more? (So maybe 'Putting so much pressure on myself in considering the long-term impact of everything I do actually makes it more likely that I'll shout! I'll try to focus just on what's going on right now. If I'm shouting because I'm stressed out, what do I need to restore some calm?')

And, just in case this one is keeping you stuck on this path, a really *really* common reaction to realising you're here is that little voice at the back of your mind (probably that Critic showing up) saying, 'yes yes I get that for *other* people but *my* child *is* going to be all of those things if I try hard enough.' In which case, why? And what is that belief costing you? And could it be costing them anything too?

If you need a bit more of a hand off this pathway:

- Think about your aspirations for your child – what are they? Are they realistic?
- Do any of those aspirations conflict with each other? Or with your actual child and what they are like? Or with you and what you are like?
- If you could pick one aspiration for your child, something you want for them in their life, what would it be? (If you have written 'happy' then please think again – not one of us can be happy all the time and the pressure to be so can in fact increase our levels of anxiety! A more realistic alternative might be 'accepting of themselves' or 'a sense of purpose', which can contribute to overall feelings of well-being.)

This dead end is a really powerful one too because it is kept well lit by the people around us and their expectations. A judgemental look when your child whines in public, a loaded 'will you *please* quieten your baby', an image on Instagram of a calm, smiling family in matching outfits, the realisation that everyone else's child is doing something that feels out of reach for yours, or even just the sheer number of targets that our children are measured against throughout their education add to this. It can be incredibly difficult to step off this path and look at how this might impact on you and your child, let alone to change direction.

Yes, parenting is influential, but so is our character, our environment, our other relationships, our exposure to new information. And, as we'll learn in the next part, our children have a lot of say in how they turn out. Instead of raising perfect children, how would it feel to just raise YOUR child?

The Second Dead End: The Pressure to Be Perfect Parents

As you brush yourself off that path, we find ourselves on the second one: the pressure to be a perfect parent. We think this pathway will lead to competence. But the longer we walk it, the more we realise that it never ends, and that competence feels harder and harder to reach. We might have glimmers here and there, but there is always more path to follow, and new obstacles that appear in our way.

You might not realise you're on this one. When I talk about perfectionism with my clients I often hear something along the lines of: I can't be a perfectionist because I'm not perfect (in other words: I still have so much I'm not getting right, I still have so much to strive for, I never manage to meet my expectations). If that resonates with you, welcome to the perfectionist path.

Every day we receive huge amounts of (often oversimplified) information about pregnancy, birth, parenting, child development and mental health from myriad different sources. Of course this can be beneficial up to a point, but it can also add pressure. It creates the impression that there is a 'right' way of doing things – but this 'right' way changes constantly. If in the 1980s parenting was focused on development and intelligence, since the mid- to late 90s parenting has emphasised self-esteem, emotional expression and connection – and the idea is that these will be gained by changing parenting behaviour. Our role as parents is not just to nurture, or to guide . . . it's to enhance child development. We are no longer just parents, we are the creators of optimal adults.

And if we have more than one child, we might feel we are being pulled in different directions, not able to meet anyone's needs fully. But that is family life and part of the problem with the way we talk about parenting – because if we need to meet everyone's needs COMPLETELY then we can never 'succeed'.

To give you an example, if I google 'how to be a good parent' I'm given pages and pages of lists: 9 steps to more effective parenting; 5 positive parenting skills; 10 commandments of good parenting; 50 easy ways to be a fantastic parent. Without even realising it, these might become markers to measure ourselves by, especially if we have an active Critic and Fretter working together and especially if our Lover is getting lots of validation when we meet these requirements.

Yet. If we drill down into just one of them – one commandment is to 'love your child unconditionally'. But how do we do that? What if we've never experienced unconditional love? What if there are things we find challenging about our child? How do we set boundaries and encourage behaviour that we find acceptable without making a child feel unloved? What is love anyway? A simple statement like that – which we might read without really engaging – brings with it enormous questions about what good parenting is and how we show it. And what it can often lead to is multiple small questions about whether what we're doing is OK.

I've really seen this in the kind of questions that come up with parents I speak to, in an increasing number of queries about the long-term impact of momentary parenting actions. Anything less than perfect brings guilt, shame and anxiety. 'I shouted at my child, what will that mean for them?' 'My kids are watching over the recommended two hours of screen time a day, what damage will that do?' 'I'm so bored of playing but I don't want my child to feel rejected, how do I keep going?'

And, as information gets increasingly specific, our capacity to get things wrong increases too. So I might have a conversation with a parent such as, 'My toddler had a tantrum and I read a script that I saw on Instagram and they didn't stop tantrumming, now what do I do?' or even 'I said the word "no" but I've read that we shouldn't be saying "no" any more, how do I make this better?' And behind these questions are the real questions of 'Have I messed up?' 'Am I a bad parent?' 'Will my child be OK?' And as we walk further down this path, our anxiety increases and leaves us feeling that the responsibility of parenting is insurmountable. It becomes harder to see our children as whole humans and not just a series of tasks to complete.

But hang on. Because, at the same time, it's not OK to be anxious – because how will that impact on optimal brain development? Back on to that first path we go.

And of course, people and their expectations light this path too. If you've ever been overwhelmed by the quantity of emails from a nursery or school, you might relate to that. Again, it takes a lot to walk off this path, look at what is lining it and question what will work for your family without getting pulled back on that same path again.

Something I've noticed in modern parenting advice is that it's not just advice on parenting practices and strategies that add pressure. Even guidance on parental well-being can drag us under. One example of this is the 'good enough parent' – a phrase coined by psychoanalyst Donald Winnicott in 1953 when he spoke about the 'ordinary devoted mother'. The concept of the good enough parent is not just that we, as parents, can disappoint our children, make mistakes, tolerate that they might become disillusioned with us. It's that we actually *should* do this so that they can gradually learn about themselves as separate people, and feel OK about making mistakes and disillusioning others too! If we allow them to see our messy humanity, they can be messy humans too. Yet, as this concept has turned into book titles, social media memes and even online parenting courses, 'good enough parenting' has become another pressure. How much should we fail our children? In what way? Isn't 'good enough' just an excuse? In essence, how can I be a perfectly good enough parent?

Another example is being a cycle breaker, which appears empowering on the surface but can be a heavy burden. Breaking cycles of trauma is a complex concept that encompasses years of theory and refers to childhood trauma and adversity, racial trauma and intergenerational trauma. And it has become a TikTok-trending hashtag – with over 50 million views for the hashtag #breakingthecycle as I write this today.

While there are many ways we may wish to break the cycles of generations past, the idea of being a 'cycle breaker' can feel overwhelmingly hard.

The thing is, and this is really how change happens as you go through therapy, cycles might change but they don't break. As we change one thing, we find something else that we might want to change. Our children grow and need something different from us. Our circumstances change. It is a beautiful thought, that we might hand our child a clean, smooth piece of paper on which to write their own map their own way, but much as we would like to we can't erase our experiences, and the complexity of our lives. The idea that we can transform ourselves so completely is not only overly simplistic, it also brings such feelings of failure when we inevitably repeat what is automatic to us.

Remember the record player that was in the family room, playing the song to accompany your dance (page 89)? Our ways of reacting, relating to people, our feelings about ourselves and the world – they are all a bit like a groove in that record. When we have played the same song for many years, the needle on a record player will easily slip back into that groove. When we are making changes, it will take a lot of playing of those new songs before they feel familiar – and when we're knocked, that needle will fall back into that familiar groove until we've been playing a new song enough to create a new groove. That's not failure, that's just learning.

If you can relate to any of these ideas, let's find our way off that path by considering these questions:

- What do you think an ideal parent should be doing? Get it all in a list if you can.
- How do you feel looking at that list?
- Where do those ideas come from, for you?
- If your child is old enough, ask them what they think a 'good' parent is. Compare your lists. Are they very different?

And again, if that little voice pops up saying, 'OK, that might be fine for other people but I am going to keep working my socks off at my parenting,' ask yourself – if you could let go of any pressure to be an ideal parent, what would that free you up to do? To feel? To be? How would your day look different? And if it's hard to imagine, have a think back to Part II and get a bit curious about why you're pushing yourself so hard, and what that might be costing you. We can bring your guide in here too, and invite them to offer some alternatives.

Another (Invisible) Dead End: The Pressure to Not Feel Any Pressure

As you step off these paths, wondering how you got stuck on them, suddenly you hit another dead end. This one is an invisible one – the pressure to not feel any parenting pressure at all.

This is a bit different to the other two, and it relates to lots of the things we've talked about already. It comes from stories about how parenting is natural, so it should be easy. That if we look like we're not coping we'll be judged unfavourably. It comes from stories about how children should behave, so that we smile at people in the supermarket while hissing at our child to stop whining. It comes from all those other stories we've talked about, so maybe we aspire to be an unflustered parent who always has tissues in their bag, or a cool, collected one who is always up for some fun. It can come from our real experiences of being criticised by others – or even those imagined experiences of judgement that we may feel in comparing ourselves to other parents (whether in real life or on social media).

It can also come from somewhere a bit deeper, that makes it hard to show our feelings, or from inherited stories about how children should behave. This means that we find it hard to parent face to face with our children; we sort of have to look at them side on. We live with them but can't quite connect with them. And we stay on this path because if we were to face our true feelings about parenting, maybe we worry that we would be truly lost.

Remember when we were sitting in the kitchen with our porridge bowls, and we talked about power? Or at the beginning of this chapter when we talked about competence?

We try to appear calm so that we feel we have control. Because we need to feel we have control, and we need other people to see we have control. Sometimes because we don't have power, and haven't had power, and feel powerless. Why does this arise so strongly in parenthood?

Firstly, because parenting is about love. And, as you are probably very aware by now, love is really complicated for us. Becoming a parent brings up so much about our own experience of how we were loved and how we love. Our feelings of love – and our feelings in general – can be shockingly powerful as parents. So having parameters to 'prove' that we love well – that we are good parents – can feel safe, even when they add pressure.

And secondly, because kids are CHAOS.

And they make us feel utterly helpless, multiple times and in multiple ways.

Children shatter any illusion that we have control over, basically, anything – especially other humans. We can try, so hard, in so many ways, to create a sense of control and order over the chaos. We go to pregnancy yoga, we sleep-train, we instil routines, we follow parenting manuals, we try to shape them and mould them and give them ALL the right things to become – as we discussed above – optimal human beings. And then they end up in a weird position in utero and we have a tricky birth, and they puke on the new rug, and they leave peanut butter in your hair, and they swear at your mum, and they climb over the school fence, and they don't come home when they said they would, and they go out with people you can't bear, and they drop out of uni, and they don't say thank you for your support with any of it.

And we can either try harder, and read more tips, and try new things, and speak to new people to find new solutions. Or we can let go of those very adult concepts of power and pressure, and welcome their chaos, and try to understand it better.

I'm not talking about giving up all sense of control. We can control environments, we can control ourselves, and we might have some control over our plans. But what we can never control are other people, including our own children. What we *can* do is get to know them. Because we're not creating optimal children. We're raising whole, complicated, often exasperating human beings.

As we step off that last path, let's go and meet them. Let's just check in before we move on.

1. How are you feeling? (How is your heart rate, your energy levels, how do you feel in your body? And how are your emotions? Are you feeling anxious, sad, excited, curious, something else?)
2. What has reading Part III raised for you? (In terms of information, ideas, memories, feelings?)
3. What one thing would you like to remember from these chapters?

PART IV

The Story of Children

CHAPTER 11

Tools for the Journey

'All grown-ups were once children . . . but
only few of them remember it.'

Antoine de Saint-Exupéry, *The Little Prince*

I
t's time to roll up your map. Take a look on there and think about how far you've come on this journey since we started the book. Hopefully you've got to know much more clearly why you work the way you do, some of the characters that have been influencing you, the real people in your life who affect how you are as a parent, too. You might have a stronger sense of who you are at the heart of it all, and the sort of parent you are aspiring to be – one based on you, your own values and your unique life rather than the stories and expectations around us all.

And, as we said right at the start, you might have lots more questions, and feel a bit wobblier too, because things that felt certain might now feel a bit less certain. Through this journey – as so often happens during a therapeutic process – there might be a feeling of lots of things (the linen from inside the cupboard, perhaps) being thrown up in the air. We might have to pause to see where it all lands before we can decide how we want to put it away again. If things are feeling a bit unsettled for you, just a reminder here that it's

OK to put this away for a while until you have a clearer idea of your own map and how you want to rewrite it.

Keep your map close because we might need it again. But we're not returning to normal life, with its routines and dishes to wash and bums to wipe or dinner to make, quite yet. We're going to go a little deeper into our adventure. Bring your guide with you for support, because I'd like to lead you into a whole new map. We don't tend to go here, because we quickly lose the ability to follow this map as we get older. As children, we are often desperate to get out of this map and into the adult world. As adults, we superimpose our maps on to children's. Or, especially when we have maps we want to rewrite, we look at other adults' maps. We look at the maps around us, the maps we think our kids' friends have, the maps of our childhood friends, we look at the maps that are laid out in parenting books, we steal glimpses of other people's maps from TV, social media, film, books.

But your child has come with a map too.

In the chapters that follow, we're going to learn how to get to know your child's map – especially when it is (as it inevitably will be) different to yours, different to your partner's or co-parent's, different to those of other children around you, different to how you expected, different to what their community expects of them, different to what society expects.

And, just so we're clear before we enter into this next part of our journey, and you might be thinking, 'Finally, she's going to tell me what I actually have to do now' . . . I'm not. Let's just talk about why.

Because I don't know you, and I don't know your child.

Instead, I'll give you some really broad strokes about children that might help you understand them a bit better, but it's pretty likely that you're going to read this next section and be left with even more questions than you started with. And that's fine. I mean, actually that's great. Because, as we saw in the introduction, our role as parents is not to mould our children but to hold them – to support them in discovering their magical selves and their own unique way of being, and to offer a solid foundation they can rest on when they need to.

Just as we did before we looked at your map, we're going to need a few things before we can look at your child's. So, in this Neverland where we find ourselves, between your map and theirs, we're going to receive five tools to help us read their maps. These are tools that you can use at any time in your parenting journey, and in your other relationships too. And, as we've said all along, they might seem simple enough written down but, when you come to use them, you'll find that you need to practise using them – just like any other tool – before you will feel skilled. And then things might change again, and you'll have to learn to use them in new contexts. Forever a beginner.

Parenting Tool 1: Repair

When we are spending hours (often many hours) with our children, how can we not make multiple 'mistakes' and do things that we didn't intend to do, or say things that we didn't want to say? And how can they not make multiple mistakes too?

One of the most helpful tools we can carry into our parenting (and all of our relationships) is repair. It is like a force field around us and our family that protects us from difficult moments of rupture and disconnection. The more we accept that we are flawed, messy, imperfect humans, and the more we can accept that in our children too, the less we resist the evidence of those flaws. And the easier it becomes to move through sticky moments.

We need to learn to be OK about the times we are not in sync, and to accept being told about this. To be able to think, 'Ah crap, I got that wrong' and be open to what is needed to move forward. To also be able to say, 'Hey you got that bit wrong and I still love you.' These ruptures aren't failures. They are *essential*. It is not in the perfect moments of connection that we build relationships, it is in the making up.

To be OK with repair, we also need to be comfortable with conflict. By 'conflict' I don't just mean the obvious stuff – arguments, shouting matches, butting horns over something. Our day as parents is full of conflict, which we might avoid or shut down. Conflict with ourselves ('Is it OK if I go out tonight even though my child is crying?), with our children ('Oh don't be silly, the sauce is fine, just eat your dinner') and of course between our children, with our partners, and with others in our supporting cast and wider community.

Being comfortable with conflict can challenge a lot of the things that came up in the previous sections of the book. Maybe it doesn't meet our expectations, or the stories that we have carried about parenting and family life, so we question ourselves, or our children. Perhaps a conflict sends us stumbling into those dead ends of the last chapter, so we avoid upsetting our children because it takes us away from those ideals of perfect parents and children who always get along. Our relationship with conflict is formed in those dances we learned about in Chapter 6. Families used to an Argentine tango might feel very comfortable screaming at each other one minute then laughing the next, while if you have been brought up in an Irish dance sort of a home an argument might feel catastrophic.

But we also come to our parenting with our own internal world. So maybe our Critic comes in and says, 'See, look what a mess you've made' and we have to Float away from our difficult feelings of shame and pretend it never happened. Or the Lover tells us that we need to soothe any rifts as quickly as possible, even if that means swallowing our own needs and avoiding a confrontation with our child. The Fretter might work hard to prevent any possible conflict from arising, while the Stoic doesn't take heed of such pesky quarrels. Or we blame our child for causing the conflict, turning our Critic on to them and seeing it all as their fault so that we don't need to feel bad.

We also bring our past experiences of conflict, of course. Maybe the little kid inside us pops up and remembers being punished severely for minor misdemeanours, or how frightening it was to hear arguments in our home. The feelings this can evoke in us – such as fear that our child might feel like we did – can stop us from addressing difficulties and differences of opinion.

We can be so afraid of conflict for so many reasons, but when we avoid conflict it does pop out in other ways, like snapping at a partner or feeling low or uneasy in our body. When we feel that conflict has taken over and repair is too difficult, it can seem that we don't know where to begin.

And repair itself can feel really hard – not just the repair itself but being the one to step forward and offer the olive branch. If we've had a salty porridge bowl of authoritarian parenting (see page 74) to contend with, then repair – admitting we might have got it wrong – is so counterintuitive to what we know. It involves admitting that we're not all-knowing authority figures but fallible humans. We might think that offering repair and apology will remove our parental power and take away our children's respect for us.

If we ourselves have had, or have been working from, the sweeter bowl of permissive parenting, or spoon-feeding porridge as a helicopter parent, then any mistake on our part or our children's might not feel acceptable. It would mean we have to acknowledge our children's flaws and might lead to conflict.

So this tool, repair, gives us the knowledge that it is part of our human experience to learn through our mistakes, not avoid them. Just as our children learn to walk through falling over, we learn about our relationships and each other through the times we get it wrong. We as parents, and our children, will make countless mistakes and there will be immeasurable small rifts in our relationships. But we, as the adults, have to be the ones to repair and to model what repair looks like. At some point, our children will follow our example because they'll learn from us that it's easy to reconnect. To repair we don't need to establish who was at fault. We can see our conflict as another troll under the bridge – and solving our conflict or disconnection becomes a problem to overcome together.

What does repair look like in reality? Firstly, we need to feel OK ourselves – and we're going to come to that in Chapter 13. Secondly, we need to step forward in a way that feels right for us and our child. You will find hundreds of scripts online about how to repair after a rupture with your child: that is, how to make up when you've lost your cool, or acted in a way that felt out of sync with your child's needs, or noticed that you haven't been getting along well. And those scripts might give you some good ideas, but repair has to come from the heart not the head. I'm from Newcastle upon Tyne in the hardy north of England, and phrases like, 'I'm so sorry I got angry, you didn't deserve that. Sometimes it's hard for Mummy to stay calm and I need to work on that. I imagine it's scary when Mummy yells. I love you very much and I'm so sorry I hurt your feelings' will just never roll off my tongue (and nor should they because they're not the ones that come naturally to me). But it's OK to experiment and figure out what feels most comfortable and most effective in your home. You can start by thinking about what you might like to hear in the same situation, or what you might want to happen. But remember that your child is a very separate human to you – so what might work for you might not work for them; but it could give you some ideas to start with.

An important part of repair is forgiveness – for ourselves too. Parenting can be relentless, and done in the context of many competing demands. That's why having your guide along to find words of compassion for you can be essential as you enter your child's map (see page 45 if you need a refresher on this).

So, to take this tool on your journey, see what you think of these questions:

- What is conflict like in your home?
- Why do you think conflict is shown in this way, in your family?
- How do you feel about repair? What makes it easier?
- What do you need to feel that a conflict has been repaired? What do you think your child needs? How about other people in your family?
- Being responsible for repair can be really difficult for people – how do you feel about that being part of your role as a parent?

Parenting Tool 2: Empathy

Let's get a bit soppy for a moment. Because repair comes from our adult selves, but to really tune in to our child we need empathy. To try to remember the experience of being a child, and what the world is like for them. Because, just as we talked about differences with our own parents, our children are growing up in a world that is so different to the one we grew up in. And unless we are curious about what that is like for them, we can't meet them in it.

As we take on this tool, we gain the power to see the world through the eyes of our child.

The first thing you might notice is that everything is really high up. When adults talk to you, it might be hard to hear what they're saying unless they look you in the eye and get to your level. Lots happens, all the time, that you don't quite understand. You might lose yourself in a game only to realise your frustrated parent is standing over you waiting for you to get dressed with a frown on their face. Another thing you might notice is that you're so often queuing for something – to join a toddler group, or to enter the playground, or to eat. And if you get impatient then you're admonished. And if you express individual choice you might be told something like, 'You get what you get and you don't get upset,' or maybe that catch-all 'Children should be seen and not heard'. So often you're being jostled on to the next thing with a 'Come on! Quick!' And you're told to share your things even though your parents keep their exciting things – like their phones, keys and the best snacks – all to themselves.

We can so often see children as little adults, but really they are not like us at all. One of my favourite facts about children is about brainwaves. Up until around the age of eight, the brain is most often in a theta state, which, in adulthood, we may enter into only when we are daydreaming or meditating. Small children are often lost in a world inside their minds – and it is in this flow state that children (and adults!) gain huge benefits – from expanding their imagination to a greater sense of confidence. But we as adults spend a lot of the day pulling them out of that dream and into this big, noisy world that we live in. And the world we live in isn't very friendly to our children.

In the UK, and other cultures that value individualism, there is a separation of the adult world and the world of families and children that just doesn't exist across the globe. In 2010, the then Children's Commissioner Sir Al Aynsley-Green talked about the UK being hostile to children, and, as we found in Chapter 1, it also ranks among the lowest for family-friendly policies.

Often our children are pushed and pulled around on our adult maps in our adult worlds. One example of how our adult expectations can stop us seeing through children's eyes is around holidays. We might arrange activities we think are fun, like taking them to visit a funfair, then find that they are terrified of all the rides, or find it too noisy, or just want to watch the rubber ducks bobbing on the water – and then we might feel that they are being ungrateful.

Our children may become conduits for our own needs and desires, or objects that we need to control. They are so often pulled down those dead-end pathways of adult expectations. If they are not compliant, they are difficult. If they interrupt an adult conversation, they are impatient. If they question us, they are rude.

This permeates our expectations about family life too. Often 'fun' is what happens to us when we are away from our children, who are then presented as energy drains. Yes, we see sanitised images of families with super-white teeth laughing around a board game. But we so rarely see representations of families just knocking about together. As parents the prevailing story seems to be that we must pour our energy into our children and then recover away from them. Of course we need a sense of ourselves away from our children, but, as we've discovered, these images become what we see as 'normal' and aspirational even if they don't fit with our experience.

In minor ways every day we might as parents also feel the impact of this, even just going into a more 'adult' space like a restaurant or museum with a small child, no matter how quiet they are. This can often add such pressure to us as parents, with this real or imagined hostile gaze impacting on how we interact with our children.

Some researchers have likened our treatment of children to discrimination against them. The Childism Institute, a global network, uses the term 'childism' to equate it to other movements such as feminism, recognising that children are often marginalised in adult-centric worlds, and emphasising the role of children in creating a more equitable world.

You might think it is far-fetched to talk about discrimination against children, but consider that in 2022 England has still not banned smacking children, and that the USA, having signed the

Convention on the Rights of the Child, has not yet ratified it. Children's services – in local authorities, the NHS and youth clubs – have been decimated, affecting vulnerable children the most. And in 2018 – before the Covid pandemic, Brexit and the cost-of-living crisis worsened the financial impact on families even further – the UN Special Rapporteur examined poverty in Britain and reported that, despite it being the world's fifth largest economy: 'The bottom line is that much of the glue that has held British society together since the Second World War has been deliberately removed and replaced with a harsh and uncaring ethos.' In the UK, 27 per cent of children were living in poverty in 2020–21. That's about 8 children in a class of 30. This increases to nearly half of children in lone-parent families, and nearly half of children in racially minoritised groups.

One of the ideals we so often have of our children, in that pathway of being perfect, is that they will be happy all the time. And, if they are sad, or angry, that they should quickly return to being happy. But, just as we do, children feel a huge range of things, often all at the same time. One of the biggest gifts we can give them is to understand that being a child in the modern world isn't always easy – and allow them to express how they feel about that.

You can take this tool of Empathy with you into your daily parenting by holding on to two ideas.

Firstly, we as parents just need to remain open to hearing about the experiences of our children. To listen open-heartedly to their reality without questioning it. Sometimes they will not meet our expectations or assumptions, but being able to hear them gives us insight into the world on their map. And, even if they aren't able to tell us in words, they will let us know through their behaviour – by dissolving after the pressure of behaving all day at nursery or school, for example.

Secondly, if they are old enough to ask, we can also wonder what things are like for them. These aren't always the questions we ask our children, but questions like, 'I haven't been a child for a long time now, what's it like for you?', 'What are the differences you see between my life and yours?', or simply, 'Tell me what's going on for you at the moment?' can open conversations. Some children might find conversations like that tricky, and it's their choice about how much they want to share. But simply holding on to a curiosity about what life is like for them can keep this tool in use. Something that can help us with that is the third tool.

Parenting Tool 3: Collaboration

We've spent a lot of time talking about different family dynamics – who holds the power in your household, who is leading the dance, the ghosts you've inherited. But when we see family life as a collaboration, and the members of the family as a team (even if we are ultimately the team leaders), it makes it easier to look at our children's maps without imposing ours on top. This brings us a bit closer to the 'just right' porridge too – where children are aware of what is expected of them (and there are clear expectations on them) but are supported to meet those expectations.

Collaborating brings together the needs of you and your child, and all of the members of the family, with equal importance. It can be the tool that we need to let go of those stories and really clamber off those paths we looked at in the last chapter because, when we're working as a team, and tuning in to its individual members, we just have to let go of a lot of stories and ideals. It also rings the final death knell on those power struggles because we're working with our child; we're not trying to control them nor are we accepting their control of us.

Sometimes this can involve a lot of unlearning too – and figuring out a new way of communicating, especially as our children grow into the school and teenage years.

Just like adults, children may grapple with something for some time before they can begin to articulate their internal experience. And, more than anything, they need us to be ready when they are. This can be the hardest part of parenting – stepping back and opening up spaces for your children to fill when they are ready. And this rarely happens when you have prepared for it, but more often when you are waiting to watch the last episode of the series you've been loving, or getting ready to go out for the evening, or (ahem) trying to finish writing a chapter.

This can feel really difficult for parents. When a child who has seemed totally fine suddenly starts collapsing, or whining, or getting aggressive it can feel very out of the blue. We might meet this with problem-solving – wanting to find quick solutions rather than just listening (which can enable them to find their own solutions). Or we can get into a back-and-forth argument – what psychotherapist Philippa Perry calls 'fact tennis' – where we focus on winning points instead of understanding each other. Sometimes it might take us a while to be able to pause and wonder what's being communicated.

There's another skill that can give you a quick route into helping you collaborate: active listening. This will aid you in reading your child's map and understanding their experience. The bonus is that the more you practise this skill with your child, the more they will learn it too and use it in their other relationships.

Active listening is exactly what it sounds like: listening with intent. I think of it a bit like putting a laser focus on to someone, and tuning out distractions, to fully absorb what they are saying. It's one of the first things we learn in therapy training and it's remarkable how much it can bring to the way that we communicate with others. It sounds simple – it just involves paying attention (to words and non-verbal communication), really listening to what is being said and the meaning behind it and reflecting back what you've heard without ascribing your own judgement or assumptions to it.

What that might look like in a family is when a child says, let's use a classic, 'It's not fair!' You might turn to them, show that you don't have any distractions (like putting down your phone, turning away from your desk, switching off the TV) and invite them to tell you more (in whatever words fit for you – 'What's not fair?', 'Ah, tell me more!', or just a silent invitation with open body language). Then just give them space to talk, with a few sounds of encouragement if you need them. And, when they've run out of steam, just reflecting back what you heard: 'It's really unfair that Ms Lowe keeps the whole class in when just a few people have been noisy. You feel really annoyed about that.' And, rather than jump in with our opinion, or a solution (because it is *really* hard not to want to fix things for our child), just pausing and letting them continue to talk and reflect can often help them find their own solutions before we offer any. We can do this with little ones too, just by trying to tune in to what they are attempting to tell us – which can allow them space to figure something out on their own.

Of course, this doesn't happen every time. Sometimes we might say, 'Tell me more' and our child will stomp out of the room because they're not ready to talk. Sometimes you reflect back and your child will say, 'Oh my God you don't understand *AT ALL*' because they just need to rage. Some children find those sorts of conversations too difficult, and might prefer to have them walking side by side, or busy doing something, if eye contact feels intense to them. Again, we can test out what works in our family.

And of course, this is a skill that sounds simple but is *incredibly* hard to achieve in family life. Our children make multiple bids for our attention that are answered with, 'Hmmm?' or, 'Yep, absolutely' or, 'In a minute.' And children are with us for large chunks of the day, and they can sometimes talk a lot! Of course there are many times that children don't feel really heard by us, and perhaps their emotions escalate. In family life it is so easy to go through days without *really* paying attention because we are doing the washing up, or waiting to get back to our laptop, or trying to get out the door on time. Our children's needs can sometimes – often – run counter to our adult responsibilities. It can be hard to stop what we're doing. Being able to pause and turn your high beams on to your child feels like it slows everything down – but it can also help emotional storms pass more quickly and build that collaboration between you in figuring things out together. And when you're not able to listen deeply, even just focusing on paying full attention for a few minutes can offer some connection. And when you can't listen at all, or can't help but jump in with an unwanted solution that leads to a 'You NEVER listen!', then you have that tool of Repair to use.

To take this tool with you into reading your child's map, I'd invite you to consider:

- What do you think about the idea of collaborating as a family? What concerns might you have about this? What could get in the way?
- Have you ever had the experience of being really, deeply listened to? What was that like for you?

Parenting Tool 4: Boundaries

That collaboration should always be used together with our fourth tool: boundaries. We often don't think about boundaries until they've been crossed – in other words when we are losing our temper unexpectedly, or bursting into tears without knowing why, or realise that our jaw has been clenched for days, or bristle when our child touches us. It's when we start saying things like, 'No one appreciates what I do for this family!' or, 'I've had enough of the lot of you' or, 'You're all so ungrateful' or, 'I don't know why I bother.' Or if we don't say those things but feel awful inside our bodies. And we also know when our child isn't sure of their boundaries because they start spilling over too – with crying, or whining, or shouting, or that special thing children sometimes do when they flop on the floor and make moo-ing noises.

You might have read or heard about boundaries; in parenting the word tends to be used to refer to creating boundaries around our children, particularly their behaviour. But boundaries – for all of us – are buffers between us and the world. They create space between where we end and others, and the world, begin. They help us hold on to who we are. They allow us to exist in the world as unique people with our own unique needs. And we are creating and following these boundaries all the time, for us as individuals, for our children and for our families. Whether that is (collaboratively) building them for our children, following daily routines so everyone knows what is expected of them, considering our own needs, or deciding how the family can have a particular need met.

If we're aiming for a 'just right' porridge bowl, that means clearly letting our children know what we expect of them, or what we (and society) see as acceptable. We often find it much easier to set boundaries around things that feel really certain to us – like, 'Hold my hand when you cross the road,' or, 'Don't put your finger in the plug socket.' If our children push back, or protest at our setting that boundary around their behaviour, we might feel more able to hold it steady because we have no doubt in our mind that it's right. But as a parent we are making countless decisions about boundaries every day, and often our boundaries become a little wobbly and change in different contexts. And it's really easy in a family for the boundaries to get shaken.

Those pathways of intensive parenting that we got off in Chapter 10? The stories about what a good mum is and what a good dad is? They make it really hard to figure out what our boundaries might look like as a parent. Often our boundaries get tied up in ideas of power, and who is wielding it. The parents

I speak to often reflect on how much advice there is in the early days of parenting – how much encouragement there is to give it your all, to meet every need (even when you're beyond exhausted), to be ever-present. And then when babies grow and need to learn a bit more about how to become, well, citizens of the society we live in, the advice kind of . . . dries up. We are *really* good at telling parents how to nurture their children. We are not so good at helping parents figure out how to create limits in clear ways. And we are terrible at helping parents nurture themselves.

As parents, we have more demands on us and fewer resources. It's really hard to hold consistent boundaries with your children when your attention is required in four different places at once (and children are really good at spotting a permeable boundary!). It is not surprising, then, that parents are experiencing high levels of burnout. And that this is most common in countries where intensive parenting has become the norm.

Parental burnout takes us away from the very goals we are trying to meet. It not only affects our own mental health – leaving us feeling emotionally and physically exhausted – but also leaves us feeling less able to enjoy our children, and distancing ourselves from them in order to cope. We end up feeling like we're going through the motions, finding little pleasure in our children and finding reasons to be apart from them. Our children, needing to stay close to us (because that's how they stay in our dance), then may feel more demanding to us, creating a vicious cycle. It can also look very similar to depression. When we're not getting our needs met, we simply can't find joy in our parenting.

Often boundaries get shaky because we feel afraid of conflict or because we have simply never experienced boundaries ourselves. Especially if we have the Lover in our cast of characters and learned this role through putting others' (like our parents') needs before our own.

Our boundaries can also be too inflexible, if we have a Stoic or an Ogre who is centre stage, or if we feel a bit afraid of connecting with someone else too closely, as in the Irish dance. In this case we might refuse to move them even when the situation has changed – for example continuing the usual bedtime routine when a baby is feverish and crying, or insisting on a child doing their homework at the usual time when they've just found out their best friend is leaving the school.

You already have some tools to use with this one. Repair might help you feel more certain about the boundaries you are creating with your child and family. Gaining the insight into yourself that you have now can also help you think about why boundaries might feel tricky. Letting go of the ideals and stories that you have about how parents and children should behave can help you consider what you want.

Something else that can help us use this tool is one piece of knowledge – and that is that your child is their own person. That might sound obvious, but we forget it so often when we try to use our own maps to read them.

One of the things that is so confusing about parenting – and that we might have really mixed feelings about – is that one of the biggest drives children have throughout their development is to be themselves. Totally, uniquely, them. If you have carried this person in your body, the process of separating from them – turning from a one into a two – can be mind-twistingly strange. We might also long for the day when our child is self-sufficient, missing life before parenthood, while also feeling loss when our child lets us know they don't need us.

For the first six or so months of their lives, infants don't realise that they are an 'I'. They don't have a sense of themselves as separate from us. We can clearly see this in the first three months, when little babies like to feel that they are still in the womb. Throughout history, even as far back as 50,000 years ago, babies would be carried in a sling or wrap, and the majority of cultures still demonstrate proximal care, where infants and babies are physically close to a caregiver.

But once a sense of self develops, even babies start to strive towards independence. We as parents quickly start to be used as a point to orient from – like 'Homey' in a game of tag. Of course this varies from child to child, with some children preferring to stay close for longer. This varies culturally, too, and some children are raised to continue to consider the common needs of their communities over individualism.

This can feel like a struggle throughout childhood and adolescence – this feeling we have as parents of being needed sometimes very urgently, but then our presence being pushed away just as suddenly. As our children gain independence, they may simultaneously need us and resent their need of us because they want to be bigger, an internal conflict that we might even hold into our adulthood.

We talked about how our caregivers act as our sanctuaries when we were discussing our internalised parents. But, just like our actual homes, we return to those secure bases less and less as we grow. We might need to check they're still there now and then. We might bring our dirty laundry home and hope we get some help doing it. But then at some point we only come home for the holidays.

The steadier our dance is, the more our children internalise that sanctuary, the less they will need to return home to us. They just need to know that we're there when they need us.

And if we are to understand that our children are their own, unique people, we have to know that about ourselves too. If we are to have some buffers around our needs, that means recognising our own needs and finding ways to meet them.

Parenting can be BRUTAL. These years can be marked by emotional turmoil – not just for children but for those around them too. So we need not just our own boundaries but people to help us hold them up.

Often we don't just have one child in the home to consider.

We might have a toddler and a baby, or two children, or a baby and older children, or teenagers. Even if we do have one child at home, we might also be back at work; and this might also be a time of financial hardship, or we might be caring for other family members. The demands of the daily routine of caring for small humans are great.

Many of the parents I speak to are so focused on their children, and often so weighed down by feelings of guilt about what they are not doing, they completely forget about themselves. While each phase brings new joys, it also brings new challenges where physical demand might be replaced by emotional stresses.

For that reason, it is in these years that it becomes especially important to have boundaries around yourself. And give to yourself too, at least as much as you are giving to those around you. Bring your guide in to help you. Easier said than done, I know, but giving might not mean a weekend on your own. It may just be placing your hand on your heart and checking in with yourself. Taking a few moments in your resting place. Listening to music that is *yours*, not a Disney soundtrack. Lying on your bed in the dark in a starfish position while the rest of the family are occupied elsewhere. Anything that reminds you that there is a space between you and the little humans around you.

We need to receive too, which is where those other humans come in. Even just sharing our experiences with others and hearing them say, 'Yes I'm exhausted too' can boost us a little and allow us to read the maps of our children, and see their spark.

Parenting Tool 5: The Spark of Childhood

The last tool is not really a tool at all, but a lantern to light up your child's map. It is a reminder of the wonder of your child, or children.

These little beings come into the world, this marvel takes place where an actual human is created and is then born. I know it happens 21 times a minute but that's a WHOLE NEW HUMAN. A person who will exist on this planet and will change it, in some way. Maybe not a big way, and maybe only to a few people, but just by being here they change the course of history. They come with a spark, a flame that is theirs alone, and so much of the world dampens that spark.

Do you remember that happening to you as a child? Perhaps some of the reflections you made back in your childhood home might help you think about this. You might remember a moment when you felt your spark, your spirit was . . . squished a bit. Or a lot.

One of our jobs as parents is to help our children keep that flame going. That spark that is unique to them. And one of the ways we can do that is remembering what makes them . . . them. Not the child we expected. Not the child society tells us is the right kind of child. Just them.

Remember the first time you knew you were going to have this human in your life? Or humans? Maybe the first time you saw a scan photo, or when you met them for the first time. Remember how you felt then, about them, and everything that meant about how your life was going to change? How you knew that meeting this new human was going to turn your world upside down? You maybe didn't know *just* how much but you knew it was going to be massive. We forget that so quickly, don't we? The wonder that we felt at the prospect of this new human.

I'm not going to talk about enjoying every moment, because (as we've said) parenting is hard, and defined by mixed emotions much more than plain old enjoyment. This isn't about thinking that every single part of your child is amazing, all the time. We are, by now, fully aware that us humans – both the adult and the child ones – are flawed. But sometimes, especially on the harder days, remembering the wonder we felt at them coming into our lives can help us tune back in to their world.

- Who is your child?
- What are they like?
- As you think about them now, what do you notice?

Over the next few days, I wonder if you might just observe them a little, these curious creatures who share our space. You might notice a few things.

- What do you see that you didn't see before?
- What do you think they've learned recently?
- How have they changed in the last few weeks?
- What's the best thing about them, right now?

Where Are You Now?

I said that I wasn't going to give you easy answers, and I've just landed five weighty ideas on you all in one go, which may have left your head spinning. Some of those tools might feel like common sense to you, depending on what you have on your map and what you learned from the previous parts of the book. Some of them might have flipped some ideas you held right on their head. You might be feeling a bit cynical, or over-whelmed wondering how you're going to put all of that into practice. Perhaps I've fed the Fretter and the Critic, giving you new standards to aim for. 'OK, so I *shouldn't* be an intensive parent but I *do* need to collaborate, and set boundaries, and also look after myself, and apologise and . . . when do I just sit on the sofa and watch Netflix?!'

As always, remember that this isn't a recipe book. These tools are not a model to follow, they are broad-stroke principles that you can apply to your life however you choose. Everything in here, hold it loosely. If there's one thing you can take from this chapter, it's that this isn't about doing more for your child; in fact often parenting isn't about doing at all. Our children are not ours to shape – we're just talking about holding them gently as they discover the world for themselves.

Some of this might make sense to you now, and some of it might not. You might go off and, in a few weeks, have a conversation with your child that reminds you of something that I've said in here and have a lightbulb moment. Or maybe you'll read something elsewhere and that will help you apply this to your own life. Or your partner will talk to you about something and you'll find yourself discussing how to be more collaborative.

And if none of it resonates, that's OK too. This is about getting to know you better, and getting to know your child as they are. And maybe you have a different way of getting there, and some different tools to use. These tools are here as and when you are ready to use them.

As we place all of these tools in our pocket (there's quite a lot to go in there, so it's a good thing they're imaginary), finally we can get to look at the thing that brought us on this journey in the first place: our child's map.

CHAPTER 12

Our Children's Map

*'If the person you are talking to doesn't appear
to be listening, be patient. It may simply be
that he has a small piece of fluff in his ear.'*

A.A. Milne, *Winnie the Pooh*

The first thing that you'll see as you take a look on this map is that it's a bit barer than yours, depending on how old your child is. Some pathways are really clear, whereas others are barely there yet.

There may also be some similarities. Their childhood home, of course, maps on to your current home where you met your cast of characters, and you might have already identified whether your child has a few characters of their own. Some of the ghosts we met in Part II might be floating around, perhaps a little more transparent, and there will be some angels too, who might be brightly sparkling.

Can I just draw your attention to some of the pathways around the map? These are pathways to help you understand how your child works, what sort of human they are and why they do the things they do.

The Monkey Mind

If you take a look on your child's map, you'll see some pathways running across it, just like on yours. And, if you look closely, you might spot a little monkey. It's here to teach us a bit about the brain.

We talked in Chapter 10 about how much more we know now about neuroscience, and how influential (and pressurising) this information has become. You might already have read a lot about the brain, especially how it changes in the toddler and teenage years. But understanding how brains work, especially under stress, can really support us in understanding why children – and adults – behave the way they do. In essence, how we can sometimes be at the mercy of the survival systems of our children's brains (and our own).

What follows is a tremendous oversimplification of neuroscience. Our brains are far more complex and hard to fathom than this implies, but think of this more like a metaphor that helps us understand how we work.

Your prefrontal cortex, the part of the brain behind your forehead, is responsible for executive functioning. We can think of this as the Wise Elder of our mind. The prefrontal cortex is the sensible part of us – it helps us make decisions, it understands time and consequences, it holds our working memory, helps us plan, inhibits our impulses and moderates how we express our emotions, and allows us to be flexible.

Little kids don't really have much of a Wise Elder in their minds. It makes sense, doesn't it, because they're not very 'Elder' yet. Throughout the early years, our brains go through enormous transitions, with connections being fine-tuned, and those that are not used being discarded. Our brains develop this over the first 25 years of their life, and our Wise Elders finish last. Some people struggle with executive functioning long into their adulthood (this might be due to neurodivergence, hereditary factors, neglect and adversity, high levels of stress, and poverty – all of which can manifest in diverse ways).

We also have our limbic system – which starts to develop quickly within weeks after birth. The key parts of this system for us to understand are the amygdalae (our alarm system – the monkey!) and the hippocampus (our linen cupboard, storing memories as well as helping to control our emotional responses). It won't surprise you to know that emotion and memory are linked, as thinking of a memory can evoke such a strong emotional response in us. In the early years of our life we are working largely from the limbic system, then we have a period of relative stability until the limbic system takes over again in the teenage years, when it grows faster than our Wise Elder can keep up with. There are other parts of the limbic system too – the main thing for us to remember is that it is this part of the brain which contains our stress responses.

This is where the Ogre (our fight response) and the Fretter (our flight response) live. In children there may not be so much a Floater as an actual freeze response – you might recognise this in a rigid body that will not be manoeuvred into a buggy or car seat. And the Wounded Soul is less an emotional collapse than a complete, full-bodied, physical and emotional one.

Our monkey – the amygdalae – is paying attention all the time, like a radar for threat. This happens to us adults too; these parts of our brain are very involved in keeping us safe, but most of the time information gets passed to that Wise Elder and we're able to stay pretty calm. But for children, in the toddler and preschool years as well as in the teenage years, when something happens that feels threatening in any way, the monkey completely takes over and the Wise Elder parts of the brain pretty much switch off. This is so that they can get to safety quickly – a time when they don't need to think, they just need to act. But a threat may not be a real threat to survival, of course; it may be something that is simply experienced as threatening – a threat to their sense of autonomy, or a threat they have thought of. And, as you'll know if you've raised a toddler or a teenager, the monkey can take over numerous times a day.

The Wise Elder feels a bit more accessible in the middle childhood years, then in the teenage years the brain goes through another huge reorganisation. That Wise part of the brain is still very much developing, while the emotional centres of the brain are not only maturing but are at their most active. For example, dopamine – the neurochemical that is linked to reward-seeking – peaks in adolescence. This leaves the monkey very much in charge.

Knowing that our children are little monkeys in the guise of humans can really help us to use those tools to understand them:

- Empathy that they are as overwhelmed by their responses as we might be.
- Collaboration to support them in developing that Wise Elder (more on that in the next chapter).
- Boundaries to reduce that sense of emergency.
- Compassion to try to keep their spark alight in the face of that raging fire.
- Repair when we – inevitably – forget that we're talking to a monkey, or turn into monkeys ourselves. It's not uncommon for a home to be full of monkeys sometimes.

Becoming Human

As well as that monkey swinging between pathways, you will see on that map a huge array of different pathways leading to your child's house. These are all the different paths that help them form themselves, who they are. You'll see that at the end of one is *your* childhood home, and their other parent's child-hood home is at the end of another, because we've spent quite a few chapters now exploring how our own childhoods influence our children's. There will be pathways to the swamp of ghosts and angels too, and some of those pathways will already be established, and there might be others there that haven't been opened up and may remain closed. And there will be loads of pathways that are signposted with all the many things that make up a human. These might be paths about your child and what they arrived with – with signs like 'temperament' and 'personality'. They could be signs about the environment they have come into that influence who they are, like 'womb environment', 'financial situation', 'conflict', 'birth order'. They might be signs about the body they are in, which of course impacts on how we develop a sense of who we are – like 'race', 'gender', 'disability'.

Remember back when we visited your swamp of ghosts and I talked about the ways in which our responses to things (like stress) can be inherited? And then we've talked about all of the different ways our relationships can influence how we see ourselves and relate to others in the world. And we've talked a bit about environment too.

This is really the essence of being human, and what we lose when we try to simplify our child (and how to parent them) into a series of strategies or tasks. Becoming a human with a sense of self is an enormously complex process that we are constantly learning new things about.

Psychology as a subject, the study of humans' minds and behaviour, gains new understandings of how we become ourselves all the time. We now understand that, while many traits can be inherited, they can also be switched on or off depending on our environment. And as our knowledge grows, sometimes we cast off old stories that we thought were truths.

There are many pathways we could explore in more detail, but let's just choose one to look at, to see one example of what our children bring to their relationship with us.

Temperament

This pathway is about how our children come as unique people from their earliest days. Especially if you have more than one child or have had lots of children around you, you will be aware that children just arrive different to one another. One reason for this is temperament. There has been some controversy over what temperament is and how it develops, but it can be loosely summarised as an inbuilt set of characteristics that influence our responses.

Temperament is pretty stable over time, especially after the age of two, and is linked to the development of our adult personality. Our temperament defines how deeply we feel our emotions (how easily we are frustrated, how we experience discomfort, how easily we are soothed), our ability to regulate our state (how distractible we are, how much we have an inbuilt routine, how adaptable we are to new situations, how easily we become overstimulated) and how active we are (how impulsive we are, how shy we feel, how much we smile and laugh, how sociable we are). Temperament and emotion are not the same thing but are closely linked – our temperament will define how we express our emotions. Traditionally, temperament has been grouped into 'easy' (the majority of children), 'slow to warm up' and 'difficult' (this only applies to about 10 per cent of children, even though your child might feel incredibly difficult to you at multiple points throughout the day!).

So the reason why some babies will nap and eat at regular intervals is often not because of anything you're doing but is heavily influenced by their inbuilt sense of rhythm. One reason why some babies are hard to settle is because of their inbuilt intolerance of discomfort. One reason why some children love a party while others stay on your lap is because of inbuilt differences in sociability. We might blame ourselves – or our children – for these traits but they come from a place not of choice, but of their innate them-ness.

And, of course, there are pathways leading off this one too, to demonstrate the other things that influence temperament, such as gene variation, epigenetic factors (the ways that these genes might be expressed), womb environment, as well as environment after we are born. As we discussed in Chapter 4, there is growing interest too in the ways that temperament (in particular our reactivity to stress) is influenced by parental and intergenerational trauma even before conception. And one pathway goes directly back to us – because how our children's temperament is expressed depends very much on how we feel it 'fits' with us and their environment. So if a 'slow to warm up' baby lands in the arms of a chilled-out parent who is happy to drift through the day with few demands, this might feel like an easy pairing. But if a 'slow to warm up' baby lands in a loud, hectic family they are likely to begin to feel more difficult to those around them.

Your Unique Human

This is not something that tends to be acknowledged when we're given parenting advice – that what works for one child will not work for another. So, we might comfort one child from a tumble with a big cuddle – while another child won't even notice that they've fallen over.

Often this can become very clear to parents whose children don't fit the 'mould' in some way. Those with health issues, disability, specific educational needs, neurodivergence. We often then have to let go of our expectations and preconceptions and figure out what works for our child and family, even when this is completely counter to mainstream advice. For example, admonishing a child who is having an aggressive outburst becomes less fitting when that outburst is caused not by a power struggle but by the overwhelm and anxiety caused by existing as a neurodivergent child in a neurotypical world. Even common 'gentle' parenting approaches – like validating feelings through soothing words – can become unsuitable. When someone is in a highly dysregulated state, having to interpret our words will just add to feelings of stress and demand.

This is where the parenting tool of Collaboration can really come into its own. If we move towards collaborating with our children, we let go of singular expectations of who they are and who they will become. This doesn't mean being permissive, with that sweet porridge; it is simply seeing your child as a human in their own right – just one who doesn't have the skills, knowledge and physical and emotional development that you do.

All this said, there are so many different pathways that we will never fully explore. Sometimes we might spend a bit of time really getting to know one path – such as our child's interests – only to find we're blocked off all of a sudden by another path crossing over it, such as our child's friends (who might then be the only ones allowed to continue on that journey with them while we are only occasionally invited along). And these pathways are not linear – because our development is often two steps forward, one step back – so that just when we start to think the pathway of emotional regulation is nice and smooth, we enter the teenage years and realise we have a lot more journeying to do.

What has this brought up for you? It can be a bit overwhelming to realise just how many components there are involved in being a human. But in many ways, this can release the pressure to know it all. Instead, we can just look at what is in front of us – holding on to that sense of wonder if we can – and help them to protect their spark.

What Is a 'Child'?

I'm not going to go into huge amounts of detail here about children at different ages and stages – there are other, brilliant books available for that. But there are a few concepts about child development that will help you to see your child as they are and understand their experience. Considering how much we learn about fractions at school, and how to ask for the train station in another language, it's pretty astonishing that we don't learn anything at all about how we develop as humans.

Let's step on to the doorstep of our child's home. As we arrive here, let's just consider three things that we are bringing as we step through this door. Because we're not coming here empty-handed.

Children Carry Our Baggage

I know we've talked about this a lot already, but one of the things about child development that we so often leave out is that we bring all our baggage to parenting. And our children carry it. They have to hold everything that we see in them as well as those traits that they are bringing.

They carry our hopes and expectations.

By the time we have a baby we might already feel we know them – we might be holding that perfect image of a baby and what a baby will do, how they will be and how they will make us feel. So our babies and children might have to hold our disappointments – our realisations that they are not our ideal child but a complicated, real, whole person.

We've also talked about our own little babies and how they can pop up in us when we have our own baby. What can often then happen for our actual little babies – and as they grow, our children, teenagers and adult children – is that they have to 'hold' these younger parts of us, on our behalf. This is called projective identification – we project parts of ourselves into others, they absorb these, and then we respond to them (either how we would have liked to have been responded to, or how we actually were responded to). And then we are responding to parts of us, rather than to our actual child. But what happens at some point (and maybe what's happened to you for the first time in reading this book) is that our child realises, 'Hey! That's not mine!' and they cast off the parts of us that we have imposed on to them.

I know that's kind of a tricky concept, so let's put it like this. Let's say that maybe when we were little, our parents had a lot of different stresses going on, and maybe we were the youngest of many siblings and as a baby we just had to go along with whatever was happening – perhaps we were carted around with our siblings, or had to stay in a pram while our parents worked. If we cried, and everyone around us was busy and just couldn't respond, we quickly learned that it was better for us and for everyone to keep those cries in. We learned that traditional Irish dance. But what also stayed inside was a feeling of being alone, with no one around to come when we called. And then, we grow up, and we have a baby of our own, and when we hold that baby in our arms we – somewhere deep within us – say, 'This baby is *never* going to feel alone.' So we carry that baby everywhere, and respond at the first sign of a grizzle, and we prevent them from feeling discomfort, and we come running as soon as they call. And then, when they're 3, or 10, or 17, or 30, they say, 'For God's sake, would you *leave me alone!*' Because in looking after the abandoned little baby we projected into them, we didn't realise that they never felt abandoned themselves. In fact, they were feeling pretty suffocated.

They might also hold parts of other people too. So those internalised parents, or the cast of characters? We might see them reflected back in our babies. So when they cry we might, in our minds, hear them say, 'You're so useless' (hi, Critic!) or,

'You're letting me down' (hi, Wounded Soul!). And then we might respond to those parts, and we might bring in others from our cast of characters (so perhaps the Lover comes in to respond to the Critic, or the Ogre comes in to stamp out the Wounded Soul) so our dance becomes really complicated.

Remember, we're not aiming to break cycles here – there will of course be times we project things from our own past and experiences on to our children and other people. And of course our own views, experiences, mood and so on will absolutely impact on them sometimes and stop us from being able to understand them. And there will be times when they, for many reasons, just feel unfathomable to us.

When we untangle the stories that we've carried, and get to know all of the past and present parts of us, we can take some of that load back from our children. We know those parts of us – so we don't need to hand them over. And, together with our tool of Empathy, this helps us see who they truly are.

Children Are Built for Relationships

More than anything else, humans are relational. We are born within, and for, relationships. Children start dancing with us while they're still in the womb. And all of our children's relationships – with us, with others and with the world around them – will shape who they become. Not just now; they will continue to be shaped for their whole lives, just as we are. We are a foundational part, but there are many other pathways too.

Even the tiniest of humans relate to others. Babies communicate, from day one. In the 'conversation' of holding our gaze (starting a conversation) and then breaking that gaze (pausing the conversation for a breather). They cry, in order to communicate their discomfort and frustration.

As parents we encourage this relationship-building without even realising. We do this non-verbally, mirroring our baby's expressions in exaggerated ways, looking concerned when they are distressed – communicating that we understand their experience and helping them learn that they really exist, and have sensations and experiences that they will come to understand as being different from ours. We do it verbally too. When a baby babbles, parents across the world interpret what they are telling us, often using a sing-song voice (known as 'motherese' or 'parentese'), which not only helps hold their attention but also helps them learn to break down language. Over months and years, these interpretations are internalised by our children and help them make sense of their experience.

In essence, babies and children learn through their relationship with us. This is not a one-directional relationship, but about synchrony – how smooth the dance is between a baby and their caregivers. Children are tuning in, all the time, using information around them, experimenting (in the toddler years, constantly!) and adjusting their expectations and behaviour accordingly. They are reading our dance steps and learning to adjust theirs.

Although as parents we can feel that we are saying the same things hundreds of times, our children are absolute masters at reading us. They may not see the importance of brushing their teeth when we ask them to, but they always have their senses open to read our mood.

This makes sense when we remember what we've learned about those dances, knowing that babies and children need to make sure they stay close to us in order to stay safe. Even in teenage and adult years, they might continue to dance with us, even when they are learning other steps elsewhere. To know how close to stay to us, children see past our external facade – our characters – and sense what we are feeling underneath in order to know how to get the best from us. And, to help them do this, even in their earliest months they are developing their own cast of characters – what psychoanalyst Esther Bick called 'second skin defences' – so they might float off if they feel we are getting in their face a bit too much, or release unbridled fury if we don't feed them quickly. And as they grow, they might develop other characters as they learn what will get them certain responses and then, in their teenage years, experiment with *more* new characters, and relate to others in different ways.

It is the regular, consistent interactions with us and the world around them that will define the dance they get used to with the network of people caring for them – and which of these cast of characters will stick around in the longer term.

And, in our dance, children may lead us too. One beautiful study of babies, using brain imaging during parent-and-baby play, showed not only that their brains 'coupled' with each other – lighting up in similar areas as they played, particularly in the prefrontal cortex, which helped with joint attention, joint eye contact and shared emotion – but also that, fascinatingly, the infants' brains were often the ones 'leading' the adult brains – showing that the infants were anticipating what their adult would do next.

The more we can hold on to our tools of Empathy and Collaboration, the more we can allow them to shape their relationship with us, to let us know which porridge they need – and even change our steps if they need to.

Children Are Emotional Barometers

And whether we like it or not, we bring our emotions to this door. Our children are born to read our cues and know how best to relate to us (although of course they sometimes relate to us in ways that rail against the cues they've read!). This also means that children tend to read the room much better than adults can. So even if we say, 'Time to go now' in a kind, firm tone, they can hear the exasperation beneath it and see the clenching of our jaw, and they may interpret our frustration as rage and respond to that. They then communicate the emotion they're tuned in to, in subtle or hard-to-interpret ways – or very clear and loud ones!

In parenting, what so often happens is that, if children are demonstrating anxieties or behaviour we find difficult, we will start to try to figure out what is 'wrong'. Of course we want to find a solution. But sometimes, in doing so, we place the problem firmly in the child (and often hope that techniques will fix the problem).

Of course, sometimes our individual children may need particular, individual support. However, it's helpful to remember that children are also the barometers for the mood in our homes. Some more than others, particularly those who are more sensitive.

Even though children may appear more robust as they grow, they are still soaking up the moods of everyone around them, and they may then express these through their behaviour or through physical complaints like tummy aches. Just as they did as toddlers and babies, children and teenagers gain safety through their closeness with us and others who they trust. In order to stay close to us, they sometimes need to ignore the more difficult aspects of us – and in doing so they sometimes internalise those aspects (the opposite side of the projection we talked about earlier, called introjection). They may even act them out, almost on our behalf. They absorb our Ogres, our Critics, our Wounded Souls, so that they don't have to face them – and neither do we.

This emotional gauge doesn't only apply to your relationship with them, but the emotional temperature in the home too. One example of this might be the ways that children respond to their parents' relationship. By six, children already have a good understanding of the different roles in a family, and they might get drawn into regulating the 'emotional climate' between parents. Even without explicit conflict, children may feel tension and stress – and correspondingly act on this. This distracts the parents from their conflict. For example, if a child is aware that their parents have been arguing more frequently, they might begin to complain of headaches, or they might start getting tearful at bedtime. This then provides (usually completely unconsciously) a problem for the parents to solve together, which restores a sense of equilibrium to the home.

When we understand this, it helps us to widen our gaze when we are struggling with our children's behaviour. We too are existing within contexts that cause stress, and this inevitably impacts on every member of the family, both together and as individuals. Bringing in all of these different factors can lighten the pressure on a child to carry the problem. In family therapy, this is neatly summed up with the phrase, 'The person is not the problem, the problem is the problem.' When one member of the family is having a hard time, by coming together to resolve this as a shared problem (the troll under the bridge), we can find shared solutions that don't attribute blame.

In the next chapter, we're going to step into your child's home. You're welcome to bring your guide too. If you look inside that home, you might already have a sense of the dance they are learning with you, the porridge that you serve. You might have already decided that you'd like to work with your family – slowly, and collaboratively – to redraw some of the things inside that house.

Filling those rooms will be a process of many years and, don't forget, we can make changes and redraw areas at any time. But I'd like us to enter the kitchen of this house now – the heart of the home.

CHAPTER 13

Mapping Out Feelings

'He who can reach a child's heart
can reach the world's heart.'

Rudyard Kipling

As we step into our child's home at long last, something pretty strange starts to happen. It's filling up with things . . . just endless stuff, tiny toys and plastic tat and a laundry basket that magically refills every time it's emptied. And the noise! There's a high-pitched whining coming from somewhere, and shrieks of laughter, and someone is playing a recorder very loudly. We're going to get into the kitchen, holding on to the walls to stop ourselves from stumbling as the ground shifts and shakes. Because as we enter this house, and this kitchen that holds such a lot of family life, we have – for a moment – entirely left our adult world behind. We have entered a space of feelings.

This is the complexity, and chaos, and magic of family life. Sometimes you can stroke the soft cheek of a small person and feel your heart swell and wonder how this whole human is in your life, and that you get to witness them grow and change. And sometimes there are multiple people talking at you all at the same time, with the background music of the TV theme tune you've been listening to on repeat for three weeks, and there isn't any milk, and all you want in that moment is to have a minute – just one minute – without anyone making a demand on you.

Children are intense.

Oh, wow. Are they intense.

And not only that, but they are super intense because they can bring up *such* intense feelings in us.

Let's sit down together in this kitchen within your child's home. Your guide is welcome too. As we take a breath, perhaps things settle just a little. We've got to know each other pretty well by now, so I think you know what's coming next.

If we want to ride the waves of our children's intensity, we have to understand our own feelings first. To be familiar with our own emotional landscape. To hold their feelings and make sure we have someone to hold ours, too.

How We Feel about Feelings

Let's start with how intense feelings can feel. Both in facing our children's feelings – which often burst out with little temperance – and also in facing our own. Because often one of the most challenging experiences in families is how emotions can turn into a REALLY big deal.

We've talked about how children can bring up raw, intense feelings in us based on our own early experiences. And there are so many layers to this. There are the feelings our child has, and how we interpret them. There are the feelings that get brought up in us – which might be related to those historical little-kid feelings, the stories we've internalised, our feelings in the moment. And then there is how we respond to that.

Often feelings can be overwhelming in families because we simply haven't been taught the language of emotion. And yet, emotional intelligence is the building block to so many things – not just emotional awareness; it also supports us at school and in the workplace, to build stronger relationships and to meet demands of different situations, as well as being linked to more positive psychological and physical health.

While there are different concepts of emotional intelligence and what this really means, they always include the two components of: being aware of and managing our own emotions, and awareness and management of the emotions of others. Psychologist Daniel Goleman has described five components to emotional intelligence:

1. How aware we are of our own feelings.
2. How well we can regulate them in different settings.
3. Empathy (being tuned in to others' emotional state).
4. Social skills to build relationships.
5. Motivation to learn more and keep developing.

Emotional intelligence is something that we learn throughout our lives.

If this is a new concept for you, as it is for many parents of the 'seen and not heard' generation, it can feel difficult to grasp. It may not be just that emotions weren't met with acceptance, interpretation and understanding. It may be that they weren't spoken about at all. Or it may be that they were met with ridicule, dismissal or denial. So it can take some unpicking to consider even just what our relationship with our own feelings is.

There are cultural differences in the way that we are brought up to express and understand emotion too. Recognition of emotions such as happiness, sadness, anger, disgust, fear and surprise is fairly universal (although we tend to recognise these more accurately from within our own ethnic group), and across the globe we feel our emotions physically in similar ways, although we might label them slightly differently. However, expression of emotion varies depending on our social and cultural context. For example, studies comparing expressions of anger in the United States and Japan suggest that anger is an acceptable emotion in the USA, where individual desire and autonomy are goals. While in Japan, anger can be seen as unacceptable, running counter to goals of harmony. This can be seen in parenting differences – for example, Japanese parents will adjust their responses in order to de-escalate conflict, while in the United States children are encouraged to articulate their anger, and healthy expression of anger is seen as a sign of maturity.

Shall we start by noticing how you feel about feelings? This might feel clearer having spent some time in your childhood home. But if you find it hard to remember clear answers to this, you might just notice a feeling in your gut about what you think may have happened.

- If you showed your feelings as a child, how do you think that would have been responded to (as in: angry, sad, frustrated, worried but also happy, excited, joyful?)
- What feelings do you think were not 'allowed' in your home growing up?
- What feelings were encouraged?

And, of course, it gets more complicated because sometimes we not only haven't been given language to express emotions or had those emotions validated – sometimes we may have been told our emotions were actually something else, or learned quickly to shape-shift our emotions in order to get the response we needed.

A very classic example is the many messages adults tell children in order to reduce the strength of their feeling, such as saying, 'You're OK!' to a crying child, or the classic 'Big girls/ boys don't cry' (aka 'be brave', don't show your suffering externally). But parents and caregivers also do this to alleviate their own sense of shame or responsibility over having caused, or failed to prevent, an emotional response – because of their own maps and their own discomfort with conflict. So when we said to our parent, for example, 'You did that! And it was YOUR fault!' or, 'YOU didn't listen to me and I TOLD you I didn't want that to happen,' we might have been met with a combination of responses that amount to 'It wasn't my fault and don't blame me and maybe actually it was *your* fault.' We often do this as humans, not just to children but to other adults too; in order to absolve ourselves of our own possible mistakes we turn the blame on to our accuser. Sadly, this is often modelled not only by our parents or caregivers but also by bosses at work, healthcare professionals, people in the public eye and . . . world leaders.

There are benign versions of this – the sort of palms-up 'don't look at me' responses that you are probably very familiar with. This still has the result of leaving us doubting our own feelings, and can make it harder for us to label them accurately. There are common gender differences to this too. For example, for those socialised as girls and women, anger may be discouraged and relabelled as unreasonableness, hostility, demandingness, hormonal imbalance, nagging and so on. This is often then internalised and may become attached to feelings of failure and self-criticism and then turn into sadness, which is much more socially acceptable. For those socialised as boys and men, conversely, sadness may be discouraged and relabelled as sensitivity, fatigue, stress, shyness, rejection and so on. This may be internalised as weakness, isolation, self-criticism and confusion, which may then turn into anger or irritability – again, much more socially acceptable. And *this* plays out in how these experiences affect our emotional intelligence – for example, women are often found to have stronger interpersonal skills and empathy, whereas men are often found to have higher tolerance for stress. It even affects others' perceptions of our emotional intelligence – for example, women's emotional abilities are frequently overestimated.

There are also much more damaging versions of this, which

can lead to lifelong feelings of self-blame and leave us with a profound sense of unworthiness. This might be where emotional, physical or sexual abuse is experienced or witnessed and we as children have either directly been blamed for this or have blamed ourselves – so we end up feeling that we are deeply broken and even that we have the capacity to do damage ourselves. This might be expressed in different ways again, so for example in women the understandable emotional distress that this can lead to might be labelled as borderline personality disorder and in men it may lead to diagnoses related to antisocial or aggressive behaviour and substance abuse. This doesn't seem to be a difference in the way emotions are felt – it is much more about the way that emotions are not only expressed but also interpreted (by health and mental health professionals too) in gender-biased ways. Bias has also been found in the way our emotions are interpreted by others depending on our race and social class.

- Can you think of any examples of where this may have happened to you in some way in your own family? For example, times when you were discouraged from expressing particular emotions, or felt that they had to be expressed in specific ways?
- Widening that out, are there messages that you received from your social or cultural context that influenced your understanding of and expression of your feelings?
- How about now? What gets in the way of you tuning in to your emotions now? Do you receive messages that certain emotions aren't welcome from your partner, workplace, friends, community, wider society?

As you can see, feelings are complicated. They are complicated to feel, and they can be really complicated to interpret.

If you've never been taught to speak the language of

emotion, how on earth can you be expected to support the development of emotional intelligence in a child who expresses emotion at full force and in ways that are designed to get a response from you?

Learning to recognise, interpret and express our own emotions is the first step in helping us recognise, interpret and respond to the emotions of our children. And it can help with so many other things too – like how to answer questions, how to have difficult conversations and how to reconnect after an argument.

How can we begin to do this? OK, as we sit here together, let's travel a little deeper into *this* moment.

Recognising Emotions

It's likely that, having read the last few pages, you might have a greater sense of how you recognise (or don't) your own emotions. Often we don't even know just how many emotions we have and we may have tried very hard to learn how to ignore them.

How can you tune in to emotions? If we think of our feelings as messengers, which are universally shared but culturally constructed, then we can bring some openness to understanding our feelings. And some curiosity too to our feelings about feelings.

Firstly, we need the language to learn how to label what we're feeling. But even that is up for debate – various models present this in different ways. These often depict core emotions (such as fearful and happy), as well as different combinations of emotions that produce other feelings (for example, contempt arising as a combination of anger and disgust) or clusters of emotions that are linked together (such as disappointment and regret). They also depict emotional intensity (for example, a spectrum from rage to mild annoyance). One recent study used a mathematically based framework to conceptualise 27 distinct categories of emotion, some of which are closely related to each other (such as anxiety and fear) and others that are further apart (such as awe and disgust). And, as we've said, context matters too – anxiety and excitement can often feel very similar in our bodies, so our interpretations add an extra layer here.

Let's just spend a little bit of time getting to know emotions in *your* body. See if you can spend a few minutes – even just three – in a quiet space without any interruption. Sit down somewhere without distractions, as much as possible. If you live in a vibrant family home, this might be pausing for a few moments before you return home, or taking a few minutes in a different room while the children are watching TV.

If you just turn your attention inwards, what do you notice? You might notice physical sensations like an ache somewhere, or hunger, or tiredness. Read ahead a few lines so you can then close your eyes and really tune in.

Just notice what, of those physical feelings, might be connected to your emotions. And as you start to tune in to your emotional experience, see if you can label what floats up. Often we see our emotional experience as one-dimensional, but we might also be experiencing lots of different feelings at the same time. We're never just focused on one thing; often, especially as parents, we have many different experiences simultaneously so that we are dealing with resolving multiple problems all at once – from how we're going to respond to a work demand to what we're going to make for dinner, all while navigating the emotional landscape of our family. So once you have labelled one or two feelings, see what else floats up. The longer you sit, the more you might notice that feelings pop up that actually surprise you (and then you might have feelings about the feelings).

As you label your feelings, just notice how you know to use that label. What signals in your body help you to identify that emotion? Perhaps a tightness in your chest, or a heat in your belly, or a tingling in your head. How did you learn to identify those signals in that way?

Try not to judge whatever comes up. We so often do this about our feelings, especially if we've been encouraged to shape-shift them into something more palatable to those around us. So if we notice feeling anxious our Critic might come in and disparage that, bringing in another feeling of shame. In Buddhism this is depicted in the parable of the second arrow. The first arrow is our suffering, whatever has happened to cause us pain. The second arrow is our response to that suffering – and this is the part that we have some control over. If our second arrow strikes us with judgement, fear, embarrassment, shame then our suffering will inevitably increase. If we bring in a shield of acceptance, kindness, compassion for ourselves, then we just have the first arrow to recover from. So notice that too. Consider what are your first arrows, and the second arrows you add to them. Where did you learn to do that?

It can be surprisingly moving, and sometimes confusing, to tune in to your emotions like that if you've never done it before. And often we can mislabel them, for all the reasons outlined already. Just as you are learning about the emotions of your child, perhaps it might be OK to apply that same curiosity to your own.

You might be able to tune in to your emotional experience and label your feelings while sitting somewhere quietly. This in itself is often a new experience for us as adults. It's really helpful to practise that skill of emotional recognition by checking in with yourself multiple times a day. I often suggest that my therapy clients find particular times to do this regularly, such as every time you shut the front door, or every time you walk into your actual kitchen.

But what about recognising our emotions while in a highly charged situation with our child or children? And then being able to manage them enough that we can recognise and support our child with their emotions? And often, more than one child at the same time?

Accepting Emotions

One of the biggest pitfalls in parenting is that we enter into it cognitively. We think that we can *think* our way through it. But parenting, from its very beginning, is so physical. Really, we need to *feel* our way through it. As we've done throughout this book, we need to be clear about the obstacles that stop us from connecting with our child – not on a rational level, but by allowing ourselves to tune in to what they are feeling, using that tool of Empathy we talked about in Chapter 10. Not just showing up, but being in it with them. Remember empathy as one of the components of emotional intelligence? Brené Brown sums this up beautifully, saying, 'In order to connect with you, I have to connect with something in myself that knows that feeling.' We have to be able to connect with that something in ourselves that will help us understand, but not superimpose.

By now, you might be more familiar with some of the obstacles that get in the way of that.

Our first obstacle to recognising our child's emotional experience is our own very natural stress response – getting to know our own monkey (see page 211). For some of us, because of our heightened stress responses (whether these are caused by recent traumatic events or stresses, or historical or intergenerational events), some expressions of emotion will be read by our bodies as a threat that we need to survive in whatever way we can. Just as happens in the brains of our small humans, when we're faced with something that is threatening in any way (that might include a child punching you on the arm and causing physical pain, but it might also be an exuberant baby discovering their own voice and shrieking loudly and unpredictably throughout the day and overloading your sensory system), then our monkey brain will take over and our Wise

Elder will disappear. Other things that make it harder to keep our Wise Elder present are tiredness, stress, decision fatigue, hunger – all things that we often experience as parents, where the needs of our children can so often consume our own. Tiredness is a big one here – one study found that even just one night of sleep deprivation has been linked to changes in brain function, including a 60 per cent increase in the amygdala response to emotionally negative pictures.

We might respond to this perceived threat in different ways, depending on where we are, how we're feeling in the moment, and the ways we learned to respond as children. So, as we outlined a little when getting to know our cast of characters, we might run around trying to fix it, or run away (the Fretter flight response), we might get snappy, shout or physically aggressive or overpowering (our Ogre fight response), we might get tense and feel unable to think (that Floater freeze response coming in), we might shut down emotionally and just go through the motions to get through it (our Wounded Soul collapse or 'flop' response) or we might do whatever we need to pacify our child regardless of the consequence to us (our Lover – also called the fawn response).

- Do you notice familiar ways that you might respond when faced with your child's emotions?
- Do you notice differences in your stress response depending on different situations? What makes it different for you?
- Do you have a usual 'go-to' stress response?
- Why do you think that is?
- Is there anything that you've already noticed helps you come out of that response and get your Wise Elder back in the room?
- Is there anything you might add in to help you with your own stress response (e.g. deep belly breaths mid-meltdown, earbuds to reduce noise, regular breaks from

being touched, someone to offload to when the storm has passed).

There are also our historical obstacles – the things from our own experiences that fill us up with our own little-kid selves and stop us from seeing the kid in front of us. And there are obstacles to do with the relentlessness of everyday life. The preoccupation with our other relationships. This can all interact too, for example if you are in a supermarket with a small child (in itself a stressful experience!), hungry, underslept and desperate to get home – that makes it harder to tune in to *anyone* else's emotional landscape. And then if your child – in absolute joy at being among all these shiny new things – starts asking for those shiny new things, and you keep saying no, and they are getting increasingly upset. There is the obstacle of having little resource to respond with empathy. There might be other obstacles too, like how many people are looking at you right now and what sense of shame or judgement they bring.

Can I tell you an obstacle that is so present in our lives but one that you almost certainly won't want to hear? One that gets in the way of us recognising our children's emotions but also gets in the way of connecting in our relationships more generally? Your smartphone. There is now a wide body of research that shows how smartphone use can create a barrier between us and our children. One such example is with infants. You might have heard of the 'still face' paradigm that psychologist Ed Tronick created in 1978. During the experiment, a parent and baby or toddler are interacting, the parent then turns away just for a moment and then when they turn back, they have a blank, unresponsive face. Even babies as young as four months old will try for some minutes to evoke a response from their parent, become distressed and then become flat and withdrawn. A 2022 study found that (sorry, deep breath) mobile phone use had the same impact on infants as the still face. When parents reported greater phone use in general, it also took longer for the baby and parent to reconnect as the baby remained upset or withdrawn, was less likely to be sociable with the parents and also less likely to explore toys.

Other studies looking at mobile phone use when parents or caregivers are with children have also shown that our own behaviour changes when we are absorbed in our phones – one study looking at the very common behaviour of parents being on their phones in a restaurant found that the more absorbed a parent is in their phone, the more likely they are to respond harshly to their child's bid for attention.

Essentially, when we are on our phones a lot, our babies and children will try their best to get our attention and then, when we don't give it, they are more likely to show their distress either externally (with tantrums, aggression, restlessness) or more internally (with whining, sulking, withdrawal). And, the more our children behave in these ways . . . the more likely we are to turn to our phones to help numb our feelings about their behaviour, causing an absolutely spectacular vicious cycle.

Reading this book, perhaps you've come across a number of points where you've reflected on wanting to make a change. Phones are incredibly addictive – they are designed to encourage compulsive use – and there may be times when you've felt completely at the mercy of your phone. Before you start questioning whether you've broken your child, just ask how you would like things to change. We don't need to add a second arrow of guilt.

- Thinking about your own child or children – are there things about their emotions that have surprised you?
- Are there things about their emotions that you find particularly difficult?
- How do *you* feel when they are expressing positive emotions like excitement, joy, love?

- How do you feel when they are expressing negative emotions like anger, distress?
- Are there any emotions that you wish you just didn't have to deal with? Why do you think that is? Does that create other problems? Like what?

Emotional Storytelling

Feelings is one area where stories can really help us out. Especially if we haven't been familiar with our emotions, telling stories about emotional experiences can allow us to create a little distance from them. This can also have the added benefit of bringing our Wise Elder back in when emotions are high, because we need those frontal lobes of the brain to help us turn our raw emotions into complicated language.

So, if our child becomes very upset because, let's say, they've lost a toy train, we might tell them this story – 'You're crying because you're upset. You lost your train.' They might, especially as they get older, correct or expand on these stories so, if we interpret their emotions inaccurately, they might retell this story emphasising how it felt for them.

Outside of those more highly charged moments, we can also bring more meaning into stories by having conversations with our children about their feelings – again, this can be helpful for us too if we are learning it for the first time. This might look like asking a child to describe the feelings inside their body, such as 'How do you know you're excited? What does that feel like in your body?' or explaining the feelings in your own body.

A lovely technique in therapy is to tell stories about emotions themselves, by talking about them as if they are objects, creatures or – for example – a cast of characters! Especially when we or our children are feeling really tangled up in a feeling, describing it in this way can create a little bit of distance between us and this overwhelming emotion. With small children we might draw out what a feeling could look like, like a dark cloud of sadness or a red firework of anger. For older children – and for us – creating characters to describe our emotions can support us in managing our feelings and bring some creativity to our understanding of them. So, if our Critic is getting a bit noisy and making us feel bad about ourselves, we might play around with them a bit – perhaps call them Mrs PricklyKnickers and talk back to them as if they are a grumpy Roald Dahl character. Or we might bring our characters together – so if our anger is an Ogre then we might be able to consider what that Ogre needs so that we can act in a way that might be more helpful for us in the moment. So perhaps allowing our Ogre to write furiously about how angry our partner made us will enable our Warrior to step forward and come up with some solutions for them, or empower our Lover to remind us to bridge-build instead of smash everything to pieces.

You can have a practice if you'd like to:

- Bring to mind an experience that raises some emotion in you – not something too distressing, just a mild irritation or upset.
- Try to tune in to that feeling in your body. Notice where in your body it is.
- If it were an object, or a creature, or a thing, what would it be?
- What would it look like?
- Imagine taking it out of your body and holding it in your hands. How does it feel? It is warm or cold? Heavy or light? Soft or hard?
- Is it making any sound?

You can also experiment with what happens when you visualise different ways to deal with this feeling – such as talking to it and asking it what it wants, shrinking it, putting it in your pocket, or attaching it to a balloon and letting it float away.

The Fairy Tale and the Reality

We've talked so much about fairy tales already but I wonder if you carry some stories about what expressing emotion should look like. Because our unconscious ideas, as always, can get in the way of us accepting what is in front of us.

One of the common things I hear from parents is that they've done 'all the right things' and their child is still hitting/shouting/crying/pinching their siblings/lying on the floor wailing. Sometimes this may just be because they are overwhelmed with their own emotions, and nothing we say can reach them in that moment. But sometimes this is because we may have *said* things that sound empathic or soothing, but because of our own fear, impatience, worry – whatever – this doesn't match up with our actual feeling. And our little emotional-barometer children sense that, which adds another layer of confusion to their own feelings. In our doing of 'the right things' we might also add stress to ourselves because we're trying to remember that perfectly written script we read online, or kicking ourselves because our wording wasn't quite what we were aiming for – again, working from the cognitive rather than the felt and inadvertently adding in an obstacle to the human-to-human connection that our child might be in need of (and that we need too, of course).

It may also be that our expectations of the conclusion to those 'right things' – like validating, expressing empathy, interpretation of emotion – are not accurate. Our child's feelings may leave us unsettled. Especially if we have had to suppress our own feelings, we might never really have experienced or witnessed what it looks like for a feeling to arrive in our body, be immersed in that feeling and allow it to pass through. Many adults who come to therapy are amazed at what can happen when they stop second-guessing or restricting their own feelings, allow them to emerge and – with very little guidance or interpretation – find that their Wise Elders just arrive back and they can problem-solve.

What we often do to children (and to adults too) is that we explain, or interpret, or problem-solve . . . all of which tax their already taxed monkey brain and prolong the emotional mael-strom. And then, because we're also working on regulating our own emotions and frankly it's all just getting a bit much and maybe starting to feel like an assault on our senses, we might then start to distract, or shut down, or suppress. And this might cause confusion, taxing their monkey brain further – or the emotion looks like it's disappeared for now but it might pop up in the form of tears at bedtime, or a tummy ache, or shouting at a sibling (again, whether we are children or adults!). So when we think we are accepting and allowing an emotion, we're actually just changing its shape without realising.

The conclusion of connecting on that emotional level isn't for the emotion to disappear. In fact, what tends to happen is that the emotion will grow. And, depending on the child (or adult), it might take a while to be worked through – and then it'll pass on. The Wise Elder might then come back into play and, at some point, you can talk over what happened. At that point you might be able to help your child recognise their emotions – noticing what caused a feeling to arise, labelling it and, as they get older, reflecting on the emotions of others around them too.

Again, that point may not be when *you* want it to be (because you'd like some damn resolution yourself, thank you very much) – but hours or even days later when your child can look at it with more objectivity. Even young children will be able to come up with creative ways to solve any problems that might have arisen if we can give them the space to do so. For many families, there might then be some dilemmas to consider about how to marry up a child's feelings and viewpoint and the feelings and views of others – with boundary-based questions to resolve in your family such as, 'How do we feel about saying sorry when we've done something wrong?', 'What do we think about sharing?', 'How important are manners to us?'. I'm sure you have a number of other examples that will come to mind.

Emotional outbursts can feel never-ending, especially if we're trying so hard to respond to them perfectly. But tantrums often come like storms and pass through quicker than we imagine. It's when we feel like our emotions haven't really been heard, or can't be accepted by someone else, that they stay with us for much longer.

Another way that our ideals about parenting can get in the way of emotional connection is a belief that, if we are emotionally connected to our children, they won't feel sad, angry, frustrated or upset. If that's something that resonates with you, just reflect back on what we've talked about so far because there's something in that which indicates that 'happy' is really the only acceptable emotion. Humans are multidimensional, and some humans more so than others. Some of us have wide-ranging technicolour emotions – whether this is due to our temperament, personality, neurodivergence or cultural acceptability. We can't experience happiness unless we have something to compare it to. And this underlying belief can add yet more pressure – with a common phrase I hear being, 'But I'm giving them *everything* and I'm *exhausted* and they're *still* not happy.' We've talked over the costs of this sort of intensive parenting already (see page 76). In fact, it is often when our children feel most connected to us and safe in our presence, and aware that we have the space in our minds, bodies and diaries to absorb their emotions that they will feel able to express them (this is why, when we've had some lovely one-on-one time with them . . . they have a meltdown on the bus home).

One final thing in terms of our expectations, as we saw in Chapter 11, we just don't live in a very child-friendly world. We also happen to live in a stress-inducing world for us adults too. Our children will inevitably have feelings about that. Trying to keep up with these demands in order to conform can, in fact, take its toll on our bodies and minds.

- Does this sound familiar to you? How does this show up in your own family?
- Based on some of the information you learned in the last chapter about their development, how do you see your expectations now? Do you think they are realistic?

In learning about our own and others' emotions, there will inevitably be times that we get it wrong. In fact, in parenting there will be millions of times we just don't quite gel with our child. And, as we've discussed, we will make countless mistakes. If you're not comfortable with acknowledging your missteps, your children will point them out. And if we still don't feel comfortable, we'll get into an unwinnable battle about whose fault it is – and we may end up placing our own mistake on our child's shoulders to salvage our sense of infallibility.

There are also phases in family life where we just all rub up against each other the wrong way. Especially around transitions or times of stress, when parents might be preoccupied and children feel less present in our minds. We can't always prevent these phases of discord – nor would we want to, because we can offer our children 'good enough' lives as well as good enough parents – but we can support our families (including ourselves) through them.

So another skill we may need to learn is being able to acknowledge our own development. To use our tool of Repair to let our children know that we are flawed human beings who frequently stumble and don't have all the answers. And, in doing so, to allow them to explore their own flaws and mistakes and embrace the possibility that this can lead to development too.

Supporting Emotions

So what are we going to do with this information? Seeing as we're in the kitchen, let's see what is around to help us through all of this emotional work – preventing, containing, repairing and buffering.

PREVENTION

Tuning in to our emotions, particularly getting to know our stress response, will help us to figure out how often we are feeling overwhelmed ourselves. Let's get a saucepan out; I like to use the analogy of a pot of water on a hob. The water is our nervous system and the heat under the pot is the stressors we are under. When the water is cold we're using what is called the parasympathetic nervous system (otherwise known as being in 'rest or digest'). We feel safe, calm and relaxed, and all of our physiological processes are working smoothly. The more we turn the heat up, adding stresses, the faster the water boils, and eventually we might boil over (and go into our monkey threat state – the sympathetic nervous system of fight, flight, freeze, flop or fawn). Some of us, because of historic or current stresses, might always be on a simmer.

Being aware of our emotions, and tuning in regularly, means that we can spot when we're close to boiling over and find ways to turn the heat down.

Given how fast-paced the world is and the expectations we have of ourselves in it, alongside the stories about parenting being a form of martyrdom, we can often see looking after ourselves as a luxury – it might even be something you see as selfish. The kids come first. But meeting our own needs, and asking others to meet them too, is a form of prevention.

The more stress our bodies are under, the more likely it is that our Wise Elder will find it harder to stay present in times of stress – and some of us come with bodies that are more sensitive. Just those basics of sleep, regular mealtimes, quiet spaces (preferably outdoors) and movement can feel hard to access but are so important. You might have some go-to heat-reduction techniques that you use – we often hear the standard ones like meditation, dancing or running but you might prefer something more like Marie Kondo-ing your drawers, putting in some earplugs or getting on your skateboard. Whatever works – just find something that does.

You prioritising prevention means that your children also see how important it is. When children are more up and down than usual, often these are the things that go for them too – with disrupted sleep, perhaps less movement than usual, feeling cooped up at home, low blood sugar all contributing to their own emotional outbursts. Having calm and quiet spaces to decompress is often one that we forget about – for all of us – but children (and adults) need to have these safe places to wind down. For toddlers and children you can create snuggly calm corners for them, for older children having a private area to unwind is important too, and for adults knowing that we can find a regular space, even for a short time, without interruption is crucial.

At those times of discord, when you can see that your child needs connection from you, often we can end up down those dead ends – feeling ashamed and guilty, setting our standards super high again. But because we're depleted, an attempt at reconnection feels difficult – because our child might need to express their dissatisfaction with how things have been through their behaviour, which we might become impatient about, which adds to that disconnect.

Prevention also means you first. We can't fill up our children's hearts when ours are empty, it will just feel like a burden. So rather than saving 'self-care' for after things feel better, make that the first step to ensuring things get better. That's why this book is arranged like this. You first, always. Understand yourself, and you'll understand your child better. Show yourself love, and you'll be able to do that more easily for them.

And one of the best things we can do for prevention is everything you've done in reading this book – getting to know yourself. Wondering whether our expectations match reality, accepting the messy bits and embracing imperfection.

CONTAINMENT

Let's turn the heat off under that pan, and put a lid on it. Containment is how we create a cocoon around our children's feelings throughout their development. When feelings are overwhelming, containment offers that sense of safety that someone bigger and safer will just hold them for you. Again, often this is less about what we do, and more about how we feel in the moment.

We might need to contain our own feelings first. We might call upon that guide to help us in these moments, offering a metaphorical arm around our shoulders – or we might channel their qualities to support us. When things are really stormy, one way of doing this is to use methods that can quickly turn your own heat down. This might be telling yourself something to remind you that you are safe, such as, 'This is not an emergency' or simply 'I am safe.' Or it might be showing your body that you are safe, by elongating your out-breath, or clasping your hands tightly, or focusing on the feeling of your feet on the floor – all of which will allow you to counter a stress response. When the heat is really high, with little ones, you might even just lie down on the floor, eyes closed, palms up – surrendering to the situation and silently inviting them to join you (be warned this can end in laughter and small people climbing on you). Or you might need to discharge a bit of energy (which can so easily come out in a shout) by giving your body a wriggle, or letting go of a deep sigh, or vigorously shaking your hands.

We might not always know exactly what our child needs in the moment. We are likely to get it wrong, often. But it can help to hold in mind that they may be using you to help them get hold of themselves again – something called co-regulation, where they use your calm to bring calm to their storm. Emotional barometers, remember (page 223)? It is through co-regulation that children learn how to self-regulate. In the baby and toddler years they will use us a lot; in their early school years they have a little leap in their ability to do this for themselves; and then there is another big leap after adolescence (depending, of course, on other stressors too). Just keeping your body calm can help the storm to pass for both or all of you. And as your child grows, you can ask them – in calm moments – what they need from you when they are feeling stormy.

Sometimes our children need us to do more than just contain. Sometimes they are asking us to absorb them completely – for a short time, until their feelings have passed and they can problem-solve. And sometimes they might express this in the strongest terms – telling us how much they hate us, how much they wish they had a different family, even how they wish they weren't alive. Such strong feelings can just feel too powerful and, in many ways, children are asking, 'Please can you take this from me?' When we are stung with the unfairness of this, it's so easy to hand it back to them by saying, 'Don't talk to me like that!' or, 'You don't really mean that.' Which might pause their unleashing from our point of view but doesn't allow them release.

Sometimes it's OK to hold these unmanageable feelings for a little while. Letting them rail against us (the tool of Collaboration might help here), not even needing to say very much at all and being ready with a hug, or just your quiet presence, when the storm has passed, the monkey has calmed and – usually – tears start to flow or they sag into exhaustion. And then, when your child is ready (and that might be hours or days later), those active listening skills (see page 199) can be put to use to support them in problem-solving with the help of their Wise Elder (and yours).

REPAIRING

As we've already discussed, we are going to get it wrong. Often, and in surprising ways. In these dances we will often stumble. This is where the tool of Repair comes in – to help us acknowledge our human errors and allow and accept the messier bits of our children. Seeing as we're in the kitchen, and we've had a pot boil over, perhaps this could be a towel to mop up the spills.

It's useful to note that Repair isn't always right after the moment. It can come days later, or need to be repeated. Sometimes in the reconnection we might make mistakes too – especially if we have a different perspective on what happened. But keeping in mind that conflict is our Troll can help us focus on how to work together to rebuild our bridges.

You might need to repair with yourself too, through forgiveness or just restoration. We are often pushing ourselves hard as parents and can be physically depleted. We then often get ourselves back up to zero but never actually restore ourselves to feeling like a whole human. I suggest seeing the kind of things we usually do under the guise of 'self-care' – a dinner out, a walk alone – just as maintenance work. On top of that we need to find ways to restore, with deep rest that allows us to switch off our minds and bodies. That might mean sitting briefly in a dark, silent room alone, or ideally having a nap with an eye mask and some earplugs. Bringing stillness into an active day.

BUFFERING

Perhaps the most important step – let's get that cup of boundaries out of the kitchen cupboard. Offering containment and repair doesn't mean being a punching bag. It can be really hard to know the line between allowing children to express their emotions and a boundary becoming wobbly. When monkey brains take over in small children, it's not unusual for this to come out in the monkey-est of ways – hitting, scratching, spitting, biting. And in big kids too, they might be verbally aggressive (or, for some, still physically aggressive). But where you draw your boundary will depend, again, on your unique situation. There are lots of factors that might determine this – the size of your child, how safe they/you are in a situation, whether you can physically separate yourself, how you feel about what's happening, whether there are other children around to buffer, how overwhelmed they are by their feelings. The clue is if that cup of boundaries is spilling over and you are feeling resentful, overwhelmed or impatient – or even unsafe. The line of what you feel is acceptable might need to be drawn more firmly. And that line might be different to others' around you. We can discuss this in our bridge-building meetings (see page 255) – again without judgement of how monkey emotions can sometimes feel for us.

As well as considering our own boundaries, and what we need to feel whole and human, we also need somewhere to express our own feelings about the storms that sometimes batter us. Because 'containment' is a nice word, but it can be the hardest thing to do and it can pull on every fibre of our being. We need other people to co-regulate with and contain us. And we might also need to repair with ourselves.

I wonder if learning about emotion in this way feels new to you, and if so, whether having that understanding itself can create a buffer around the emotionally charged nature of family life?

As we sit here in the kitchen, let's imagine that we're using all of those parenting tools we received to just lower the temperature and get the ground more stable again. This time drawing on how we might need to bring compassion to our own internal conflicts and repair with ourselves, opening up to collaborating with the different members of our family and all of the different parts of us, having empathy for our own experience, allowing ourselves to receive what we need to do this whole parenting thing and maybe even getting a little bit of our spark back too.

CHAPTER 14

Family Stories

*'Would you like an adventure now, or
would you like to have your tea first?'*

J.M. Barrie, *Peter Pan*

W e've well and truly established by now that parenting is complicated. We started this book talking about parenting as a one-directional task. A parent (in charge) moulding a malleable child, and an idea that there are foundations we can lay down early on, and then our parenting job is done. Move on.

We're coming to an end with the knowledge that humans are messy, families are messier and being a parent is a lifelong relationship with a child or children that may also involve lots of different people.

So we can't leave our child's map quite yet, because we haven't added in the many other people who might be in their lives. Before we leave this house, let's head over to the Family Room and see who is in there. You might have a partner there, your child and possibly their siblings. There might be other important people from your family life in there too – other people who are important to your child. Where do they fit into all of this? Let's take some of the ideas we came across back in Chapter 8 when we were talking about your partnership, and see how they can bring us a clearer sense of how we work as a family.

The Family Dance

We have lots of stories about families, don't we? Perhaps the most prevalent one is the story of the happy family. Although there are many stories we might hold a little more quietly – our own family stories, which might include rifts, heartache and obligation.

A while back, we brought together the attachment dance that you learned with the dance steps of your partner or co-parent. We talked about how children get brought into these dances, and sometimes get swung between parents in convoluted, competitive moves.

There may be many people dancing with your child, and within a family home those steps are complicated. I wonder if we could take a moment to think about how the members of your family fall into step with each other?

You might notice that different people are dancing in couples – perhaps in your family people tend to pair up but coming together into a whole family dance feels difficult. Or maybe there's a steady waltz going on with some of the family, but when another person – a parent, or one of the children – enters the dance everyone loses their rhythm and trips over each other's feet.

It can feel a bit overwhelming to imagine that we're aiming for a steady dance with the whole family. How can we have a consistent relationship when life can feel so hectic? We might, for example, be aiming for a waltz but then deal with a work crisis, or an unwell grandparent, or a house move, or just a sleepless night, and feel that we've forgotten how to dance at all.

But remember that we're aiming for steady most (not all) of the time, and that, as life happens, other members of the family or community might be able to come in and keep that dance going.

- Bringing together what you know now about attachment dances – and watching out for dead ends – what are you (and your co-parent if they are present) aiming for in your family dance?
- Where are the moments that you feel things are out of sync for you as a family? Is there anything else you need to know about to help you find a rhythm?

Just as we do as a couple, sometimes we might need to get a bit of support to dance together as we negotiate the very different needs of our family members and figure out how our other responsibilities fit into our dance patterns, so that our children get a (relatively) steady tempo.

There might also be times when we want to dance separately. Especially if we have more than one child, having time together to fall into simpler steps can be essential. This can feel hard to achieve if you have competing demands, or if it's hard to find someone to care for your other child or children. But keeping those tools from Chapter 11 to hand can allow you to have even small moments of greater connection with the individual humans in your family. Deeply listening to a story about their friend at bedtime, or asking them about something they've become interested in, bringing out that Spark of Childhood to meet them in a game, inviting them to help you with a task that you can do side by side – we don't always need to *do* spectacular feats to meet our children where they are. Sometimes we just need to slow down a moment with them.

Family Bridge-building

As your children grow, you may also choose to bring them into discussions about what is on that bridge that connects all your maps together. Having a shared family set of values, expectations and hopes – created with the help of Collaboration – can actually create a boundary around your family. As well as your own boundaries within the family and relationships with each other, this can enable you – as a family – to preserve your integrity, and hold on to the things that feel important to you all.

One way of keeping this as a regular conversation, so that bridge-building (and mending) is a part of family life, is having family meetings. These can change as your children develop, but knowing that you will all be coming together regularly not only keeps these exchanges alive but also provides opportunities for repair, to check in with each other and hear about each other's experiences. So that we can remind ourselves that we are a family, but made up of individual, unique humans.

Having a family meeting to do this – including the children, even when they're little – can offer an anchor to the week when everyone knows they have a voice in the way their family works. And this isn't for meal planning or organising who is taking who to which kids' party. It's for airing gripes, talking about the things that feel important, deciding whether any changes need to be made. How we want to be as a family, and also what we want to do when it feels like everything is going wrong. This doesn't mean that we'll come up with solutions in the moment – sometimes it might also just be about active listening, acknowledging that things are tough and discussing what we might need to weather that together.

You can use some of these questions as a conversation starter, but this will be a process of experimentation, and will need to be adapted over time and depending on the capacity of different family members. It can be useful to have a question in there about protecting boundaries, so that it is part of your family conversation that we all have different needs and that it's important they are met (including our own). Some of those 'talking about talking' questions might come in handy, too, so that you can learn about what kind of communication will work for the different humans in your family.

- What's important to you, at the moment?
- What do you think should be important for us as a family?
- Where are these similar? Where do they conflict?
- Do you think we need to make any changes to how we do things at the moment?
- What do you need at the moment?
- How can we stay a team even when times are tough?

Having learned more about children, and yourselves, over the course of this book, if you are parenting with someone else you could also have a conversation about some of the things you are aiming for having read this book.

So you might speak to your partner or co-parent about some of the ghosts that you are struggling with at the moment, and ask them to just give you a (very gentle) nudge when they notice that a ghost has popped out. Or if you are working on changing the porridge you're serving, being able to discuss what that would look like in your home and what you might need to get there.

Especially as children get older, a family meeting might also mean hearing about the impact of our choices on them. Depending on how old your children are, you could share some of these ideas with them – especially if you are hoping to make some changes. We can struggle to name this to our children – bringing us back to those ideas we talked about around how we feel about conflict, and admitting our mistakes. This can be part of creating a more collaborative family environment, and allows us to open up conversations about how our children might have felt about how family life has been. If things have been difficult, those conversations can feel very painful – so as well as keeping a focus on repair, it might be worth having your guide close to hand and watching out for if that Critic decides to join in.

There will, of course, be phases when we need other regular times – sometimes many of them, sometimes fewer – to hear from our children (and sometimes partners) about how they feel about the other members of the family. Sometimes this might just be the need for an offload. But sometimes members of the family can get stuck in a difficult dance together. We might need to create space so that the biggest of emotions – anger, resentment, frustration – can be aired out of earshot of the perceived cause of them, without judgement and without blame. So many stories can get in the way of this – stories like 'never undermine the authority of your partner' or 'siblings should love each other all the time' or even 'hearing the frustrations of one child is disloyal to another'. But, in order to support Repair between family members, we can use those same principles we talked about in the last chapter. We can allow our child or partner to rant a little so that the monkey can let off some steam, which will allow their Wise Elder to come in and bring those tools of Empathy with them. We can do a bit of emotional storytelling about what we're hearing – or share the experiences we have had that resonate.

Sometimes as parents we ourselves become the bridge between family members, holding them together so that they can fall apart. And of course, we then need those around us to hold us up when that load is heavy and we need to fall apart too.

At its heart, building these spaces for communication and collaboration enables us to build strong bridges and tackle trolls together. And these spaces will be messy and complicated too – we might imagine family meetings with cookies and milk, then find ourselves with a wandering toddler, a frustrated child, a monosyllabic teenager, a distracted partner. Or maybe we want to give our children one-to-one time and a family meeting but the days are running away from us and we barely have time to breathe.

Don't forget we're not idealising anything here, just creating opportunities for conversation and connection when we can. This stuff isn't easy, and family life is often complicated and challenging. Sometimes if problems arise or we're just not quite getting along it can take time to find a place of relative harmony – and I'm talking weeks and months, not hours or days. We might grapple with something, chew it over, get frustrated with each other. Often this is because we're not quite 'getting' it or feel like we're not being 'got'. But then we find a new insight, resolve something and come back together again with a new understanding of ourselves and each other. We sometimes need to push through those messy bits with compassion and patience, in order to find that reconnection.

This is how we get to write our own family story – one that is not a fairy tale but has every member of the family as its hero.

CHAPTER 15

Children Are Mapmakers

*'We can't save the world by playing by the rules,
because the rules have to be changed. Everything
needs to change and it has to start today.'*

Greta Thunberg

As the dust settles on our journey, with a tired brain and (hopefully) a fuller heart, I just want to remind you of one of our parenting tools: the Spark of Childhood (see page 206). As we say goodbye, I'd like to add one thing to that. The knowledge that children are, in their very nature, mapmakers. And that these maps we've been exploring are the tiniest little part of a very big world.

We're not just raising children who will become adults within our homes. We're raising humans who are going to be part of the big, bad world.

We often worry as parents about how our children behave with other children. Do they share, are they kind, are they well-mannered, do they say sorry when they've done something we feel they shouldn't have?

But what about how they are in this global community of ours? Do they care about the planet? Are they aware of their neighbourhood and their impact on it? Do they look after the things and people around them? Do they know how different and similar they are to others in the world? The world is changing, quickly and sometimes in frightening ways. We've established that parenting is an enormous task, raising these little humans. We've focused on their feelings and ours, helping them feel seen as whole, messy people and allowing them to see our whole, messy selves.

But what else are we handing down to them? The world we have brought them into? The vast land and ocean that expands out of our own maps? Sometimes wanting the best for our children can also translate into wanting the best for our communities, and the world – if we can allow this to happen.

Often we think of parenting as something we do in isolation. The tasks that we complete, the messages we give. But humans are social creatures, and the way we live often works actively against our human needs to be connected to others and to thrive in communities. Having children can be a perfect opportunity to turn this around. To bring others into our lives and our homes and allow ourselves to learn from each other. Parenting so often is done behind closed doors, sometimes even in secretive ways if we are feeling in any way ashamed of how we're raising these humans. But if we can imagine that we're raising global citizens, maybe we'll feel more able to throw our doors open and share our stories.

Having children can be the first time in our adult lives when we take a pause from the modern world and notice what else is out there. We might feel able to take the opportunity to slow down and rediscover the magic that is so present in the world of children. This is one of the lessons we can take from our children – who so often teach us more than we can teach them. To see the world through their eyes.

A Pause for Pressure Release

I know, this is meant to be a book about parenting and we've already pulled apart layers of your self, looked at your relationships and gone through a load of information about children themselves. Now I'm asking you to think about the whole world? No pressure, right?

My all-time favourite quote about parenting is from Dr Charles Raison, who wrote, 'One generation full of deeply loving parents would change the brain of the next generation, and with that, the world.' So actually if all you take from this book is that you're going to try to understand where your children are coming from a little bit more, that is more than enough. Especially if you're trying to do something very new in your own home, even considering anything else might just feel like too much to think about.

But, if we have the capacity to consider it, we can make small changes in our family lives – which might not only help our children think critically and compassionately but help us too, to reconnect with the things that make life feel meaningful.

Widening Our Gaze

What often happens when we start thinking about the kind of world that is out there for our children is that our panic starts to rise. These are some of the topics that can keep us up at night: Climate change, government, global conflict, inequality, technological change, war, trafficking ... and what about financial instability and lack of access to public services, gender-based violence ... it's too much, isn't it?

We tend to either turn towards this and feel overwhelmed by it, or we might turn away and busy ourselves elsewhere.

Throughout this book we've talked about slowing things down, and how readily we can set ourselves unreachable standards and then feel shame when we don't meet them. We often do this in dealing with our place in the world too. So we may feel we have to do everything we can to, let's say, reduce the impact of climate change in our own homes, but then when we put a milk bottle in the wrong bin we feel like failures and feel defeated and that it's all too much.

Just as we learned about accepting our parenting mistakes, we can expand this to the other areas of our lives too. To know that we will stumble and fall many times, but crawling slowly in the direction we want to go in might be enough. We don't need to do it all now, or at once, we can start by merely thinking about our direction of travel.

Our children, being the magical and curious creatures they are, will begin to bring this to us in their own time. They will learn their own stories – through their friends, through school – especially when they become teenagers and start to explore their own values, identity and beliefs.

Our generation of children are set to be world-changers. This generation – known as Generation Alpha (can we just take a moment to consider how totally cool that is) – began in the same year as the first-generation iPad and Instagram were launched. Following the trend of millennials and Gen Z, our children will grow up faster but live with us for longer than previous generations – so we are going to be parenting them for a long time. They will be the generation that will be most globally connected, and racially and ethnically diverse than any that have preceded them. They are already socially engaged and politically active, with 20 per cent of those aged five to nine having already taken part in a protest. They may also be the 'post-stereotype' generation, judging people on their personal qualities rather than social groupings. The Covid-19 pandemic will be a defining moment in their lifetimes, potentially amplifying this generation's goals for a more connected and sustainable world.

Our views as adults will be challenged, many times over, as we as a whole family learn about what is important to the individual members and, in turn, what becomes important to all of us. As adults we might get indignant, get that salty porridge out, find it impossible to understand some of the things that our children experience, think and feel. But, as comedian Wanda Sykes puts it: 'Here's the thing, kids get it . . . if you don't get it, if you get hung up on shit like this . . . you just sound fucking old, that's all. These kids are on 5G and you are on AOL dial-up.'

We are going to be confronted, with Generation Alpha being well-prepared to challenge authority – both inside and outside the home. Perhaps we need to become more comfortable with saying, 'I don't know, but I think we can find out together,' (and, let's face it, most five-year-olds can find out information from Siri faster than we can . . .)

- What stories do you think your child is carrying within them, from others around them? About the world, and the people in it?
- Do you think any of those stories conflict with each other? (For example, perhaps in your home your children may get on well, but they have stories from books, films and their friends that younger siblings are annoying and not to be tolerated. Or maybe you are a vegetarian family and talk about animal welfare – but your child's best friend has a family of meat-lovers?)
- What further thinking or discussions might you like to have so you can clarify your thoughts, ideas or beliefs about some of the stories your child is introducing you to?

Small Steps

In the last chapter, we talked about the family bridge –setting up some shared values or guidelines to remember what is important in your own family. These were related to how it might feel within your home, the ways in which you are aiming to relate to one another.

- Is there anything you might want to add about the values that you would like for your family, about what happens outside your home? And how you want to live as a family in this vast world?

Some of these values might feel really clear in your life already. There might be ideas about charity, community care, hospitality, compassion that are very familiar to you. These might be ideas that you have integrated into your family life.

Or, these values may not have been so explicitly established in your life, but it is likely that you do have clear ideas about how you want to exist in the world that have come from your family, friends and all the other influences around us. How you want to be treated and how you want to treat others (whether they are animal, vegetable or mineral).

These don't need to be complicated ideas – because we alone aren't going to solve the world's problems. But we can find ways within our own families to at least explore and acknowledge them. We don't even need to 'teach' our children how to address the things we feel are important. Children are such natural justice-seekers that they will find their own missions – often our role is just to support this and be curious about learning alongside them.

What might you do together as a family to take some steps to learn about the world or make changes? This might be reading a book together – and we are so lucky to live in a time where books are reflecting the questions we are asking about inequality and injustice. It might be getting to know the natural world to enhance our appreciation of it – this might be growing something together, or just finding a spot to sit in and watch the world around you. Perhaps you might make a family commitment, like no-meat Mondays or raising money for a charity. Or maybe it is just being open to conversations – embracing questions about difference and finding out why this is a topic that is important to them.

What's Ours, and What's Theirs

We've talked about how hard it is to separate our feelings and experiences from our children's. What about when they start calling us out on our inconsistencies in our values? Or when they bring their open minds to us and point out our small-mindedness, or bigotry?

How will we accept that they might come to thoroughly different conclusions to our own, in their politics, behaviours and beliefs?

When we view our children as humans in their own right we can respect their opinions as much as our own. They may not have the lived experience that we do, but they do see the world through fresh eyes. Of course they are influenced by the messages they receive from us and those around them, but they bring their unique position and will exist in this world in a different way to us – because they are fundamentally different people.

There are many times this will bring up discomfort in us. Just as allowing our children to show their anger when this is something we didn't experience ourselves can encourage us to change our own relationship with anger, allowing our children to express all of their views and questions to us can alter the very meaning that we make of the world. And sometimes this will feel deeply uncomfortable, and we may wish to do some learning and unlearning on our own so that we are able to welcome their difference. And sometimes, if we're lucky, it will allow us to experience some of that Spark of Childhood that we might have lost ourselves many years ago.

And one last time . . . let's just check in before we move on.

1. How are you feeling? How is your heart rate, your energy levels, how do you feel in your body? And how are your emotions? Are you feeling anxious, sad, excited, curious, something else?

2. What has reading Part IV raised for you? (In terms of information, ideas, memories, feelings?)

3. What one thing would you like to remember from these chapters?

4. What five things would you like to remember from this book?

The End

As we arrive at our ending, let's go to your resting place together and sit ourselves down.

- Where are you? What's going on around you? Is there anyone there with you?
- How does it feel being here, in this place?
- What are you sitting on? What does that feel like in your body? Settle a little deeper into the surface beneath you. What are your feet on? Just focus on them for a moment.
- What's the temperature like? What does it feel like against your skin?
- What can you hear? Tune in to those sounds.
- Can you smell anything? Anything else?
- And if you reach around, what can you touch? How does that feel? Anything else nearby you'd like to touch?
- Do you have a taste in your mouth?

Have a good look around you, really notice what you see. Turn up all the colours in this image so that it becomes even more vivid and vibrant.

How does it feel in your body to be here? Where do you feel that, in your body? Really tune in to that feeling and let it expand in your body.

We've been on quite a journey together, and as we say good-bye you're taking a lot with you as you continue this journey on your own. Perhaps you'll come back and walk some of these pathways again, when some time has passed and your curiosity brings you back to see if you can explore a little further. But, for now, thank you for coming on this adventure with me.

As we come to the end of the book, I wonder where you're left after all of this. It's been a lot to take in, I know, so I wonder if we can bring your guide in here with you. What might you need to hear from them, as you allow these ideas to settle?

I just want to highlight one final fable, which might have been forming as you've been reading this book. You've read a lot, and we've covered a lot of ground together. But there might be a story there still about quick fixes. Or straightforward answers. Or paths that just go forward and not all over the place.

As you put into practice some of the things you've been reading about, you might find that nothing really changes at first. Or, even, you might find that things feel harder.

Some time ago, when we were on our own map and talking about our own families of origin, I told you about the equilibrium in families. And that applies in your family too. Even when you have been desperately wanting things to change, or family members haven't been getting on and you're keen for things to feel different – everyone in the family is really familiar with how things have been. It takes time (sometimes a long time) for change to happen, both for us and within our relationships. If, for a long time, you've responded to a child's angry outbursts with, 'Right, that's it! Go to your room!' and suddenly you meet this with a long deep breath, an open face and curiosity, that is going to be *really* confusing for your child! Our child has learned one dance, and we're showing them new steps. So initially, they will try to pull us back into our familiar dance – because they know those steps. So they might shout back at us, as they usually would, or go to their room and slam the door anyway. And then we might feel a bit bleak, like it isn't working and we don't know where to go next. If your partner and you have been struggling over your dance steps, pulling your children between you, as you learn to dance in sync your children might not understand where they fit in any more (and, if they have been choosing a side of the Couple Canyon to stand on, might even feel reluctant to cross over the bridge to their other parent). It might feel like no one knows any steps for a while, as we figure out a new dance together.

This is why it can help to have tools up your sleeve instead of specific strategies. Because if our goal is to try to empathise with our child's feelings, collaborate with them, hear more about their experience, then we're more likely to be able to withstand that shout, or go and knock on the door, or wait until our child is ready to talk. And the more we do this, just as when we disentangled ourselves from our cast of characters, the easier it gets to keep moving towards our destination and not get caught up in storms. In doing so, this breaks through that pull back to the familiar family balance, and allows the family to begin writing new stories.

Change is hard. And parenting is hard. So this brings us back to considering what we might need to be able to create something different in our homes. But, as we've established, parenting isn't just a relationship between a parent and a child. Parenting might mean having many other people to support you, and your child, especially in times when you need more buffering. We can put so much pressure on ourselves to offer everything, but our children will form attachments to many others – some inside their home and many outside it. And some of those people will influence them just as much as we do. Other adults offering safe, supportive and nurturing relationships to our children can also buffer them against the times that we're not able to be the parents that we want to be.

Our children have the potential to create the most

colourful, wide-ranging maps that we could ever imagine. Our role is pretty simple: to allow them to create their own maps, and show interest in their journeys; to watch them explore, and occasionally help them up if they stumble; to talk to them about what they're uncovering, and tell them about our own maps; to protect that Spark of Childhood if we can.

In doing this, we might have the privilege of becoming a guide that they will carry inside them as they leave our homes.

And then they'll never have to read this book.

~~And they all lived happily ever after~~
And they all somehow muddled on together.

Further Reading

References

These are some of the key citations. For a comprehensive list of works and theories influencing this book please see the 'Further Reading' list at www.dremmasvanberg.com.

Chapter 1

'Children simply *don't* make us happy' (p 26)

Deaton, A., & Stone, A. A. (2014). Evaluative and hedonic wellbeing among those with and without children at home. *Proceedings of the National Academy of Sciences*, *111*(4), 1328–1333. https://doi.org/10.1073/pnas.1311600111

'In a country like Greece . . .' (p 27)

Smith, Helena, 'It's National Preservation: Greece Offers Baby Bonus to Boost Birthrate.' *Guardian* (4 Feb 2020).

'yet 3 in 10 children in the UK are growing up in poverty' (p 28)

https://www.actionforchildren.org.uk/support-us/campaign-with-us/child-poverty/
https://cpag.org.uk

'alongside 1 in 6 children globally who live in extreme poverty' (p 28)

https://www.unicef.org.uk/press-releases/1-in-6-children-lives-in-extreme-poverty-world-bank-unicef-analysis-shows

'The minimum cost in the UK to raise a child . . . highest it has been since records began in 2012' (p 29)

Hirsch, D. & Lee, T., 'The Cost of a Child in 2021.' Child Poverty Action Group (Dec 2021).

'our childcare system is the most expensive in the world' (p 29)

https://data.oecd.org/benwage/net-childcare-costs.htm

'UK fathers worked some of the longest hours in Europe' (p 29)

Modern Fatherhood, 'Parental Working In Europe: Working Hours.' (2016).

'And in the USA, where there are "childcare deserts" ... leaving work' (p 29)

> Childcaredeserts.org
> American Progress, Childcare Deserts series.

'A devastating statistic from a 2022 survey by Pregnant Then Screwed ...
chose to have an abortion' (p 30)

> Pregnant Then Screwed. Press release: '6 in 10 Women Who Have Had
> an Abortion Claim Childcare Costs Influenced Their Decision' (2022).

'10 per cent of Brits and 17 per cent of Americans who state they don't have
children or plan to have them in the future place cost as one of the reasons'
(p 30)

> Brown, Anna, 'Growing Share of Childless Adults in U.S. Don't Expect
> to Ever Have Children.' Pew Research Center (19 Nov 2021)
> Ibbetson, Connor, 'Why Do People Choose Not to Have Children?'
> YouGov, UK (9 Jan 2020).

'Unless you are part of the Aka tribe of Central Africa ...' (p 31)

> Hewlett, Barry, *Intimate Fathers: The Nature and Context of Aka Pygmy
> Paternal Infant Care* (Ann Arbor: University of Michigan Press, 1991).

'Or you live in Finland' (p 31)

> European Commission, Finland – Maternity and Paternity.

'inequitable and failed policy' (p 31)

> Quote attributed to Adrienne Burgess, Fatherhood Institute in: Topping,
> A., 'Want Gender Equality? Then Fight for Fathers' Rights to Shared
> Parental Leave', *Guardian*, 11 Feb 2020).

'50 per cent of new mothers who experience hypervigilance in the weeks
after birth (rising to 75 per cent in new mothers who have birth-related
PTSD)' (p 32)

> Ayers, Susan, Wright, Daniel & Ford, Elizabeth, 'Hyperarousal
> Symptoms after Traumatic and Nontraumatic Births.' *Journal of
> Reproductive and Infant Psychology, 33* (2015): 1–12.

'10 per cent of new fathers who experience post-natal depression' (p 32)

> Misri, S.K., *Paternal Postnatal Psychiatric Illnesses: A Clinical Case
> Book* (Springer International Publishing, 2018).

Chapter 2

'National Childbirth Trust (the UK's largest parent's charity) even has an
article helping you choose your camp.' (p 36)

> NCT, 'The Most Popular Parenting Styles and How to Identify Yours.'

Chapter 3

The concept of a map (p 45), used throughout the book, draws from John Bowlby's theory of attachment relationships as internal working models, Byng-Hall's concept of family scripts, Larry Ludlow's 'family map', Bronfenbrenner's systems theory and the 'paracosms' of children's imaginary worlds.

The downward arrow technique (p 48) is from cognitive behavioural therapy:

> Beck, J.S., *Cognitive Behavioural Therapy, Basics and Beyond* (New York: Guilford Press 2020).

The concept of a guide (p 49) is drawn from Deborah Lee's concept of the perfect nurturer:

> Lee, D. A., 'The Perfect Nurturer: A Model to Develop a Compassionate Mind Within the Context of Cognitive Therapy.' In: P. Gilbert (ed.), *Compassion: Conceptualizations, Research, and Use in Psychotherapy* (London: Brunner-Routledge, 2005), pp. 326–51.

The concept of a resting place (p 53) is used in different models, including eye movement desensitisation reprogramming, trauma-focused cognitive behavioural therapy and hypnobirthing – as well as having been used in meditation for many years before any of those models were conceptualised, perhaps as early as the thirteenth century.

I learned about quick grounding techniques ('The Quick Version', p 55) from Babette Rothschild:

> e.g. Rothschild, B., *The Body Remembers Casebook: Unifying Methods and Models in the Treatment of Trauma and PTSD* (New York: W.W. Norton, 2003).

Chapter 4

The Swamp of Ghosts (p 59) draws from Selma Fraiberg's work:

> Fraiberg, S., Adelson, E. & Shapiro, V., 'Ghosts in the Nursery: A Psychoanalytic Approach to the Problems of Impaired Infant–Mother Relationships.' *Journal of the American Academy of Child Psychiatry*, *14*(3) (1975): 387–421.

'Our bodies have a form of knowledge that is different from our cognitive brains . . . what is safe and what is dangerous' (p 62)

> Menakem, Resmaa, *My Grandmother's Hands* (London: Penguin Random House, 2017), p. 5.

Carrying our angels (p 64):

> Lieberman, A.F., Padrón, E., Van Horn, P. & Harris, W.W., 'Angels in the Nursery: The Intergenerational Transmission of Benevolent Parental

Influences.' *Infant Mental Health Journal: Official Publication of The World Association for Infant Mental Health*, 26(6) (2005): 504–20.

Chapter 5

For a summary of how memory works and the association of memory and emotion (p 68):

> Barrett, L.F., *Seven and a Half Lessons about the Brain* (London: Picador, 2020.)

On brain reorganisation in parenthood (p 70):

> Conaboy, C. 'Mother Brain: How Neuroscience is Rewriting the Story of Parenthood' (New York: Henry Holt and Co., 2022)

The ~~Three~~ Five Bears of Parenting (p 74):

> Baumrind, D., 'Child Care Practices Anteceding Three Patterns of Preschool Behavior.' *Genetic Psychology Monographs*, 75(1) (1967), 43–88
>
> Maccoby, E.E. & Martin, J.A., 'Socialization in the Context of the Family: Parent–Child Interaction'. In: P. Mussen and E.M. Hetherington (eds.), *Handbook of Child Psychology, Vol IV: Socialization, Personality, and Social Development* (New York: Wiley, 1983).

Chapter 6

The idea of the nursery (p 79) draws from nearly 70 years of attachment research, including the growing field of infant mental health, which is where I began my interest in perinatal mental health.

'with more than two-thirds of children reporting their experience of at least one traumatic event before they reach age 16 . . .' (p 81)

> SAHMSA (2022) Understanding Child Trauma web page: https://www.samhsa.gov/child-trauma/understanding-child-trauma

'Emotional abuse is a common experience too – with over a third of people self-reporting this, as well as around 18 per cent of people experiencing emotional neglect' (p 81)

> Stoltenborgh, M., Bakermans-Kranenburg, M.J., Alink, L.R.A., Van Ijzendoorn, M.H., 'The Prevalence of Child Maltreatment Across the Globe: Review of a Series of Meta-Analyses.' *Child Abuse Review*, 24(1) (2015): 37–50.

The concept of the baby self (p 83) comes from Joan Raphael-Leff's concept of 'contagious arousal'.

> Raphael-Leff, J., 'Healthy Maternal Ambivalence.' *Psycho-Analytic Psychotherapy in South Africa*, 18(2) (2010): 57–73.

The understanding of the baby's experience (p 83) comes from the work of Donald Winnicott., e.g.

Ogden, T.H., 'Fear of Breakdown and the Unlived Life.' *The International Journal of Psychoanalysis*, 95(2) (2014): 205–23.

'Psychoanalyst Joan Raphael-Leff calls these our "wild things" – 'the "formless" things without names, the untamed, unprocessed, passionate, chaotic things that seethe deep below the civilized surface and erupt at times of greater permeability' (p 84)

Raphael-Leff, J., 'Where the Wild Things Are'. In *Parent–Infant Psychodynamics* (1st Edition (London: Whurr Publishers, 2003): pp. 54–69.

'Donald Winnicott went so far as to say, "there is no such thing as a baby"' (p 86)

Winnicott, D.W., *The Child, The Family & The Outside World* (London: Penguin Books, 1967).

'many different influences . . . research looks at attachment "networks", not just that parent–child couple' (p 86)

e.g. Dagan, O., & Sagi-Schwartz, A. 'Early attachment networks to multiple caregivers: History, assessment models, and future research recommendations'. *New Directions for Child and Adolescent Development*, 2021, 9– 19.

'The father of attachment theory, John Bowlby, called this our "internal working model" of relationships – this is our blueprint' (p 88)

Bowlby, J., *The Making and Breaking of Affectional Bonds* (London: Tavistock/Routledge, 1979).

The Four Dances (pp 89–92):

Ainsworth, M.D., 'Patterns of Attachment Behavior Shown by the Infant in Interaction with His Mother.' *Merrill-Palmer Quarterly of Behavior and Development*, 10(1) (1964): 51–8.

Crittenden, P.M., 'A Dynamic-Maturational Model of Attachment.' *Australian and New Zealand Journal of Family Therapy*, 27(2) (2006): 105–115.

Main, M., & Solomon, J. (1986). 'Discovery of an insecure-disorganized/ disoriented attachment pattern: Procedures, findings and implications for the classification of behavior'. In T. B. Brazelton, & M. Yogman (Eds.), *Affective development in infancy* (pp. 95–124). Norwood, NJ: Ablex.

'One study found that, of children who had been raised in institutions where they suffered from "structural neglect", 17 per cent still managed to have a secure attachment relationship with their favoured caregiver' (p 94)

van Ijzendoorn, M.H. et al. 'Children in Institutional Care: Delayed Development and Resilience.' *Monographs of the Society for Research in Child Development*, 76(4) (2011): 8–30.

'Having even one warm and supportive adult in our lives can help us learn to waltz against all the odds' (p 95)

Afifi, T.O., MacMillan, H.L., 'Resilience Following Child Maltreatment: A Review of Protective Factors.' *The Canadian Journal of Psychiatry,* 56(5) (2011): 266–72.

Chapter 7

The idea of a cast of characters draws from many models. For a full list of influences within this Chapter, please see the Further Reading list at www. dremmasvanberg.com.

Chapter 8

For further information on the couple relationship and couples becoming parents please see the Further Reading list at www.dremmasvanberg.com.

The idea of family dances (pp 134–6) comes from both attachment research and family systems theory:

Hill, J., Fonagy, P., Safier, E. and Sargent, J., 'The Ecology of Attachment in the Family.' *Family Process,* 42 (2003): 205–221.
Richardson, H.B., 'Classic Reprints: The Family Equilibrium.' *Family Systems Medicine,* 1(1) (1983): 62–74.

Chapter 9

'Psychoanalyst Wilfred Bion described this most accurately in his concept of containment' (p 154)

Parry, R., *A Critical Examination of Bion's Concept of Containment and Winnicott's Concept of Holding, and Their Psychotherapeutic Implications.* Doctoral Dissertation, University of the Witwatersrand (2010).

'. . . 40 days to restore maternal well-being and health after pregnancy and birth), in our modern world many parents find that these rituals simply add pressure in the absence of wider family support' (p 155)

Dennis, C-L, Fung, K., Grigoriadis, S., Robinson, G.E., Romans, S., Ross, L., 'Traditional Postpartum Practices and Rituals: A Qualitative Systematic Review.' *Women's Health,* 3(4) (2007):487–502. doi:10.2217/17455057.3.4.487

'one cross-cultural study across 11 countries found that the role of the mother-in-law was often cited as a source of unhappiness for new parents . . .' (p 155)

Oates, M.R., Cox, J.L., Neema, S., Asten, P., Glangeaud-Freudenthal, N., Figueiredo, B. & Yoshida, K., 'Postnatal Depression across Countries and Cultures: A Qualitative Study.' *The British Journal of Psychiatry, 184*(S46) (2004): s10–s16.

'If we have become estranged – which is more common than we often realise, affecting around 1 in 5 families in the UK' (p 156)

StandAlone, *The Prevalence of Family Estrangement* (2013).

'and 1 in 4 in the USA' (p 156)

Pillemer, K, *Fault Lines: Fractured Families and How to Mend Them.* (London: Hachette UK, 2021)

'with around 40 per cent of grandparents in the UK and Europe' (p 157)

Age UK, *5 Million Grandparents Take On Childcare Responsibilities* (2017)

'There are similar cultural differences too . . . their adult children' (p 158)

Silverstein, M., Gans, D., Lowenstein, A., Giarrusso, R. & Bengtson, V.L., 'Older Parent–Child Relationships in Six Developed Nations: Comparisons at the Intersection of Affection and Conflict.' *Journal of Marriage and the Family, 72*(4) (2010): 1006–1021.

'. . . our own experience of being a sibling . . . their position in the family' (p 160)

Blair, L., *Birth Order: What Your Position in the Family Really Tells You about Your Character* (London: Hachette UK, 2011).

The concept of family equilibrium (p 162) draws from family systems theory and ideas of homeostasis and coherence, which is discussed in more depth here:

Dell, P. F., 'Beyond Homeostasis: Toward a Concept of Coherence.' *Family Process, 21*(1) (1982): 21–41.

John Byng-Hall's concept of replicative and reparative family scripts is also relevant here:

Byng-Hall, John 'The Family Script: A Useful Bridge between Theory and Practice.' *Journal of Family Therapy, 7* (1985): 301–5.

Chapter 10

There is a growing body of literature from both popular culture and psychological research into the impact of intensive parenting culture (p 170), including how excluding these parenting norms can be. Please see Further Reading list for more information.

'So, if you follow a clear bedtime routine . . . your own history of sleep' (p 172)

Fadzil, A., 'Factors Affecting the Quality of Sleep in Children.' *Children (Basel, Switzerland), 8*(2) (2021): 122.

'If you had a C-section . . . none of which are conclusive' (p 172)

Darabi, B., Rahmati, S., HafeziAhmadi, M.R. et al., 'The Association between Caesarean Section and Childhood Asthma: An Updated Systematic Review and Meta-Analysis. *Allergy Asthma Clin Immunol,15* (2019): 62.

'If you had post-natal depression . . . extraordinary challenge)' (p 172)

Murray, L., 'The Impact of Postnatal Depression on Infant Development.' *Journal of Child Psychology and Psychiatry, 33* (1992): 543–61.

Netsi, E., Pearson, R.M., Murray, L., Cooper, P., Craske, M.G. & Stein, A. 'Association of Persistent and Severe Postnatal Depression with Child Outcomes.' *JAMA Psychiatry, 75*(3) (2018): 247–253.

'And there are other factors too . . . considered too' (p 172)

Coast, E., Leone, T., Hirose, A. & Jones, E., 'Poverty and Postnatal Depression: A Systematic Mapping of the Evidence from Low and Lower Middle Income Countries.' *Health & Place, 18*(5) (2012): 1188–97.

'And your teenager . . . stay in a difficult relationship' (pp 172–3)

Cartwright, C., 'You Want to Know How It Affected Me?' *Journal of Divorce & Remarriage, 44*:3–4 (2006): 125–43.

'One example of this is the "good enough parent" – a phrase coined by psychoanalyst Donald Winnicott in 1953 when he spoke about the "ordinary devoted mother"' (p 178)

Winnicott, D. W. (1953). 'Transitional Objects and Transitional Phenomena—A Study of the First Not-Me Possession'. *International Journal of Psycho-Analysis*, 34, 89–97.

Chapter 11

The parenting tools outlined in the chapter are those which I share most frequently in my therapeutic work, and come from both family and child development literature, as well as my clinical experience. I've chosen some key resources for you in case you would like to read more about any of them, which you can find on the Further Reading list at www.dremmasvanberg.com.

'In 2010, the then Children's Commissioner Sir Al Aynsley-Green talked about the UK being hostile to children' (p 194)

Wardrop, M., 'Britain Is One of World's Most Unfriendly Countries Towards Children.' *Telegraph* (2 Feb 2010)

'the UN Special Rapporteur . . . harsh and uncaring ethos' (p 196)

United Nations General Assembly, Human Rights Council, 41st Session, 24 June–12 July 2019, *Visit to the United Kingdom of Great Britain and Northern Ireland Report of the Special Rapporteur on Extreme Poverty and Human Rights.*

'In the UK, 27 per cent of children were living in poverty in 2020–21 . . . racially minoritised groups' (p 196)

Child Poverty Action Group, *Child Poverty Facts and Figures*

'what psychotherapist Philippa Perry calls "fact tennis"' (p 198)

Perry, P., *The Book You Wish Your Parents Had Read And Your Children Will Be Glad That You Did)* (London: Penguin Books 2019).

'For the first six or so months of their lives, infants don't realise that they are an "I" . . . (p 204)

Winnicott, D.W., 'The Theory of the Parent–Infant Relationship.' *Essential Papers on Object Relations* (1986): 233–53.

'Throughout history, even as long as 50,000 years ago . . . close to a caregiver' (p 204)

Little, E.E., Legare, C.H. & Carver, L J., 'Culture, Carrying, and Communication: Beliefs and Behavior Associated with Babywearing.' *Infant Behavior and Development*, 57 (2019): 101320.

'This varies culturally, too, and some children are raised to continue to consider the common needs of their communities over individualism' (p 204)

Behrens, K.Y., 'Reconsidering Attachment in Context of Culture: Review of Attachment Studies in Japan.' *Online Readings in Psychology and Culture*, 6(1) (2016).

Chapter 12

The Monkey Mind (p 211) draws from different writers on neuroscience and emotional regulation, including:

Peters, S., *My Hidden Chimp* (London: Studio Press, 2018).
Siegel, D.J. & Bryson, T.P., *The Whole-Brain Child: 12 Revolutionary Strategies to Nurture Your Child's Developing Mind.* (London: Robinson, 2011).

'Some people struggle with executive functioning . . . all of which can manifest in diverse ways)' (pp 211–12)

Rodden, J., 'What Is Executive Dysfunction? Sign and Symptoms of EFD.' (Updated 11 July 2022) *ADDitude.*

On different factors in child development please see the Further Reading list at www.dremmasvanberg.com.

'using a sing-song voice (known as "motherese" or "parentese")' (p 221)

Fuller-Wright, L., *Uncovering the Sound of 'Motherese,' Baby Talk across Languages*. Princeton University News (19 October 2017)

'psychoanalyst Esther Bick called "second skin defences"' (p 222)

Bick, E., 'The Experience of the Skin in Early Object-Relations.' *International Journal of Psychoanalysis* 49 (1968): 484–6.

'One beautiful study of babies, using brain imaging during parent-and-baby play . . . their adult would do next' (p 222)

Piazza, E.A., Hasenfratz, L., Hasson, U. & Lew-Williams, C., 'Infant and Adult Brains Are Coupled to the Dynamics of Natural Communication.' *Psychological Science*, 31(1) (2020): 6–17.

'"The person is not the problem, the problem is the problem"' (p 224)

This comes from Michael White's narrative therapy work (see https://dulwichcentre.com.au/michael-white-archive)

Chapter 13

Please see the Further Reading list at www.dremmasvanberg.com for a full exploration of the theories and evidence behind these ideas of emotional intelligence, regulation and co-regulation, gender and individual differences in emotional expression and interpretation and different models of emotion.

'Recognition of emotions such as happiness, sadness, anger, disgust, fear and surprise is fairly universal' (p 228)

Barrett, L.F., *How Emotions Are Made: The Secret Life of the Brain* (London: Pan Macmillan, 2017).

'studies comparing expressions of anger in the United States and Japan suggest that anger is an acceptable emotion in the USA . . . anger is seen as a sign of maturity' (p 229)

Boiger, M., Mesquita, B., Uchida, Y. & Feldman Barrett, L., 'Condoned or Condemned: The Situational Affordance of Anger and Shame in the United States and Japan.' *Personality and Social Psychology Bulletin*, 39(4) (2013): 540–55.

'In Buddhism this is depicted in the parable of the second arrow' (p 234)

You can hear more about this in this talk by Jonathan Foust (2018) https://www.youtube.com/watch?v=KAv619nQcbM

'Brené Brown: "In order to connect with you, I have to connect with something in myself that knows that feeling"' (p 235)

This is from her talk on empathy, recorded on RSA Shorts: https://www.youtube.com/watch?v=1Evwgu369Jw

Smartphone use and children (p 238):

Konrad, C., Hillmann, M., Rispler, J., Niehaus, L., Neuhoff, L. & Barr, R., 'Quality of Mother–Child Interaction Before, During, and after Smartphone Use.' *Frontiers in Psychology*, 12 (2021): 616656.

Radesky, J.S., Kistin, C.J., Zuckerman, B., Nitzberg, K., Gross, J., Kaplan-Sanoff, M., Augustyn, M. & Silverstein, M., 'Patterns of Mobile Device Use by Caregivers and Children during Meals in Fast Food Restaurants.' *Pediatrics*, 133(4) (2014): e843–e849.

Tidemann, I.T. & Melinder, A.M., 'Infant Behavioural Effects of Smartphone Interrupted Parent–Infant Interaction.' *British Journal of Developmental Psychology*, 40 (3) (2022).

On Emotional Storytelling and telling stories about emotions (pp 239–41):

Siegel, D.J. & Bryson, T.P., *The Whole-Brain Child: 12 Revolutionary Strategies to Nurture Your Child's Developing Mind.* (London: Robinson, 2011).

White, M.K. & Morgan, A., *Narrative Therapy with Children and Their Families* (Adelaide: Dulwich Centre Publications, 2006).

'But tantrums often come like storms and pass through quicker than we imagine . . .' (p 243)

This is based on Michael Potegal's research, summarised here:

Klass, P., 'Managing the Storm of a Toddler's Tantrum.' *The New York Times* (30 Oct 2017). https://www.nytimes.com/2017/10/30/well/family/managing-the-storm-of-a-toddlers-tantrum.html

Chapter 14

The concept of family stories is from John Byng-Hall's work on family scripts (see previous citations). Please see Further Reading list at www.dremmasvanberg.com for more background on the theories and strategies in this chapter.

Chapter 15

'with 20 per cent of those aged five to nine having already taken part in a protest' (p 262)

Beano Brain, *The New Rebellion: Generation Alpha, Changing the World by Stealth* (2021)

'Wanda Sykes puts it: "Here's the thing, kids get it . . . if you don't get it, if you get hung up on shit like this . . . you just sound fucking old, that's all. These kids are on 5G and you are on AOL dial-up"' (p 263)

Quote from: *Stand Out: An LGBTQ+ Celebration*, Netflix.

Influences

I have drawn on the work of many brilliant people in the writing of this book – to whom I am infinitely grateful in helping me (and us all) understand the complexity of human existence, behaviour and relationships.

I'm thankful for the guidance of those who supported my learning and influenced my thinking in my formative years as a psychologist. My dad P.O. Svanberg, who taught me to wonder at babies, my mum Rani Svanberg, who spoke the language of social justice and my sister Jenny Svanberg, who introduced me to chaos (theory).

As well as Avshalom Caspi, Patricia Crittenden, Alessandra Lemma, Temi Moffitt and Susan Pawlby. To Tamara Gelman, Jane Gibbons and Harriet Higgins, who taught me that you can do therapy while crawling on the floor and Isabelle Ekdawi, who taught me the importance of stories. And the two mother-psychologists in my life who helped me find my voice and encouraged me to use it – Julianne Boutaleb and Michele Roitt.

This book has been influenced by many psychological models and theories. This is a non-exhaustive list, but including: attachment theory (particularly that of attachment networks and cross-cultural attachment models) and wider psychodynamic theories and approaches (especially the work of Mary Ainsworth, Jay Belsky, Wilfred Bion, John Bowlby, Patricia Crittenden, Peter Fonagy, Selma Fraiberg, Melanie Klein, Joan Raphael-Leff, Alessandra Lemma, Elizabeth Meins, Susie Orbach, Abraham Sagi-Schwartz and Donald Winnicott), systemic and narrative approaches (in particular Rudi Dallos, John

Byng-Hall and Michael White) and compassion-focused approaches to trauma (especially the work of Emily Holmes and Deborah Lee). I am grateful to those who have educated me on infant and child mental health, and family dynamics (particular thanks to the Association for Infant Mental Health, the Anna Freud Centre, the Parent–Infant Foundation and authors and therapists such as Susan Golombok, Alison Gopnik, Robin Grille, Amanda Jones, Becky Kennedy, Janet Lansbury, Philippa Perry and Daniel Siegel). It also draws on the work of trauma therapists such as Yael Danieli, Janina Fisher, Judith Herman, Bruce Perry, Babette Rothschild and Pete Walker. And the work of countless authors who have written on feminism, parenting, gender roles and race, including Pragya Agarwal, Brené Brown, Simone de Beauvoir, Kimberlé Crenshaw, Betty Friedan, Charlotte Perkins Gilman, Jessica Grose, Suman Fernando, Patricia Hamilton, Sarah Blaffer Hrdy, bell hooks, Audre Lorde, Paula Nicolson, Liz Plank and Virginia Woolf. I am also grateful to those in and outside of the psychology and therapy world – such as Sanah Ahsan, Richard Bentall, Joeli Brearley, Anya Hayes, Mars Lord, Craig Newnes, Nova Reid, Lama Rod, David Smail and AJ Silver – for widening my gaze and continuing to educate me.

Acknowledgements

There are so many other people who I have to say thank you to:

Eitan. Thanks for holding up the bridge and troll-hunting with me.

A & Z, all the very best stories start and end with you.

Mum & Dad, my wonderfully good-enough caregivers.

Jenny, my fellow adventurer.

Cass Fairweather, my guide.

Leona, my resting place. Loves it.

The Jankels for opening whole new lands on my map.

Lance for raising questions.

All those who heard my ideas, read my early drafts, helped me turn them into a book, told me to keep writing it and gave me space to do so: Julia Silk, Anya Hayes, Lucy Parkin, Avital Tomes, Rachel Fraser, Sophie Mort, Beccy Hands, Penny Wincer and Rebecca Schiller.

All the brilliant women in my life who work alongside me at the Collective and Make Birth Better. You are a true source of inspiration. Thanks to Laura for being a constant container and Nikki for accepting flights of fancy.

Enormous thanks to Sam Jackson, Julia Kellaway and the team at Ebury for their holding of raw emotional expression so that I could find my own solutions with gentle guidance.

Thanks to all my non-blood-related aunties and uncles and brothers and sisters who are meandering on my map, all over the world (from Spanners).

Thank you to all of those who have supported me in my own parenting.

Most of all, thanks to all of my clients over the years, big and small, and those who have shared their lives with me on the Village and elsewhere. Thank you for letting me walk some of your journey with you and showing me a multitude of maps.

Index

Note: page numbers in **bold** refer to diagrams.

abandonment issues 4, 85,
102, 219–20
abortion 30
abuse 126–7
see also childhood
abuse
acceptance 235–9
achievement orientation
21
active listening 198–200
activity levels 215
adulthood
ideals of 100–1
stories from 99–119
Africa, Central 31
aggression 102, 109–11,
198, 217, 231,
236, 238,
250–1
Aka tribe 31
amygdala 212
ancestors, experiences of
62, 63–4
Angelou, Maya 79
angels 64–6, 69, 210, 214
anger 109–11, 229, 230,
265
anxiety 107, 171, 177–8,
234
arguments, 'fact tennis'
198
assumptions 2, 133–4
asthma 171, 172
attachment (dances)
87–95, 134–7, 190,
203, 205, 252–3,
268–9
anxious attachment
(Argentine tango)

91, 93–4, 135–6,
190
avoidant attachment
(Irish dance) 90–1,
93, 108, 135–6,
190, 203, 219
disorganised
attachment 92
networks of 86, 87
secure attachment
(waltz) 88, 89–90,
93–5, 134–5, 253
attention, children's
bids for 200,
238–9
attunement 39
Aynsley-Green, Sir Al 195

babies, and relationship-
building 221–2
Baby Boomers 170
baby self 83–5, 158–9,
168–9
babyhood, stories from
79–98
Barrie, J.M. 252
Baumrind, Diana 74, 76
Bick, Esther 222
Bion, Wilfred 154
blame 55–7, 81, 84, 145,
230–1
Boundaries (parenting
tool) 201–6, 213,
250–1, 255–6
brain
development 171,
211–13, 222
HPA axis 63
plasticity 171

reorganisation during
pregnancy and the
postnatal period 70
and sleep deprivation
236
and threat perception
212–13
and transgenerational
trauma 63
brainwaves 194
bridges
between partners
127–35, 138, 140,
142–3, 145–8, 152
family 255–8, 263–4
Brown, Brené 235
Buddhism 234
buffering technique 250–1
burnout 142, 203

C-sections 171, 172
care, tuned-in 84
Carroll, Lewis 17
change 173
and communication
150
dislike of 35
and family
equilibriums 162–4
change – *cont.*
fear of 148–9
incremental nature 149
organic process of
117–19
resistance to 148–9
slow and steady
148–51
see also transition
characters, cast of
104–18, 220

children's 222
the Critic 104–5, 114,
    117, 190–1, 208,
    220, 224, 234,
    240, 257
the Floater 112–13,
    115, 191, 212,
    236–7
the Fretter 106–7, 114,
    191, 208, 212, 236
the Lover 105–6,
    114–15, 191, 203,
    220, 237, 241
the Ogre 109–11, 115,
    149–50, 203, 212,
    220, 224, 236, 240
the Stoic 107–8, 191,
    203
the Warrior 108–9,
    114–15, 240–1
the Wounded Soul
    111–12, 116, 212,
    220, 224, 237
child development 171–2,
    211–13, 218–20,
    222
child–parent relationship
    76, 158
    barriers to 237–8
    ruptures in the 189–93
childcare 29–30, 141
'childfree by choice' 27
childhood
    stories from parental
        67–78
    see also babyhood
childhood abuse 81–2
    emotional 81, 92, 110,
        231
    physical 92, 110, 231
    sexual 231
childhood amnesia 68–9
childhood trauma 80–3,
    112, 179
Childism Institute, The
    196
children 138–9
    and attachment 135–6
    attentional bids 200,
        238–9
    barriers between
        parents and 237–8
    chaotic nature 181–2

and 'collapse' 198
connecting with 47,
    181
containment 154
costs of raising 26,
    29–30
difficulties connecting
    with 181
effects of parents on
    60, 87, 102,
    115–16, 134,
    218–20
as emotional
    barometers 221–4,
    241–2, 248–9
and feelings/emotions
    196–7, 221–4,
    235–8,
    241–51
idealised 196
identity 81, 204
inexperience 204–5
influences on 123–4,
    134
intensity 227
as mapmakers 259–66
modelling for 147
needs 200
neurodivergent
    ⁃ 216–17
and parental bridges
    131–2
and the parenting
    myth 21–7, 21
parents' ideas about 2
personhood 265
pressure to raise
    perfect 170–5
and relationships
    220–2
rewards of raising 26
self-sufficiency 204
societal hostility
    towards 195–6,
    244
story of 185–266
temperament 215–16
and The Warrior
    108–9
as they really are 3–4
uniqueness 216–17
and your internalised
    parent 87

see also babies
children's maps 197, 206,
    209, 210–25, 270
    tools for 189, 193
children's services 196
child's homes 213–14,
    224–5, 226
    family room 252–3
clinical psychology 6–7,
    58–9
coercive control 127
cognitive behavioural
    therapy (CBT),
    trauma-focused 53
Collaboration (parenting
    tool) 197–201, 213,
    217, 222, 249, 255
collapse 111, 154, 198,
    212, 237
collectivism 91
communication 150
compassion 213
conflict
    between partners
        127–9, 136, 138–9,
        144–8
    and the child–parent
        relationship
        189–93
    comfort with 190–1
    fear of 190–1, 203
    and parenting styles 75
    and the Repair tool
        190–3
connection 10, 47, 176,
    258
    and avoidant
        attachment 90
    difficulties 181
    emotional 243–4, 247,
        250
    need for 154, 242, 247
    and paying attention
        200
    with the self 47, 83
    see also disconnection
consumerism 29
containment 154, 248–9
control issues 77, 107,
    127, 181–2, 195,
    198
Convention on the Rights
    of the Child 196

Cosby Show, The (TV show) 19
costs
of child-raising 29–30
of living 29
Couple Canyon 127–8, 132, 134–5, 139, 141–2, 144, 146, 152, 269
couple therapy 137
Covid-19 pandemic 166, 196, 262
Critic, the (character) 104–5, 114, 117, 190–1, 208, 220, 224, 234, 240, 257
cross-cultural studies 155
culture 30, 34, 35, 77
and feelings 228–9
and grandparenting 158
and parental support 155
cummings, ee 67
cycle breakers 178–9

Darwinian theory 31
daydreaming 112–13, 194
dead ends 170–82
defences, 'second skin' 222
depression, postnatal 32, 172
development 171–2, 218–20
brain 171, 211–13, 222
psychological 86
disconnection 125, 189–90, 192
dissociation 112
divorce 172–3
dopamine 213

economic issues 28–30
emotional intelligence 228, 231
emotions *see* feelings/ emotions
Empathy (parenting tool) 193–7, 213, 220, 222, 235, 257
envy, of our children 70

executive functioning 211–12
exhaustion 96, 133, 170, 203, 206, 244
expectations
and feelings 242, 244, 246, 247
placed upon parents 143–4
see also parental expectations
Eye Movement Desensitisation Reprogramming 53

'fact tennis' 198
failure 2
families
blended 28, 124, 148
bridge-building 255–8, 263–4
equilibrium 162–4
estranged 156, 157
extended 154–7
non-traditional structures 140
as teams 197–8
values 147
see also grandparents; lone parenting; parents; partners
family meetings 255–8
family stories 252–8
family therapy 162–3, 224
fantasies 3, 17, 18–20
fathers 11–12
and the financial burden of parenting 29
and gender roles 141–4
and heteronormativity 31–2
'fawn' response 237, 246
fears 46–7, 102–3
feelings/emotions
acceptance 235–9
children and 73, 196–7, 221–4, 235–8, 241–51
containment 154, 248–9
development 213

of early childhood 73
and emotional abuse 126–7
and emotional intelligence 228, 231
and emotional neglect 81
and emotional storytelling 239–41
and emotional support 155
expression 229, 230–2, 242–4, 250
feelings/emotions – *cont.*
and fairy tales versus reality 241–5
intense/overwhelming 227, 233, 241, 248
interpretation 230–2
mapping out 226–51
and memory 212
of 'not being good enough' 105
outbursts 217, 243, 247, 268
parental 218–20
recognition 228–9, 232–5
regulation 242
shape-shifting 229–31, 234
supporting 245–51
suppression 242
and temperament 215
see also specific feelings/emotions
femininity 140
fertility 28
'fight' response 109, 212, 236, 246
financial issues 28–9
cost of raising children 29–30
Finland 31
'flight' response 106–7, 212, 236, 246
Floater, the (character) 112–13, 115, 191, 212, 236–7
'flop' response 111, 237, 246

see also collapse, psychic
forgiveness 151, 193
'freeze' response 112, 212, 236, 246
Fretter, the (character) 106–7, 114, 191, 208, 212, 236
Freud, Sigmund 105
friendships 165

gatekeeping 138, 145
Gen Z 262
gender pay gap 144
gender roles 139–44
gender socialisation 230–1
Generation Alpha 262, 263
Germany 90, 158
ghosts, personal 59–64, 66, 69, 71, 210, 214, 256
global issues 261–5
Goleman, Daniel 228
'good enough parent' 178, 245
grandparents 69–70, 156–60
Greece 27
grief 119
guides 71–3, 78, 99, 104, 113, 159, 188, 225
guilt 2, 57, 81

happiness 196
helicopter parenting 191–2
helplessness 111–12
heteronormativity 28, 31–2, 139–40
hippocampus 70, 212
holding children 189
Holocaust survivors 62
homes
    childhood 72–3, 214
    cupboards 95–8
    family rooms 89–95, 95, 179
    kitchens 72–3, 94
    nurseries 79, 82–3, 86
    current 99

your child's 213–14, 224–5, 226, 252–3
hooks, bell 99
household labour, gender division 141
human beings, becoming 213–18
humanity, spark of 206–8
hypervigilance 32
hypothalamic-pituitary-adrenal (HPA) axis 63

idealised child 196
idealised parent 1–3, 18–20, 26–8, 49–51, 59–60, 110, 155–9, 203–4, 243–4
identity 165, 204
    'bad' 81
incomes, double 29
independence 30, 76
individualism 90, 194–5
inequality, gender 139–44
influences 123–4
inner child 69, 79, 227
    and adulthood 99–100, 101
    and conflict 191
    connection with 83–6
    and our partners 150–1
    projection onto our children 219–20
inner critics 104–5, 114, 117, 190–1, 208, 220, 224, 234, 240, 257
integration 115
intensive parenting 170, 202–3, 244
interdependence 30
internal working models 88
internalisation 85–8, 155–9, 205, 220, 230–1
introjection 223
intrusive thoughts 32
Israel 158

Japan 229

judgement 146, 234

Kipling, Rudyard 226

LGBTQI+ couples 140
    see also same-sex parents
life stresses 39
limbic system 212
listening skills 197, 198–200
lone parenting 29, 124, 126, 140, 143, 196
loneliness 154–5, 219
loss 2
love 124, 181
    romantic 130, 142
    unconditional 177
Lover, the (character) 105–6, 114–15, 191, 203, 220, 237, 241

magic 17
male dominance 31
marginalised peoples 12, 196
masculinity 140
masks, social 38–40
matrescence 165
memory 68–71, 212
    content-dependent recall 70
mental health, parental 172, 203
millennials 262
Milne, A.A. 210
mistake-making 76, 192, 244–5, 249–50, 262
modelling 147
monkey mind 211–13, 236, 242, 249–51, 257
monogamy 28
mother-in-laws 155
motherese 221
'motherhood penalty' 144
mothers 11–12
    and the financial losses pf parenting 29
    and gender roles 141–4

and heteronormativity
31
mourning 118–19

needs
children's 200
other people's 203
parental 195, 203,
205–6
neglect 75, 81
nervous system 246
networks 86–7, 123–4,
269–70
neurodivergent children
216–17
neuroscience 170, 211
non-judgemental attitudes
146
norms, social 28, 76
Norway 158
'not good enough', feeling
105

Ogre, the (character)
109–11, 115,
149–50, 203, 212,
220, 224, 236, 240
one-on-one time 4
other people 121–83
partners 123–52
putting their needs
before your own
203
stories from society
168–82
supporting cast 152,
153–67
overwhelm 35, 75, 146,
208, 213, 217, 227,
240–1, 246, 248,
251, 253, 261

parasympathetic nervous
system 246
parent–and–baby play
222
parent–blaming 56
parent–child relationship
see child–parent
relationship
parental expectations 195,
196–7, 218

clear and supported
197, 202
and emotional
regulation 248
and your partner
133–4
parental leave 31
parental stories 1–3, 5, 8,
9–13, 17–35, 40
from adulthood
99–119
from babyhood 79–98
from society 168–82
from your childhood
67–78
from your history
58–66
parentese 221
parenting
decision-making
regarding
parenthood 1,
22–3, 27–8
difficult nature 23–7,
39
fairy tale 18–20, 22,
30, 139–40, 241–5
and family
equilibriums 162–4
feeling cheated/regrets
over 23
and friendships 165
and gender roles
139–44
intensive 170, 202–3,
244
isolation of 153–5
life-changing nature
23–4
as love story 47
magnitude 24–6
models 20–1, **21**,
24–6, **25**
myths and legends of
15–41, **21**
as 'natural' process
125–6, 153,
180
not talking about the
challenges of 23–7
and partners 123–52
parenting – *cont.*

and the reality gap
26–7
as redemptive
experience 32
as skill 126
support for 134,
154–7, 159, 164–6,
172
see also lone parenting
parenting advice,
anxiety-provoking
nature 178
parenting experts 6–7
parenting maps 45–57,
156, 163–7, 169,
187–9, 255, 268
and the blame game
55–7
and conflict 145
and non-traditional
family structures
140
and resting places
53–4
and The Village 164–6
and your guide 49–52
and your partner 125,
127–34
see also bridges;
homes, childhood;
pathways
parenting styles 74–8,
156–7
authoritarian 74, 75
authoritative 75, 191
helicopter parents 76
permissive 74–5
rejecting/neglectful 75
parenting tools 187–209,
269
Boundaries 201–6,
213, 250–1, 255–6
Collaboration
197–201, 213,
217, 222, 249, 255
Empathy 193–7, 213,
220, 222, 235, 257
Repair 189–93, 203,
213, 245, 249–50,
257
Spark of Childhood
206–8, 254, 259,
265, 270

parents
    and abandonment
        issues 4, 85, 102,
        219–20
    ambivalence of 23
    aspirations of 174–5
    becoming 1, 22–3,
        27–8, 59, 128–9
    defining 36–40
    development 245
    and disappointment
        218
    and emotional
        understanding
        229–30
    and failure 21
    fears 46–7
    and feeling like you
        can't cope 40
    and feeling useless
        168–9
    financial losses of 29
    'good' 1, 169
    'good enough' 178,
        245
    idealised/fantasy 1–3,
        18–20, 26–8,
        49–51, 59–60, 110,
        155–9, 203–4,
        243–4
    internalised 85–8,
        155–9, 205, 220
    mental health 172,
        203
    needs 195, 203, 205–6
    and the 'old you' 37
    overburdened 134
    and personal ghosts
        59–64, 66
    primary 134
    role 10, 270
    same sex 124
    as sanctuary 205
    and self-knowledge
        3–5, 10
    sensitive
        responsiveness 88
    smug 165
    unsafe/inconsistent 80
    see also fathers;
        mothers
Parker, Dorothy 168
partners 123–52

    bridges between
        127–35, 138, 140,
        142–3, 145–8, 152
    and conflict 127–9,
        136, 138–9, 144–8
    content 138
    and gender roles
        139–44
    and our changing
        wants 129
    wishing they were
        different 128
pathways 67–78, 169–70,
    268
    children's 210–11,
        213–17
    dead ends 170–82
    early childhood 71–8
    new 163
patrescence 165
patriarchy 140
perfectionism 170–80
perinatal period 6, 70
permissive parenting
    191–2
Perry, Philippa 198
personal histories 58–66
play, parent-and-baby 222
political issues 28–9
post-traumatic stress
        disorder (PTSD),
        birth-related 32
postnatal depression 32,
    172
postnatal period 32
poverty 28, 112, 172,
    196, 212
power 181, 202
    and empathy 198
    and grandparents 157
    and the Ogre 111
    and our partners
        144–5
    and parenting styles
        74–5, 77
powerlessness 109,
    111–12, 181
prefrontal cortex 211–13,
    222
    see also Wise Elder
'Pregnant Then Screwed'
    30

pressure 128–9, 131–3,
    195
    and the Ogre 110
    to be perfect parents
        175–80
    to raise perfect
        children 170–5
    to not feel pressure
        180–2
prevention 245–7
pro-natalism 27
problem-solving approach
    198, 224, 249
projective identification
    219–20
psychoanalysis 84
psychological safety 55
    and babies 84
    and childhood
        recollections 71–2
    and childhood
        relationships 82
    and containment 248
    and grandparents 157
    and judgements 146
    lack of 82
    and personal walls
        103–4
    of the therapeutic
        relationship 80
    and triangulation 136
    and your guide 50, 51
    and your resting place
        53
psychology 6–7
    clinical 6–7, 58–9
    decolonisation of 12
    visual explanation
        of 13
purpose, sense of 21

race 35, 62, 196
Raison, Charles 261
Raphael-Leff, Joan 84
relationships
    children and 220–2
    formation 79–88
    and internal working
        models 88–9
    maps 79–80
    'sticky' dynamics 138
    see also partners
religion 28, 34

Repair (parenting tool)
189–93, 203,
213, 245, 249–50,
257
sadness 57
Saint-Exupéry, Antoine de
187
same-sex parents 124
see also LGBTQI+
couples
sanctuary 205
self 47, 83, 214
baby 83–5, 158–9,
168–9
development of a sense
of 10, 87, 204
hidden 102–3, 119
magical 189
performance of the
38–40
pre-parent 37
and relationships 87
true 79
whole 3–4
self-assessment 41
self-blame 231
self-forgiveness 193
self-knowledge 47–8, 247
self-regulation 215, 248–9
sensitive responsiveness
88
Sex and the City (TV
show) 19
shame 56–7, 59, 81, 101,
155, 230, 234
shared experience 206
siblings, adult 160–2
sleep, baby habits 22
sleep deprivation 23, 24,
70, 113, 236
smacking 196
smartphones 238–9
Smith, Zadie 123
social isolation 153–5
social media 80, 81
social networks 86–7,
123–4, 269–70
social norms 28, 76
social performances
38–40
socialisation, gender
230–1

society
and child-raising 76
stories from 168–82
Spark of Childhood
(parenting tool)
206–8, 254, 259,
265, 270
spiders' webs 138
'sticky' relationship
dynamics 138
'still face' paradigm 238
Stoic, The (character)
107–8, 191, 203
stories 1–3, 5, 8, 40
from adulthood
99–119
assessing personal
33–5
from babyhood 79–98
characters 104–18
from childhood 67–78
of children 185–266
family 252–8
heteronormative 28
mapping out 43–120
other people of our
121–83
stories – *cont.*
from personal histories
58–66
from society 168–82
unravelling 17–35
and walls 102–4
story maps 9–13
storytelling, emotional
239–41
stress 244
and the brain 211
and the Ogre 110
poor coping strategies
103–4
reflection on 55
stress response 63, 236–7
'fawn' response 237,
246
'fight' response 109,
212, 236, 246
'flight' response 106–7,
212, 236, 246
'flop' response 111,
237, 246
'freeze' response 112,
212, 236, 246

prevention 245–7
superego 105
support, parenting 134,
154–7, 159, 164–6,
172
supporting cast 152,
153–67
survival 63, 84, 88, 107
threats to 213
Sweden 30
Sykes, Wanda 263
sympathetic nervous
system 246

taboos 23
tantrums 4, 22
teenagers 23, 69, 163,
165, 169, 217, 262
and attachment
patterns 90, 91, 92,
222
and brain development
211, 212, 213
and Collaboration 198
and parental childhood
trauma 83, 84
and the parental inner
child 219
and parental
relationships 171,
172
and psychological
safety 223
temperament 215–16
therapeutic relationship
80
therapy 6–7, 53, 95, 137,
162–3, 224
theta waves 194
threat perception 63, 71,
111, 212–13, 236
Thunberg, Greta 259
TikTok 81, 179
tiredness 236
see also exhaustion
toddlers, tantrums 4, 22
transgenerational trauma
61–4, 178–9
transition 137
see also change
trauma
childhood 80–3, 112,
179

cycle breakers 178–9
and dissociation 112
racial 179
transgenerational
61–4, 178–9
see also childhood
trauma
trauma response 81
trauma therapy 95
trauma-focused CBT 53
triangulation 136, 138
trolls 127–8, 130, 133,
141, 145, 148,
163, 192, 224,
250, 258
Tronick, Ed 238
tuned-in care 84

UN Special Rapporteur
196
United Kingdom 28
childcare 29
estranged families 156
parental leave 31
pro-natalism 27
smacking 196
societal hostility
towards children
195
working parents 29
United States 28, 196
childcare 29–30
emotional expression
229
estranged families 156
parent–adult child
relationships
158
uselessness, feelings of
168–9

values 129, 157, 255, 264
vicious cycles 203, 239
vigilance 63
Village, The 164–6
visualisation 13
vulnerability 111

walls, personal 102–4,
117–18
wants 129

Warrior, the (character)
108–9, 114–15,
240–1
why? questions 47–8
'wild things' 84
Wilde, Oscar 153
Winnicott, Donald 86,
178
Wise Elder 211–13,
236–7, 239, 242–3,
246, 249, 257
see also prefrontal
cortex
withdrawal 145
Woolf, Virginia 58
Wounded Soul, the
(character) 111–12,
116, 212, 220,
224, 237